THE
WHOLENESS
PRINCIPLE

About the cover:

The globes on the cover represent various possible world views. Three are painted on wooden spheres, with the smaller ones nesting inside the larger one. Originally produced during the Middle Ages to demonstrate interpenetrating realities, the smallest represents the sphere of the sun, the deity, a single star in a blue sky. The starred globe to the right is the natural world, natural philosophy. The globe on the left is a fifteenth-century map of the world, showing the political and social spheres. The photo of the Earth from space is the view of modern science. Curiously, the Earth photo with the Sahara and the Middle East at the North Pole position echoes the golden poles on the other globes.

Cover design
by *Anne Kilgore*

THE
WHOLENESS
PRINCIPLE

Dynamics of Unity
Within
Science, Religion & Society

ANNA F. LEMKOW

*This publication is made possible with
the assistance of the Kern Foundation*

Quest Books

The Theosophical Publishing House
Wheaton, Ill. U.S.A.
Madras, India/London, England

The Theosophical Publishing House
306 West Geneva Road
Wheaton, IL 60187

A publication of the Theosophical Publishing House, a
department of the Theosophical Society in America.

Library of Congress Cataloging in Publication Data

Lemkow, Anna F. (Anna Freifeld), 1917-
    The wholeness principle : dynamics of unity within
      science, religion & society / Anna F. Lemkow. — 1st
      ed.   p.   cm.
    Includes bibliographical references.
    ISBN 0-8356-0655-4 (pbk.)
    1. Theosophy.   2. Whole and parts (Philosophy)   I. Title.
BP573.W56L46   1990
111'.82—dc20   89-40622
                                     CIP

Printed in the United States of America

To Emily B. Sellon, special teacher, in gratitude.

I will not make poems with reference to parts,
But I will make poems, songs, thoughts
       with reference to Ensemble,
And I will not sing with reference to a day,
       but with reference to all days,
And I will not make a poem nor the least
       part of a poem but has reference to the soul,
Because having looked at the objects of the Universe,
I find there is no one nor any particle of one
       but has reference to the soul.
                         Walt Whitman

To know and to act are one and the same.
                         Samurai maxim

Contents

Preface xiii
Acknowledgements xvii
Permissions xix

I. A UNITIVE FRAMEWORK

1. Wholeness—Key to Understanding 3
   An Aberrant Idea of Reality 3
   The Consequences 10
   On Philosophical Maps 16
   Science and Philosophy 19
   Toward an Unfragmented Vision 21
   The Perennial Philosophy 22
   The Perennial Consensus about Ultimate Reality 24
   The Essence of Nondualism 26
   The Unity of Opposites 29
   On Consciousness 32
   On the Human Constitution 32
   Summary 38

2. Our Powers of Knowing 41
   Some General Remarks 41
   The Mode of the Five Senses 43
   The Rational Mode 44
   Trans-Rational Knowing 45
   Mystical Experience as the Raw Material of Religion,
       Philosophy and Art 48
   The Nature of Statements about Reality 49
   On the Interrelationship of the Modes of Knowing 49

Contents

II. SCIENCE

3. Modern Science: The First Four Hundred Years **57**
The Rise of Modern Science 57
Mechanism in the Eighteenth and Nineteenth Centuries .. 63
Physics Reluctantly Refutes Mechanism 65

4. Modern Physics **67**
Introduction 67
Quantum Physics 67
Two Types of Order: Mechanism and Quantum Physics . 72
The Theory of Relativity 73

5. The Nature of Exact Science **79**
Physics Has Given Up Its Certainties 79
What the Physicist Observes 80
The Limitations of Physics 81
Science as an Art Form 82
Physics and Truth 84
Interpreting Quantum Reality 86
Wholeness and the Implicate Order 86
Physics and Holism 91
The Far-Reaching Significance of Science 92

6. The Biological Domain **95**
Introduction 95
The Science of Biology Is Still in Its Infancy 99
Biology Reveals the Impartibility of Life 101
Biological Data: Pervasive Holism 101
The Earth as a Living Entity 108
The Systems View: A New Perspective 109
The Sciences of Complexity 112
Order Through Fluctuation 113
Order, Chaos and Wholeness 115

7. Evolutionary Theory and Its Evolvement **121**
Neo-Darwinism: A Theory in Serious Difficulty 123
On the Origin of Life on Earth 126
Evolution: The Perspective of the Perennial Philosophy . 128
Co-Evolution: The Living, Creative Universe 132

Contents

The Systems View and the Perennial Philosophy 137
Self-Reference 138
Nature's Mentalist Activities 140
Morphogenetic Fields 141
Intrinsic Purposiveness 145
Nature's Surpassing Artistry—Whose Art? 146

8. Of the Brain and the Mind 149
   Introduction 149
   The Mind-Brain Relationship 151
   Implications for the Question of the Survival of Death . 151
   Implications for the Practice of Medicine 152
   The Possibility of Self-Regulation and
     Self-Transformation 155

9. Of Time and Causality 157

10. The Psi Faculties, or the Relation Between Inner
    and Outer 163

III. THE SPIRITUAL DOMAIN

11. The World Religions: Constants and Variations 171
    Introduction 171
    The Diversity 172
    Some Points of Consensus 176
    Symbolic Means of Expression 177
    The Universality of the World's Myths 179
    Faith in Ultimate Reality 181
    Exoteric and Esoteric Religion 182

12. The Essential Unity of the Religions 187
    Truth Is One 187
    What About the Contradictions? 187
    Empathizing with Different Religions 190
    Different Paths Up the Same Mountain 190

13. Religion: Past, Present and Future 193

14. **Religion and Science** **201**
    An Intimate and Beneficial Relationship 201
    Science and Mysticism 204
    Is There Such a Thing as a Mystical Science? 205

15. **Karma: The Ultimate Law of Wholeness** **209**

16. **More on the Spiritual Implications of Wholeness** **217**
    Experiencing Unity 217
    The Higher Values: Categorical Imperatives 220

IV. SOCIETY

17. **Societal Affairs: A Planetary Overview** **227**
    Introduction 227
    The Values of the Industrial Era 228
    By Their Fruits Ye Shall Know Them 236
    The Third World 237
    Technical and Financial Assistance to
        Less-Developed Countries 239
    The Roots of Hunger 244
    The Causal Chain in Poor Countries 246
    Humanity's Common Dilemma 247
    Militarization, and the Need to Redefine Security 248
    Norms of International Behavior 250
    The United Nations 252
    Redefining National Sovereignty 254
    On Disarmament 257
    Towards a Transnational Peacekeeping Force 258
    The Technological Dimension 259

18. **Toward a More Holistic Economy** **263**
    Introduction 263
    Changes in Industry 264
    Changes in the Character and Purpose of Work 268
    Less Industrial Specialization, Especially in the
        Third World 270
    Scaling Down Export-Import Relations 270

Contents

19. How Shall We Characterize the New Era? **273**
A New Trend in Politics and Political Science 273
Grassroots Movements for Social Change 275
Struggle for a Global-Local Perspective 276
International Nongovernmental Organizations 278
"Global Thinking" in the Soviet Union 279
The Emergence of Wholeness as a Guiding Principle
    in Thought and Action 283
Wholeness in the Field of Education 285

**A Postscript on the Intersection of Religion, Perennial
   Philosophy, Science and Society** **287**

20. Order Amid Chaos **291**

Epilogue **299**

References **301**

Index **309**

Preface

The task I have set myself in this book is a challenging one: an inquiry into the dynamics of wholeness as an all-pervasive principle. By its nature, this project will demand taking as synoptic and inclusive a perspective as possible, one that comprehends in some measure the multi-formed and multi-dimensioned nature of existence.

As I see it, we, the human denizens of our planet, are now involved in a whole concatenation of mutually-reinforcing developments, with far-reaching implications for all life on earth as well as for human consciousness. One of these is the unprecedented global interdependency of peoples or nations, brought about through modern mass industry, commerce, communications and transport—developments that were in turn made possible by modern science and technology. New technology now making its appearance will further intensify societal interconnectedness. The change that has already been wrought is momentous, and its most extraordinary feature is that all the different aspects of societal existence, taken singly and together (including politico-socio-economic conditions, human rights, the quality of the environment, international security and peace), are virtually indivisible. It makes of us our brothers' keepers, whether we are ready to be or not.

This globality illustrates remarkably a fundamental proposition of the perennial philosophy, namely, that the different dimensions of existence, including the spiritual and moral, the mental, emotional and physical, are inextricably and dynamically interrelated.

As yet the interdependencies seem to exacerbate discord, competitiveness and conflict among the groups and nations concerned more often than not. Nevertheless this ubiquitous condition is perceptibly influencing the thinking and behavior of nations in a positive way as well, if only out of sheer self-interest. The different nations and peoples are increasingly compelled and motivated to support the entire collectivity. In the longer run, unless we annihilate ourselves, the imperatives inherent in our sharing one small planet will serve powerfully, especially in combination with certain other profound trends, to promote and foster a tolerant, broader, more inclusive perspective—eventually a planetary consciousness.

The other extraordinary and interrelated developments I have in mind are these:

- the present reorientation of science revolving about the problems of wholes and wholeness, whereby science is, for instance, increasingly substituting organic models for mechanical models, and shifting from structure-oriented to process-oriented thinking;
- the way our burgeoning knowledge tends increasingly to coalesce;
- the advent of synoptic studies of world symbology, mythology and religious traditions—studies that strikingly reveal the transcendent universality of human thought;
- and, in virtue of these various developments, the growing perception that religion, philosophy, science and the arts are mutually harmonious and complementary.

A two-fold aim of mine will be to substantiate something of the specifics of these trends and to show their interrelationship. It is moreover my perception that these developments and insights compellingly bring to the fore the fundamental principle of wholeness, or of unity-in-diversity. Just when it is becoming imperative to recall this basic principle of our existence, by a seeming synchronicity it emerges in a new way on all sides.

What is the meaning for us of all-pervasive wholeness? We are impelled by our global conditions and the present unfoldments of knowledge to return anew to this question that has haunted religion and philosophy down the ages—to re-examine it afresh in the light of our own time.

For the purposes of my inquiry, I shall turn to the venerable nondualist philosophy—that mode of thought whose key is wholeness by definition—and which is today referred to by various names—perennial philosophy, theosophy, integral philosophy, the primordial tradition.

Merely to bring together the main propositions and principles of this enduring wisdom—which I attempt to do in the first chapter—is to see that they powerfully complement and illumine each other; that they themselves converge into a dynamic whole—just as, homologously, and on another level, the different ways of knowing as embodied in the world religions and the sciences, when taken together, yield a fuller and richer vision of reality.

One may venture to declare that nothing less than the truth of the radical unity of existence could serve now as the meeting ground of diverse peoples and nations. Irenology, or the study of peace, perhaps the world's youngest major discipline, will unquestionably have to revolve about this truth of existence and how it may be uncovered at the heart of every mode of knowing we possess.

Truth with a capital T is ineffable, as all the religio-philosophical traditions have understood. Yet truth is humanity's touchstone. The more inclusive our vision, the closer we get to truth or reality.

How, then, *can* we achieve a more inclusive vision? A major and indispensable means, I suggest, is via an integration of the consensual insights of the different means of knowing/feeling available to us—an integration of mystical, religio-philosophical, scientific and aesthetic insights. This is obviously a *process*—a dynamic, affective process which goes far beyond mere cognition or knowledge.

There is, however, the serious problem that the present educational environment, by and large, scarcely promotes such a process. Educators themselves are still mired in the "value neutrality" and relativism that are diametrically opposed to holism.

Remedying this situation will be crucial, I believe, for world peace and justice. For it is my conviction that these will essentially depend on the attainment of an adequate degree of wholeness on the part of a critical number of us. The present book is animated by my wish to contribute, however slightly, to this integrative process.

I am bound to acknowledge that this book hazards traversing a far broader terrain than is customary in a single volume by a single writer—including something of the large domains of philosophy, science, religion and societal affairs planet-wide. A resultant shortcoming, I fear, is greater textural density than one might wish. On the other hand, this concentrated and synoptic approach may by its very nature serve as an effective means of providing an *actual* integrative *exercise*. Furthermore, to compensate in some degree, I have provided, parallel with the text, a number of selected extracts from relevant literature. These represent statements by recognized thinkers that seem to me especially instructive or eloquent, and which are intended to supplement and amplify the text itself. In this way the book incorporates, side by side with its own text, what amounts to a sort of mini-anthology on the same broad theme. Many extracts are set off from the book's text in a box.

One need not be a specialist, I believe, in even one of the large fields figuring in this book (as I am not), let alone all of them, to be able to pursue the philosophy of wholeness or holism. We have at our disposal, today, because of the spirit of synthesis in the air, a wealth of penetrating works; were it not for those that have helped me in my studies or that I have drawn upon freely and directly, I should not have been able to make the present attempt. I owe the many writers concerned a deep debt of gratitude.

Acknowledgments

In this book I cite and draw upon many writings, including current publications in a broad range of disciplines and several earlier prophetic works. Obviously, these references are extremely diverse. What makes them germane to my exploration of wholeness is their integrative approach to their subject matter. It would scarcely have been possible for me to attempt to invoke and to interrelate several large domains of thought without recourse to some of this marvellous store of wisdom and information, a reservoir which bears striking witness to an emergent spirit of synthesis. Albeit in different ways and degrees, I am thus richly indebted, to put it paradoxically, to the authors concerned, with a profounder debt, naturally, to some relatively few, as will be apparent.

In other respects, my thanks are due to the following people:

By inviting me to undertake several writing and teaching assignments in the early and mid 1980s, Joy Mills, Director of the School of Theosophy, Krotona Institute, was a catalyst for this book. I thank her for that and also for critically reading the manuscript.

I thank the following for critically reading portions of the manuscript: on religion, Robert Ellwood; on science, Patrick Milburn and Ralph Hannon. Notwithstanding these critiques, any mistakes or misinterpretations are mine alone.

I am especially grateful to Shirley Nicholson, the publisher's senior editor, for patiently reading the manuscript repeatedly in the course of the nearly four years of its preparation and for providing many helpful comments, valuable suggestions, and, in addition, an extremely important ingredient: encouragement.

I am deeply grateful to Emily B. Sellon for wise advice at different phases of the work and for her beautifully perceptive and felicitous editing of a large portion of the manuscript.

Permissions

Grateful acknowledgment is made for permission to use the following previously published material:

The poem "I came into the unknown," Willis Barnstone, translator, *The Poems of St. John of the Cross.* Copyright © 1972 by Willis Barnstone. Reprinted by permission of New Directions Publishing Corp.

Reprinted by permission of the publisher from Sloan, Douglas, Editor, *TOWARD THE RECOVERY OF WHOLENESS: Knowledge, Education and Human Values.* (New York: Teachers College Press. © 1981, 1984 by Teachers College, Columbia University. All rights reserved.): Excerpts from pages 9, 10, 14, 15, 28, 29, 52, 53.

Ten brief extracts from pp. 113, 120, 138, 138-9, 172, 173, 175, 175-176, 186-7, 194, in David Bohm, *Wholeness and the Implicate Order.* Ark Edition, 1983. Copyright © 1980 by David Bohm. Reprinted by permission of Routledge and Kegan Paul, Ltd.

The excerpt from *Nature and the Greeks,* by Erwin Schroedinger, 1954. Reprinted by permission of Cambridge University Press.

Quotations reprinted with permission of Macmillan Publishing Company and Cambridge University Press from *Science and the Modern World* by Alfred North Whitehead. Copyright 1925 by Macmillan Publishing Company; copyright renewed 1953 by Evelyn Whitehead.

Figure 2.5, p. 19, in *Elements of Biology,* by Paul B. Weisz and Richard N. Keogh, fourth edition. Copyright © 1977, 1969, 1965, 1961 by McGraw-Hill, Inc. Reprinted by permission of McGraw-Hill.

The excerpts from "The Model of Open Systems: Beyond Molecular Biology," by Ludwig von Bertalanffy, in *Biology, History, and*

Natural Philosophy, Breck, A.D. and W. Yourgrau, eds., 1974. Reprinted by permission of Plenum Publishing Corp.

The quotation from *Evolution, A Theory in Crisis,* by Michael Denton, 1986, Adler and Adler Inc. Reprinted with permission of James B. Adler.

The selections from *CHAOS* by James Gleick. Copyright © 1987 by James Gleick. All rights reserved. Reprinted by permission of Viking Penguin, a division of Penguin Books USA, Inc.

The selections from *Physics as Metaphor,* by Roger S. Jones. Copyright © 1982 by the University of Minnesota. Reprinted by permission of the publisher.

The quotations from *The Self-Organizing Universe,* by Erich Jantsch, Pergamon Press, 1980. Reprinted with the kind permission of Anne Parks, 503 Foxen Drive, Santa Barbara, Ca. 93105, holder of the Copyright.

The quotations from *SYNCHRONICITY: The Bridge Between Matter and Mind* by F. David Peat. Copyright ©1987 by F. David Peat. Reprinted by permission of Bantam Books, a division of BANTAM, DOUBLEDAY, DELL PUBLISHING GROUP, INC.

The selections from *Towards a Just World Peace* by Saul H. Mendlovitz and R.B.J. Walker, Editors. Copyright © Committee for a Just World Peace, 1987. Published by Butterworths in association with The Committee for a Just World Peace, World Policy Institute, New York. Reprinted by permission of the World Policy Institute.

The selections from *One World, Many Worlds: Struggles for a Just World Peace,* by R.B.J. Walker. © 1988 Lynne Rienner Publishers Inc. Reprinted by permission of the publisher.

The quotations from *The Economic Pursuit of Quality,* by Michael Power, 1988. Reprinted by permission of M.E. Sharpe, Inc., Armonk, New York 10504.

I
A Unitive Framework

For by one Spirit are we all baptized into one body, whether we be Jews or Gentiles, whether we be bond or free: and have been all made to drink into one Spirit.

I Corinthians, XII:13

And We shall take from every nation a witness.

Qur'ân, XXVIII. 75

Those who in the search for truth start from consciousness as a seat of self-knowledge, with interests and responsibilities not confined to the material plane, are just as much facing the hard facts of experience as those who start from consciousness as a device for reading the indications of spectroscopes and micrometers.

Sir Arthur Eddington
The Nature of the Physical World

1
Wholeness—Key to Understanding

An Aberrant Idea of Reality

Whatever one's cast of mind— whether scientific, religious, philosophical or pragmatic—each one of us desires reassurance that our lives are worthwhile, significant and meaningful. But the standards by which we judge what we mean by "worthwhile" and "significant" vary tremendously, since they depend upon our personal values. What is most important to us? Material gain? Personal gratification? Success? Appreciation? Knowledge? Or the subtler satisfactions embodied in such terms as happiness, helpfulness, compassion, spiritual growth? Obviously, our standards and values depend upon what we think of as most important and enduring in the world—in other words, upon our concept of reality.

But what reality is and how it may be sought are difficult questions. One complicating fact is that reality is far from being the same for every person, for the reason that its conception is inside one's mind: subjective. There is the further complication that everyone experiences various kinds of reality that depend on different states of mind. Again, conceptions and experiences of reality depend on cultural and historical factors, so that they vary in different parts of the world.

One generalization thus arises: every experience of reality is internalized; therefore it is intensely personal. Only its conceptualization can be shared as knowledge. This is something that must be emphasized because a contrary idea concerning reality and how it may be found is widely held today. We will begin by discussing this latter school of thought and what is wrong with it.

Western society (for although the problem is of global concern, it is Western-inspired) is a curious mixture of contradictions. For our purposes we need identify only three of these.

First of all, in terms of influence, there are the mainstream professionals and academicians, in all fields, including the sciences both hard and soft: psychology, biology, neuroscience, economics, and so forth. Let us call them Group One. How they are distinguishable from *non*-mainstream professionals will be made clear below. Since they form such an influential portion of the human population, their views about reality are particularly significant for all of us. And, unfortunately, insofar as they will even admit the validity of the question, their view is a radically erroneous one.

For on the whole such people tend to believe that reality is something altogether *outside* of themselves, not only objective, but also concrete and quantifiable. That is, they believe they can stand totally outside of what is real, be totally neutral toward it, and take its measure, thus adopting what they consider to be a "scientific" approach to reality which is "purely" objective. It is their belief, conversely, that what is not quantifiable is less than real, "merely" subjective.

Now, there is of course nothing wrong with quantification. In fact it is the essential tool of empirical science; mathematics is *the* language of physics, the most authoritative of the exact sciences. What *is* wrong is (1) the idea that reality can be something purely objective or totally outside of ourselves; and (2) that reality can be grasped solely by means of our five senses and their extensions, i.e., empirically. For while empirical science is a marvellous enterprise of the human mind and spirit, it is nevertheless a limited form of knowledge which is far from being able to encompass the whole of reality. As philosopher Huston Smith and others have said, to limit the real only to that which can be quantified is not scientific but scientistic—a perversion of science.

The assumption that reality is outside of the observer—purely objective—contradicts the basic fact that in taking the measure of anything that thing is selected, identified, and measured by the scientist's *mind,* and that the scientist's conclusions are not outside but *inside* his or her mind. Such an exercise cannot, by its intrinsic nature, *be* purely objective. Take the commonplace observation of some plainly visible physical object: the way the object appears to the person looking will necessarily be partly selective and contingent upon that particular person's vision, perspective and position, as well as what features or "facts" about the object he is predisposed to notice, and so forth.

There is unquestionably a manifested world apart from what we think its nature may be. But our perceptions of anything and everything are a product of our *interaction* with those things, not the things-in-themselves. Therefore it is illogical to negate the mind even as one employs it; illogical to omit reason in *evaluating* something, even the conception of reality itself.

Group One people do not of course go so far as to deny such a thing as mind and consciousness, but they consider them only secondary data— epiphenomena or derivatives of material reality. Accordingly, their assumption is that the human mind or consciousness and behavior, as well as reflective thought, can in principle be fully explained by activities of the central nervous system, which, in turn, can be reduced to the biological structure and function of that physiological system. The biologists among them hope to explain biological phenomena at all levels in terms of atomic physics, that is, through the action and interaction of the component atoms of carbon, nitrogen, oxygen, and so forth.

In short, Group One people reason that everything, including mind and living organisms, is reducible to what is ultimately "real" and that for them boils down to the motion of atoms in space.

The position is naive if only from the standpoint of the new physics, since atoms themselves are a somewhat mysterious category. Many Group One people are too sophisticated not to be aware of the fact that twentieth-century physics does not claim to know what matter is; that physics is not even certain that what it is measuring is physical at all; and that at the microscopic level, the observer and the observations are necessarily intertwined, so that it is impossible to stand totally outside of what is being observed. In assuming that reality is purely objective, Group One people simply ignore these basic problems of exact science, in addition to dismissing the relevent and time-honored psychological, philosophical and religious insights.

Perhaps few Group One people have ever seriously *reflected* on the problem of reality as such, or considered that it must both subsume and embrace *all* phenomena. This is the case partly because philosophy, which by definition should concern wisdom, is little concerned today with wisdom as such, and metaphysics, as a branch of philosophy, is totally out of vogue.

I recently had a conversation with an intelligent and well-educated young man who, when we chanced upon a philosophical subject, off-handedly classified himself as a materialist. On further reflection, however, he modified this self description, saying that he felt he was more a skeptic than an outright materialist. I asked if he had any convictions about such a thing as wisdom. After a moment's thought he replied that he did not, and he vouchsafed soberly that he felt himself to be living in a spiritual vacuum. I surmise that his non-conviction is mainly due to the "rational" materialism of our mainstream culture, with its narrow and shallow idea of what is real and worth exploring.

The human power of reason is wonderful and indispensable, but we always reason from basic assumptions. Group One people rightly admire rigorous thought and logic, but they start with invalid assumptions about reality. Logically, their assumptions lead to or imply a great deal of nonsense: for example, that plants and animals are nothing but molecular machines, that man is but "an insentient automaton or at most a bundle of appetites," so that, by implication at least, the authors of the greatest works of the imagination including Jesus and the Buddha were nothing but insentient automatons, but nevertheless human beings should be held responsible before the law, and that their brains (which are computers) are entitled to an education.

The computer can neither be educated nor be held responsible, nor indeed operate to practical purpose at all without a programmer, but Group One people posit no programmer.

I have noticed that Group One people confuse metaphysics with something "supernatural." If the conversation takes a philosophical turn, they instantly suspect the worst. I find myself exclaiming to such a person, "Nothing is supernatural! Everything is natural!" For although existence is full of mystery, nothing is "supernatural" or beyond nature. But "natural" does not merely mean "physical"—for example, time, number, order and love. The all-pervasive order and design which science finds in every domain of its investigation, and which make science possible in the first place, are not physical but metaphysical. It may well be described as a mystery, a wonder, but certainly not as supernatural. The mammalian brain with its connections of 10 to the 15th power is an awe-inspiring marvel, but it would be entirely inappropriate to call it supernatural. (As someone recently exclaimed, if only one percent of the connections in a single brain were specifically organized, this would represent a greater number of connections than in the entire communications network on earth!)

The spider's web, the beaver's dam, the bird's nest are all purposeful. The way the leaves of a tree are designed is extraordinarily fitting: their shape permits them to intercept light, the source of energy for photosynthesis, as well as gas and heat exchange with the air. Again, every animate form has the propensity and the astonishing ability to fulfill itself, to consummate itself, and, when necessary, ingeniously to circumvent obstacles in its way. In short, intelligence and purpose are evident throughout nature. But the very idea of intelligent design or purpose in nature is anathema to Group One people. In this they are however logical: mechanism does not cohere with purpose.

Group One biologists attribute the beginning of life on earth to a one-time accident. It is however increasingly borne in upon them that the idea is extremely implausible on scientific grounds. For example, Francis Crick, co-discoverer of DNA, is quoted (in the *Mind/Brain Bulletin*, September 9, 1985) as remarking, "an honest man, armed with the knowledge available to us now, could only state that in some sense the origin of life appears at the moment to be almost a miracle, so many are the conditions that would have had to be satisfied to get it going." It is a "miracle" to those who, by reason of indoctrination, would rather believe in blind chance or miracles than in a living, meaningful universe.

How, one may ask, notwithstanding their love of rationality and logic, do Group One people reconcile the intricate order in nature with blind, mechanical process? How do they reconcile the extraordinary beauty, variations and colorations—subtleties that often have no conceivable utilitarian purpose—with blind, mechanical processes?

Group One people value most of all "value neutrality" and utilitarian or instrumental values. They do not notice the contradictions.

Some of my own friends and acquaintances have this type of mentality. (I naturally have them very much in mind as part of the audience I would like to address.) I share their love of reason and logic. But I reject their *narrow use* of reason—their use of reason, as someone recently put it, as a purely technical faculty, a "value-free" mode of manipulating information and relationships. It is not possible to sever reason from the basic values that have always been regarded as its inseparable concomitants. The obscuration, the downgrading of basic values, is an aberration, and not a harmless one; to

The question is whether life with all its subtleties is some accidental property called into existence by events of blind chance or whether it is a more fundamental property of the world of nature. As we study the complex and interrelated aspects of planetary life, are we simply to attribute it all to random events, or are we to seek deep meanings about ourselves and the cosmos? Looking at the evidence . . . [I opt for the latter approach] . . . but that commitment to meaning only becomes apparent after one spends some considerable effort looking into our understanding of the physics and chemistry of life and the biological applications. . .

[The details] . . . establish just how intelligent cosmic intelligence really is. The argument is far more persuasive when we can see all the pieces fitting into place. And the universe is most impressive in its detailed workings as well as in its broad scope.

Harold J. Morowitz, *Cosmic Joy &*
Local Pain [pp. 104-105]

the contrary, its unhappy consequences are now assailing all of us.

For what people believe and what they do are intimately linked, and what people believe and do affects not only themselves but everyone, because *we* are intimately linked with one another.

Is it *unreasonable* to acknowledge the existence of wisdom and truth? Surely reason, except where it is powerfully blocked by prejudice, commends the human value of the fruits of wisdom. Recently many intellectuals in the Soviet Union, become freer in their expressions than they were prior to the advent of *glasnost,* have begun to allude to "the eternal verities." Mainstream disciplinarians in other parts of the world should likewise admit the validity of wisdom, abandoning value neutrality for what it is—a specious value. Then life, and the cosmos itself, will be recognized as significant and value-saturated.

Group One people, I fear, because of their deeply ingrained bias, will resist my holistic line of thought even if I succeed in presenting it with scrupulous logic.

I have already had a negative indication about this book's likely prospects with conventional thinkers from a very bright and likable young friend of mine, a Ph.D. in psychology of a mainstream school. I tried out on her only the preface to this book. She underlined every second word as "emotional," declaring that it is not the content but the style which she finds unsatisfactory—assuring me that she would even "love to see the case made." Later I scrutinized each of the words she objected to and reassured myself that they were all good dictionary words, used appropriately to reflect what I wanted to say. I could imagine this young lady herself using some of these emotional words, such as "momentous" when something startling happened in her own life. It is not inexact to say that the global interdependence of peoples on this planet *is* a momentous development.

Moreover, if every second word in my text were changed, one could scarcely say it was only a matter of style.

I surmise that what really troubled her is this: As the product, education-wise, of the prevailing school of thought that I have described, she is naturally imbued with the spirit of logical empiricism, a chief concern of which is the meaning of language. Language is to logical empiricism the only overarching criterion of excellence. Words are facts and thus a value in themselves, regardless of meaning, which is as a matter of course negligible and inadmissable. Accordingly the language it approves of is the language that conveys factual information. That is the language it considers to be the norm by which all other kinds of language must be judged.

But inasmuch as I shall be dealing with holistic (nondualistic) philosophy, I shall not confine myself to factual information or even to Aristotelian logic. To the contrary, I must include paradox. For that matter, so does exact science: for instance, quantum theory states of the electron that its position neither remains the same nor changes with time; that the electron neither stays at rest nor is in motion. What is that but paradox? Again, I shall include in my considerations the realm of ideas and values such as compassion, beauty and love, all of which are trans-rational and paradoxical, for we do not love someone simply because it is reasonable to do so. Accordingly, my language should be appropriate to all this subject matter (which is not to say that I may dispense with factual language where needed).

I would submit to those who are logical empiricists that they have a good basis for accepting my language: they need only follow the dictum of one of their most respected members, Ludwig Wittgenstein, and grant me that I am playing a different "language game," with its own rules.

At any rate, I would submit that words and their content are intimately tied, as is everything else.

The Consequences

Group One people do not live consistently as materialists; they are not invariably only acquisition-minded, utilitarian, and prosaic. On the contrary, some of them are very altruistic and caring, and capable of enjoying the fine arts; some go so far as to put their own life on the line for others, and even the most died-in-the-wool reductionist sometimes expresses a sense of awe before the wonders of nature, not noticing that it is irrational to wax emotional about blind, mechanical phenomena.

But—and here is the main point—their reductionistic, materialistic worldview is nevertheless a seriously damaging one both for themselves and, because they are influential, for the world at large.[1] For, to reiterate, our worldview and its concomitant values largely determine what kind of world we actually develop and have to live in. The kind of world we have is what we have asked for: we are *not* computers, though we each have at our disposal an incomparably marvellous computer (our brain); on the contrary, we are *creators*, individually and collectively.

Due to the materialist indoctrination, many Group One people have a positive distaste for entertaining questions concerning wisdom and eternal verities. And I have noticed that when they themselves feel or act upon altruistic impulse, they tend to rationalize their action in a way consistent with their radical bias. Or, to put it in another way, their (conscious or unconscious) mechanistic or reductionistic self-image naturally discourages recognition of their own higher faculties. All around us we see a breakdown in values, but such people automatically, routinely espouse value neutrality. They can extol unhesitatingly only utilitarian values, yet idealism often creeps in in spite of themselves, I notice. Their reductionist stance nevertheless deprives them of a *basis* for a serious commitment to higher ideals or the common good, and consigns them to a spiritual vacuum. As Huston Smith and others have pointed out, the reductionist self-

---

1. I am not inveighing against reductionist methods in science. These are useful and appropriate wherever they yield the simplest, most economical or most elegant explanation that will cover the known data. What I reject is the reductionist worldview.

For both individual and society, knowledge, whether correct or incorrect, contributes in a basic and inseparable way to what the individual or society is. . . . In most experience, the contribution of perception is limited to what fits into the overall general framework or context provided by past knowledge, both concrete and abstract. From time to time, however, challenges arise that require a creative and original response, going beyond . . . [existing frameworks]. What is then needed is *insight* . . . an inward perception . . . inward not only in the sense of *looking into* the very essence of the content that is to be known and understood, but also in the sense of looking into the mind that is engaged in the act of knowing. . . . Now it has been fairly commonly agreed that we are at present faced with the challenge of a breakdown in human values that threatens the stability of society throughout the whole world. I suggest that existing knowledge cannot meet this challenge, and that only insight can give rise to the sort of overall new approach that might meet it.

David Bohm [in Sloan, ed., p. 10]

image conduces to the *dormancy* of the higher faculties, and even their *atrophy*.

We may judge a philosophy by its fruits. The reductionistic-mechanistic-materialistic outlook has fostered numerous dichotomies, schisms, fragmentations, alienations: alienation from self (the above-mentioned spiritual vacuum) and hence from others as well, alienation from nature (automatons cannot feel much for other automatons—if we are only machines, we may as well grab for ourselves as much as we can, conquer and exploit nature to the hilt), the dichotomy between knowledge and values, between ends and means, between mind and matter, between the universe of matter and the universe of life, between the sciences and the humanities, between the rich and the poor, between industrialized countries and what is called the third world, between the present and future generations.

It will be apparent that I am suggesting that the materialistic-mechanistic-reductionistic outlook and the corresponding loss of values have not been confined to mainstream scientists. Indeed, they have not. I am not alone in perceiving this, but in fact enjoy the company of many. Since science's success and prestige are enormous, the mechanistic worldview associated with its nineteenth century formulations commended itself to the worlds of industry and business, as well as the culture at large. The image of a blind mechanical world, and of ourselves as computers, inevitably underlies the normative practice of seeking personal advantage and letting the chips fall where they may. The emphasis on individualism and competitiveness, on the part alike of individuals, business enterprises, communities, and nations, has been part and parcel of the Western-inspired scientific-and-industrial culture. It probably largely fueled the undeniable energy and accomplishments of industrialism. Yet, and this is the point, it has had a serious downside because the pursuit of personal advantage and the emphasis on individualism have been embraced as *primary* values, while the higher, less egoistic aspects of human nature and their corresponding values have been *obscured.* This configuration of thought has not surprisingly led to the present ills of unbridled egotism, greed for material acquisitions or power, rapacious ecological exploitation, cynicism, corruption and terrorism. The materialistic-reductionistic worldview has produced what is today a world living in the grip of elitism (see Part IV for details).

But there is another consequence which is both ironic and pregnant with further consequences. Empowered by modern technology and economic growth, our enthusiastic, energetic pursuit of *individual advantage* has eventuated in a condition of unprecedented global *interdependence,* which exists at every level, including the material or economic, social, ecological and moral. Global interdependence is so pervasive today that every commission and omission in any domain of human action, be it chemistry, biology, ecology, economics, social welfare or morality, no matter where it originates, sooner or later has an impact on the rest of the world.

It is a situation which takes the wind out of the idea of "value neutrality," does it not?

In another manner of speaking, our commissions and omissions now produce strong feedback from all these different aspects of existence, including Mother Earth herself. The fruits of tunnel vision, as it has been called, hit us squarely in the eye.

One message of the feedback is that everything is inescapably woven together into a dynamic whole. What leaps up at us is that the grave problems confronting us are all global and interconnected. This seems a curious anomaly. How is it that the multiplicity of questions and problems and human activities in different domains and the multiplicity of societies, with their diverse cultures and religions, all ineluctibly factor into a dynamic overall process? The situation seems to suggest something profoundly paradoxical about the underlying reality.

It is becoming apparent to us that each individual thing or entity can best be understood not in terms of its material components in isolation from its milieu, but in terms of its relationships with its environment and with other things or entities with which it interacts. More particularly, this situation applies to each one of us as individuals, as well as to the societies and nations of the world. Our very autonomy depends on our relationships!

Our global crisis has naturally induced a good deal of soul-searching. Notwithstanding the aforementioned reluctance to entertain metaphysical questions, these now arise too insistently to be brushed aside. The questions that human beings have always asked in the past now re-emerge: What *is* the nature of reality? What is *our* (man's) real nature? (I shall throughout use the word "man" generically, not in terms of gender.) What is the meaning and purpose of our existence?

We cannot look to empirical science for an answer to these questions. Its method is not suited for their consideration, and scientists have again and again held that such problems lie outside the province of their disciplines.

Traditionally, religion and philosophy have been the source of insight about questions of truth and meaning. But for many people, religion has lost its authority. One reason for this is that religions are so often part of the problem itself— sources of divisiveness, discord and conflict rather than their resolution.

As for philosophy, sad to say it has totally abandoned its traditional concerns, as noted earlier. Under the influence first of the positivist and related schools of thought, then held captive to linguistic analysis and computer science, it has repudiated questions of morality and ethics, let alone of the nature of wisdom and love. Values and the ethical choices which govern human interactions have become non-questions, unworthy of serious discussion. Moral behavior is merely personal prejudice. "Hence the descendants of the Positivists are now engaged in great efforts to save moral standards from being cast out as altogether unfounded. But their efforts are in vain. As long as

[Let us start] with the image of cultural mid-life . . . [Notice that] the central "mythos" of our recent Age of Reason was a young adult heroic story of onward and upward, achievement at any cost. But our *future* fulfillment as a culture—indeed likely our survival—will depend on our ability to move beyond the youthful hubris of our most recent age, and make passage into a more mature time. While our most recent age has had its basis in knowledge, the next must have its foundation in that quality that most defines the seeking of life's second half—wisdom.

Charles M. Johnston, M.D., "Beyond
Knowledge—Toward Wisdom,"
Noetic Sciences Review,
Winter, 1988, No. 9

science remains the ideal of knowledge, and detachment the ideal of science, ethics cannot be secured from complete destruction by skeptical doubt" (Polanyi and Prosch, 1975, p. 27).

Yet the questions arise: Is there not some meaning in the way things are put together? What is the purpose of our life?

Then, too, we are pained by the ubiquitous divisiveness, the moral decay, the extreme inequities and injustices of our world. We abhor the prevalence of violence, and brutality, and are deeply perturbed by the specter of world hunger. We yearn for a more humane world. And what is more, we are increasingly convinced that the present course of world culture is unsustainable and imperils our very survival.

Many respected intellects have foreseen the imminence of the crisis we now face, and warned of its dangers. They have all made substantially the same diagnosis: the basic problem of our times arises out of our sense of values, which governs our priorities. For instance, a report submitted some two decades ago to the international group of scholars known as the Club of Rome concluded that we must cease being so full of ourselves, that we must unlearn the habit of seeking self-advantage at the cost of others, that indeed we must undergo a fundamental change of consciousness (Mesarovic and Pestel, 1976).

Thus the solution to our world's dilemmas lies not in finding new scientific techniques (helpful as these may be) but in changing our attitudes and values and goals.

Notice that whereas Group One discounts consciousness on the grounds that it is not objectively observable or quantifiable, the viewpoint here implies the *primacy* of consciousness. There is in fact today a large and growing number of people who are flocking to various schools, retreats and workshops on techniques to effect a change in consciousness. These people may be classified for our purposes as Group Two.

This brings us to the third group, which may overlap in many cases with Group Two, but needs to be identified for itself. This Group Three consists of a sizable and growing number of scientists, philosophers of science, professionals and academics, holistic health practitioners, and others who espouse a holistic worldview. As one may judge from the rich and extensive literature this emergent segment generates, it numbers among its members well qualified individuals—even illustrious ones—from a broad range of disciplines, including physics, biology, neuroscience, philosophy of science, philosophy of religion, economics, political science, futurism, humanistic and transpersonal psychology, anthropology, and so forth. (Who some of them are will become evident from the references in this book.)

The Group One mainstream people are largely unaware of or unreceptive to the views and writings of Group Three. But we may expect this dichotomy gradually to attenuate. The mechanistic outlook was born of Newtonian/Cartesian science. Not only was mechanism disproved by physics many decades ago, but a very different outlook has already emerged at the leading edge of a whole range of sciences. The mainstream is lagging behind but this gap is bound to be bridged.

In point of fact, we now witness a whole interrelated concatenation of developments which combine to point us away from a reductionistic worldview; as the poet Yeats predicted at the beginning of this century, we may return to the human norm whose premises—and whose fruits therefore—are of quite another kind (cf. Kathleen Raine, in Sloan, ed., 1984).

In the chapters which follow, some of the specifics of these developments will be sketched into the outlines of three large domains, namely, science, religion and societal/planetary affairs.

Throughout, my primary aim is to explore the wholeness and interconnectedness of the world. In the spirit of Walt Whitman (in his poem that is the first epigram for this book), I will be concerned less with parts than with their context, Ensemble, the living, intelligible, responsive Universe.

On Philosophical Maps

A map, as has been well said by Alfred Korzybski, is not the territory. But as E. F. Schumacher remarked in *A Guide for the Perplexed*, a faithful, reliable map is a necessity. We have a great need for a reliable map of reality.

Now, as we have already suggested, the map of reality in use today by an influential segment of the population (Group One) is very deficient. Indeed it bears little resemblance to the territory, for it omits entire regions of human interest and experience.

According to the materialist-mechanist-reductionist map, the universe is an immense clockwork, an extremely complex machine made up of discrete particles and separate objects. By some random, mechanical process over the course of billions of years, this machine somehow gave rise, in a tiny corner of itself, to life, consciousness and creative intelligence.

Now this Cartesian-Newtonian map is very young, historically speaking—less than four centuries old. Parts of it are much younger (notably the neo-Darwinian notions concerning the origin of life, of species and of man, which date from the second half of the twentieth century). And the map is already partly outmoded by physical science itself, as well as by new findings of the life sciences (all this will be documented in Part II).

We are in fact returning—but in a new way as is always the case with the cyclical spiral of thought—to the ancient concept of the world that existed for millennia. It is the idea of the cosmos as organic, multi-levelled, and comprised of a hierarchy of beings—an idea found in the Christian and Jewish religions, in the Pythagorian school of thought, in ancient Syrian thought, and in Hinduism.[2]

According to this doctrine, the principle of hierarchy is epitomized in the aphorism, "As above, so below." Issuing from the Divine source/cause, the "ladder of being" or descending chain of life begins

---

2. For an extensive overview of different versions of the hierarchical doctrine, cf. H. P. Blavatsky's *The Secret Doctrine*. A digest of Blavatsky's presentation is found in *The Divine Plan*, by Geoffrey A. Barborka, pp. 43-76. A contemporary writer who espouses the principle of hierarchy, both spiritual and material, is Ken Wilber. Cf. *The Spectrum of Consciousness* and other books of Wilber's listed in the bibliography.

on the higher, invisible realms of being and extends to the visible kingdoms of nature. What is more, the ladder may be climbed in both directions: upward into spirituality, or downward into materiality. Thus each successive level is dependent on its neighbors and partakes of their qualities, but is nonetheless uniquely itself. (The word "hierarchy" is therefore not used in the sense which describes a top-down church or government or business organization.)

"The Chain of Being," writes Schumacher (1978, p. 15), "can be seen as extending downward from the Highest to the lowest, or it can be seen as extending upward from the lowest to the Highest. The ancient view begins with the Divine and sees the downward Chain of Being as moving an ever-increasing distance from the Center, with a progressive loss of qualities. The modern view, largely influenced by the doctrine of evolution, tends to start with inanimate matter and to consider man the last link of the chain, as having evolved the widest range of useful qualities."

It is understood by proponents of this doctrine that the higher—or innermost—levels of being are more inclusive than lower or outer levels, and that each rung of the ladder, so to speak, creates, comprehends and sustains the next lower to itself. Differently put, higher or more inclusive levels of organization comprehend and transcend lower or less inclusive levels but not vice versa. This is a very important point to remember when trying to evaluate the shortcomings of the reductionist model of reality.

Let us for a moment contrast the main features of a mechanistic order such as would obtain in a clockwork universe with the order that would characterize an organic or living universe. As David Bohm has written (1983), in a mechanistic context, the parts exist outside of each other and interact through forces that do not bring about any changes in their essential natures. Each part of a man-made machine, for instance, is manufactured independently of the others, and it interacts with other parts only through some kind of external contact. By contrast, each part of a living organism "grows in the context of the whole, so that it does not exist independently, nor can it be said that it merely 'interacts' with the others, without itself being essentially affected in this relationship" (p. 173). As we well know, the parts of an organism, for example, cells, tissues, organs, and so forth, not only interact but also interpenetrate each other. As Bohm would say, everything is "enfolded" into everything, so that each part contains information about the whole entity. At the same time, each part is also a sub-totality of the whole and participates in its dynamic process.

Furthermore, the ancient idea of hierarchy is today integrated with the idea of evolution: this produces the notion of a transcendent, dynamic, co-evolutionary process embracing all existents at all levels. (We shall go into evolutionary theory at some length in Part II, and will look at it both from the viewpoint of science and the viewpoint of holistic philosophy, since the question of evolution is central to both domains.)

At the terrestrial or visible level, we have, as already noted, the mineral, plant, animal and human kingdoms of nature.

"No one has any difficulty recognizing the astonishing and mysterious difference between a living plant and one that has died and has thus fallen to the lowest Level of Being, inanimate matter," writes Schumacher (1978, p. 16). "What is this power that has been lost? We call it 'life.' " Life is something that cannot be explained by any laws of physics and chemistry, he continues. We can destroy life but we cannot create it. Even if we had a formula for creating life out of mineral matter, we should still confront the mystery that something that could do nothing had become something that could extract nourishment from its environment, grow, and reproduce itself, "true to form."

Similarly, the animal kingdom is not derivable from the plant kingdom. An animal exhibits powers entirely beyond those of a plant. We can readily describe these powers, but to describe them is not to know what they are; they are a mystery.

Again, human beings are endowed with yet another new power, one of enormous consequence: that of self-reflection. As some have said, man's advent changed the very character of the evolutionary process. Human domination affects the world picture on a time-scale which is accelerating exponentially.

Whereas the hierarchical tradition regards a lower rung of existence as less inclusive than a higher rung, reductionism takes the opposite tack: that is to say, it attempts to explain the more in terms of the less—for example, plants in terms of physics and chemistry, or as molecular machines.

Admittedly, plants apparently evolved *after* minerals, animals emerged *after* plants, and humans emerged *after* animals. But the fact that the higher came *through* the lower, and the fact that it *rests* on the lower, does not prove that it *comes* from the lower (cf. Wilber, 1981 and 1983).

Indeed, putting aside for the moment the millennia-old tradition and looking at the matter empirically, since we are unable to account for emergent qualities on the basis of the preceding level, and since the higher cannot be reduced to the lower without loss, it may be more reasonable to suppose that the plant kingdom emerged when conditions were ripe for it so to do; that similarly, the animal kingdom emerged when conditions on earth were ripe for that to happen; and again, that the human kingdom appeared at the juncture when this became possible.

This line of thought is now increasingly current among a number of scientists—some are physicists, some biologists, some practicing other disciplines—who are disinclined to draw a boundary between the inanimate and animate levels of existence.

To these scientists the cosmos is more like an organism than like a machine. Or it has been likened to a thought—the thought of a mathematical thinker, as Sir James Jeans, the British astronomer, put it some decades ago. Or, again, as composed of "mind stuff" (Sir Arthur Eddington). Or, as with a contemporary physicist, David Bohm, as "a flowing wholeness."

If life and consciousness march together; if the universe is both alive and conscious; if the universe is moreover composed of a graded continuum of levels of consciousness, then may we not regard our terrestrial mineral-plant-animal-human continuum as an integral part of a vaster continuum of consciousness? Moreover, in view of the fact that the terrestrial kingdoms are dynamically interrelated and interpenetrating (in the way, for example, that my cells and I interpenetrate each other), the terrestrial continuum may be described as a dynamic unity-in-diversity.

The reader may find phrases such as "co-evolution," "spectrum of consciousness" and "unity-in-diversity" still elliptical; it is this book's purpose to explore these concepts—from the philosophical, religious, and scientific standpoints. Therefore, they should become clearer as we proceed.

Science and Philosophy

We have just been discussing the respective philosophical maps of science and traditional wisdom. But in fact the very idea of a philosophical map produced by empirical science is absurd. As already noted, empirical science does not address the aspects of existence that are not quantifiable, leaving metaphysics, philosophy, and religion to

> As the plant is formed, maintained and dissolved by the exchange of matter and energy with its environment, at which point can we say that there is a sharp distinction between what is alive and what is not? Clearly, a molecule of carbon dioxide that crosses a cell boundary into a leaf does not suddenly 'come alive' nor does a molecule of oxygen suddenly 'die' when it is released to the atmosphere. Rather life itself has to be regarded as belonging in some sense to a totality, including plant and environment. It may indeed be said that life is enfolded in the totality and that, even when it is not manifest, it is somehow 'implicit' in what we generally call a situation in which there is no life.
>
> David Bohm, *Wholeness and the*
> *Implicate Order* [p. 194]

concern themselves with ultimate questions about reality, as well as with the inner life and morality of human beings. Whereas science, in its study of its objects, looks *outward*, religion and philosophy look *inward;* their terrain is the human mind and spirit. We will examine these different modes further in the next chapter.

Even the most authoritative of the sciences, physics, finds itself unable to answer the ultimate question regarding matter: what is physical reality? That, as we said, is one reason why scientific materialism is a naive philosophy (we shall enlarge on the nature of physics in Part II).

Albert Einstein, in *Out of My Later Years,* wrote (1977, pp. 21-22) that the methodology of science does not permit it to provide "those convictions which are necessary and determinant for our conduct and judgements . . . [because it] can teach us nothing else beyond how facts are related to, and conditioned by, each other. . . . Objective knowledge provides us with powerful instruments for the achievements of certain ends, but the ultimate goal itself and the longing to reach it must come from another source. And it is hardly necessary to argue for the view that our existence and our activity acquire meaning only by the setting up of such a goal and of corresponding values."

In sum, if we want a reliable map of the world, we cannot look to empirical science alone or even primarily. I do not intend by this in the least to derogate science; I will in fact argue that it is a marvellous enterprise of the human intellect whose contributions are tremendously far-reaching. I think, for example, that Jacob Needleman makes an excellent point in his book *A Sense of the Cosmos* when he underlines the extraordinary way in which the new physics challenged our ability to understand the universe, the way it made us aware of what it is to *have* a new understanding. But as he also rightly said, physics itself does not *provide* that understanding. The fact is that empirical science is a limited form of knowledge. It can and does complement but cannot take the place of philosophical and spiritual modes of understanding. For a more comprehensive vision and for a degree of self-integration, we require the insights of our philosophical, mytho-poetical, religious, or mystical faculties. The findings of empirical science can supplement, and (indirectly) reinforce and enrich our understanding of ourselves and our universe, but the latter understanding is a function not of science's findings themselves but of what those findings suggest to our contemplative faculties.

Moreover, where empirical science undertakes to pronounce on ultimate questions—for example, the origin of life or the question Who is man? it usurps the roles of religion and philosophy and becomes not science but scientism, a perversion of science.[3] We will later show how this is so in specific cases.

Toward an Unfragmented Vision

The word "philosophy" literally means love of wisdom. Today's philosophy is, however, little concerned with wisdom as such. Academic or theoretical philosophy, as we have said, has not escaped the influence of its time; it has narrowed its range of concerns and its purpose.

Wisdom and theory are not synonymous, as all who accept such a thing as wisdom well know. Wisdom does not contravene reason, but transcends it, incorporating within it and uniting the polarities of existence. It is a state of consciousness characterized by harmony and peace. Lao Tse and the Buddha and Christ and other great Masters of Wisdom were far from being mere theoreticians. Their wisdom was

---

3. See Huston Smith (1977 and 1984); Schumacher (1978), and Wilber (1983), among other writers on the theme of reductionism versus the perennial philosophy.

above all experiential. It showed itself in what they *were*. They *demonstrated* truth in themselves.

We may well suppose that the schisms and dichotomies that beset us could only be healed by replacing the prevailing reductionist map by a truer, a more encompassing philosophy. After that thought comes another: the word "heal" is a verb: the requisite philosophy would constitute something more than abstract theories. It would be a wisdom, since wisdom, as just suggested, is not merely abstract but something that concretizes itself from the very structure of reality, and something that implies a way of life.

Truth and wisdom are not objects found in time and space; they are not measurable or quantifiable, yet they exist. Of their existence we possess ample supporting evidence of different sorts, for example, the many great works of the human imagination, and especially the many sublime passages found in sacred literature bearing upon the grandest of human concerns.

The Perennial Philosophy

Holistically minded people, including some scientists, refer increasingly today to "the perennial philosophy." Its perspective is more and more entering the stream of modern thought, something which naturally gladdens its proponents, of whom I am one. The particular name comes from Aldous Huxley's celebrated book, *The Perennial Philosophy* (first published in about 1945); Huxley borrowed the term from G. W. Leibnitz, the famous German philosopher and mathematician (1646-1716). In his book, Huxley attempted not so much to develop doctrines and principles as to present an overview of the esoteric or mystical tradition by means of a collection of marvellous extracts from sacred literature.

The main ideas and principles which are generally associated with the perennial philosophy, as I understand them, will be introduced shortly.

But why is it called "perennial" ? The reason, I believe, is this: the propositions and principles concerned have recurred down the ages, a phenomenon that becomes apparent when one undertakes a comparative study of religions and religious myths (cf. the writings of Joseph Campbell). Furthermore, scholars refer these ideas to a core wisdom tradition whose continuous existence down the ages is evident from the fact *inter alia* that every system of religio-philosophical thought

> The Hermetic chain of Greek mystical tradition, the Guru-parampara of the Hindu, the Apostolic Succession of the Christian, the Bodhisattva ladder of the Buddhist, all refer to the existence of a living tradition transmitted and communicated from teacher to disciple, teacher following teacher, in a never-ending chain the links of which are living men . . . "just men made perfect," "Masters of Wisdom and Compassion." The importance of the tradition lies less in who these teachers were or are than in what is transmitted—a wisdom that unifies all knowledge and gives purpose and direction to man's efforts to understand himself and the world in which he moves.
>
> Joy Mills, "Enduring Wisdom for a Changing World," *The Universal Flame* [p. 11]

has had its own term for it.[4] No one knows when and where the tradition began; it is immemorial, and every civilization in recorded history had the benefit of it—was leavened by it—to one or another degree; it represents humanity's priceless legacy.

Among other designations, perennial philosophy is today called also theosophy, esoteric philosophy, integral philosophy, and the primordial tradition (the last is Huston Smith's term; he prefers it precisely because we do not know the tradition's beginning).

What, then, *are* the recurring ideas of perennial philosophy? We shall try to develop them as we go along. But the principal themes are these: the oneness and unity of all life; the all-pervasiveness of ultimate Reality or the Absolute; the multi-dimensionality or hierarchical character of existence. It is postulated that the Absolute transcends all apparent separateness; it is indescribable, ineffable and unknowable. Though it lies beyond all thought, it is not remote, but resides within

---

4. "In the Hindu scriptures of the pre-Buddhist era it [the universal doctrine] is referred to as *brahma-vidya*, *atma-vidya*, and *gupta-vidya*, meaning, respectively, knowledge of the supreme, knowledge of self, and secret knowledge: also as *rahasya*, a word signifying mystery and bearing the same connotation as the mysterion of the Greeks, and the gnosis of Neoplatonism and the Gnostic schools. In Buddhism, it was and still is known under such terms as *aryajñana*, noble or exalted knowledge, and *bodhidharma*, wisdom-law or path" (de Prucker, 1974, footnote, p. 5).

the human heart, "closer than hands and feet." Thus Non-Being is the source of all being.

A paradoxical feature of the perennial philosophy is that it is perennial, a recurrent yet open-ended wisdom that develops commensurately with the evolution of human consciousness. For, as Lama Anagarika Govinda stated in another context, wisdom is not merely an intellectually formulated doctrine, proclaimed at a certain point in human history, but a movement which reveals its deepest nature in contact with different conditions and circumstances of human life and on ever new levels of human consciousness.

It will become evident that wholeness is the clue to this philosophy; that it is *nondualistic*. What is meant by nondualism will be explained shortly.

The theme of this book being wholeness, my task will be to show that all human modes of knowing and doing lead ultimately to a perception (albeit fragmentary) of shared truth and unbounded reality. Truth as we know it—even at best—is never more than partial. It therefore must give way in time to fresh formulations. Reality is still more elusive. For reality is *not*, as is so often thought, merely actuality since every actuality is ephemeral and must pass away in time. Reality must endure; it is the timeless, unchanging dimension in terms of which all evanescent phenomena and indeed all possibilities find their measure. Since the real can be felt but not described, all the great systems have traditionally referred to it in negatives—not this, not that—thereby acknowledging the impossibility of any description of that which is numinous, that which transcends knowledge and experience. But negation is not denial. And therefore we must begin by affirming that the search for wholeness is validated by its context—the impartible nature of Reality, whose ultimacy is the final test of all human experience.

The Perennial Consensus about Ultimate Reality

Comparative studies of major religions yield the insight that there is an essential consensus concerning ultimate Reality: the source-cause of the universe is infinite or boundless. The Absolute is variously called God or Godhead or *Allah* or *Parabrahm* or *Brahman* or That or the Void or *Tao* or *Ain Soph*, to mention some of its designations.

Common to this vast and ancient spectrum of thought is the further understanding that the source-cause is omnipresent and incognizable. Paradoxically, though unknowable, God or Allah or Brahman is ever-present, and as close and intimate as one's breath. As the biblical psalm (139) asks, "Whither shall I go from thy spirit? or, whither shall I flee from thy presence?"

What a striking fact, when you think about it, is this common yet uncommon understanding of all of humanity down the ages! It signifies— does it not?— that humanity is not bereft but, on the contrary, has long been and is still in possession of a profound insight concerning ultimate Reality. Contrary to today's prevailing relativism (the disbelief in the existence of truth) and historicism (the view that all thought is essentially related to and cannot transcend its own time), and notwithstanding the opposite trend which is also widespread, namely, religious fanaticism or fundamentalism (the claim of exclusive possession of truth), the different peoples, cultures and religious traditions have always shared one and the same Truth. For, as the ancient Rig Vedic verse states, "truth is one, learned men call it by different names."

To mention fanaticism is to remember the ironic fact that religions have been far more often the cause of dissension than of unity. This does not impugn the religions, any more than environmental pollution impugns nature. The fault lies not with the noble religions of humankind but with humankind's abuse of them.

The immemorial religio-philosophical conviction about the Absolute is, above all, significant in terms of the deepest meaning of unity. For what it implies is that all life ineluctably shares a common source in the Divine Reality. It signifies that each of *us* is rooted in that Reality and is therefore at core divine, "one and identical with the Oversoul of the universe," the Oversoul being "itself an aspect of the 'Unknown Root'," as H. P. Blavatsky was wont to put it. Emerson referred to it as that "Unity, that Oversoul, within which every man's particular being is contained and made one with all other." In Christian thought, at core we have our Christ-Nature; in Buddhism, our Buddha-Nature.

The fact is that the two closely interrelated teachings—concerning ultimate Reality not only in the universal sense but also in personal terms—are integral to the very definition of perennial philosophy, as Aldous Huxley (1970, p. vii) makes clear:

Philosophia perennis—the phrase was coined by Leibniz; but the thing—the metaphysic that recognizes a divine Reality substantial to the world of things and lives and minds; the psychology that finds in the soul something similar to, or even identical with, divine Reality; the ethic that places man's final end in the knowledge of the immanent and transcendent Ground of all being—the thing is immemorial and universal. Rudiments of the Perennial Philosophy may be found among the traditionary lore of primitive peoples in every region of the world, and in its fully developed forms it has a place in every one of the higher religions.

The Essence of Nondualism

The proposition that Reality is "the immanent and transcendent Ground of all being" is crucial to an understanding of nondualism, a term which is chosen in the Advaita philosophy of Sri Shankaracharya over "Oneness" since it connotes the truth that all the "pairs of opposites" which pervade the world (light and dark, good and bad, young and old) exist only in terms of each other. Moreover, the Reality wherein all the dualities are absorbed is not somewhere "out there" or "in heaven," apart from us "down here": we are, rather, *immersed* or *imbedded* in the divine Ground.

Since Reality is boundless, could it be otherwise? Could anything fall outside that which is infinite?

Stated more fully, this crucial proposition holds that ultimate Reality is impartible from the manifested world, the very "Suchness" or "Thatness" or ultimate condition of all phenomena which are indeed but its temporary presentiments. The all-pervasiveness yet transcendence of the Real is, in fact, what is meant by nondualism. Of this, Shankara said: "It is That by which the universe is pervaded, but which nothing pervades; which causes all things to shine, but which all things cannot make to shine." The Kabbalah (the mystical stream of Judaism) embraces a similar nondualism by virtue of *Ain Soph,* which literally means That without End, connoting the incognizable, boundless, transcendent and immanent Godhead.

It is further understood that although the Real shines alike through "the stone, the sinner and the saint," and "thrills through every atom and infinitesimal point of the whole Kosmos," it is not simply the sum of these parts. The phenomenal world is but a *partial* and *temporary expression* of the Absolute, whose boundlessness permits an infinity of universes that appear and disappear.

The idea of the Absolute is fundamental to philosophical think-ing. . . . Just as matter is the key notion of physics, life is the key notion of biology, mind is the key notion of psychology, God is the key notion of religion, so also the Absolute is the key notion of philosophy. . . . "The Absolute" essentially means that which is not related to anything outside of it. Whatever is related to an external entity is finite, relative and conditioned. The Absolute is infinite, all-comprehensive and unconditioned. . . . As all-comprehensive, the Absolute is essentially nondual. It embraces the one as well as the many. Therefore, it cannot be identified with either the one or the many. Some philosophers interpret the universe pluralistically, whereas some interpret it monistically. But both pluralism and monism presuppose the notion of the Absolute as the cosmic whole. . . . Phenomeno-logically, [the Absolute] is the unity of all phenomena. Theisti-cally interpreted, it is God, the creator of all phenomena. Pan-theistically, it is the underlying spiritual substance and ground of all phenomena. The idea of the Absolute is to be found in scientific thinking as well as in mystical testimony. Science envisages the Absolute as the vast space-time continuum . . . [or as] the unified field of energy.

Haridas Chaudhuri, *Being, Evolution and Immortality* [pp. 51-54]

The integral outlook . . . rejects dogmatism in all forms, whether scientific or metaphysical, religious or political. On the objective side it glimpses the mystery of Nature (*Prakrti*) beyond the scientifically revealed rational structure of the world. On the subjective side it glimpses the mystery of form-less consciousness or Spirit (*Purusa*) beyond the variegated levels and structures of the mind. Beyond both Nature and Spirit, beyond both the objective and the subjective, it envi-sions the supreme mystery of Being (*Brahman*) which is the ultimate ground of both.

Haridas Chaudhuri, *Being, Evolution and Immortality* [p.198]

Thus, nondualism never confuses the relationship between the ever-changing, phenomenal world, on the one hand, and the eternal, infinite, indefinable Reality, on the other. "The many-toned, on-going symphony of the universe" is billions of years old, yet it is but a moment in the presence of That from which all existence is insepara-bly derived.

A corollary of this tenet is tremendously important for the harmo-nization of the emergent global society: the Absolute transcends all religions, ideologies, and scientifically defined systems and philos-ophies, including, of course, statements purporting to represent the perennial philosophy itself. For—and we must underline this—*no statement, however perceptive, however profound, can comprehend final Truth;* no statement *about* Reality can be equated *with* Reality. This is why perennial philosophy must be understood as incomplete and open-ended, in need of reformulation by succeeding generations. Nondualism or perennial philosophy leaves no room for religious or ideological dogmatism.

H. P. Blavatsky, the co-founder of the theosophical movement, in her monumental treatise on perennial philosophy (which she called theosophy), *The Secret Doctrine* (first published in 1888), held that the diverse religions of the world when taken together represent more of truth than taken singly; that they are mutually complementary, but that even so they together fall short of ultimate Truth which embraces and transcends them all. (The world religions will be considered in Part III.)

Pitirim Sorokin, the noted sociologist, said that no ideology can represent an absolute value—whether it be capitalism or socialism or communism or collectivism or aristocracy or democracy or any other school of thought. This assertion made in the 1930s rings truer than ever today, in view of the current rethinking of the ideas of liberal-ism, socialism, communism, capitalism and other ideologies. Soro-kin was ahead of his time in perceiving that the nation-state and the usefulness of private property had outlived their period of greatest service to mankind.

The late philosopher Haridas Chaudhuri, in his expositions of what he called integral philosophy and integral yoga (building on the thought of the great Hindu sage Sri Aurobindo), similarly maintained that no ideology can hold good for all peoples and all times, and that a host of other ideologies, possibly incorporating some of earlier in-sights, might be devised in the future.

Philosophical understanding would reveal how an endless variety of ideologies can be reconciled in the non-dualistic structure of life. . . . Dualistic logic [equates] idea with reality, whereas nondualistic philosophy reveals the essence of reality as beyond the realm of ideas. Dualistic logic generates an exclusive, aggressive, and militant attitude, whereas nondualism produces an all-embracing, all-reconciling, peace-loving attitude. . . . An adequate comprehension of reality in its multi-form and multi-dimensional fullness can alone lay the foundation for an integrated scheme of human values.

Haridas Chaudhuri, *The Evolution of Integral Consciousness* [p. 101]

Uniqueness in time and expression is the preciousness of form. It is precious because it is transient as a flower which blossoms and wilts, but which nevertheless expresses the eternal character of all flowers and of all life. It is the preciousness of the moment, in which timeless eternity is present. It is the preciousness of individual form, in which the infinite is revealed.

Lama Anagarika Govinda, *Creative Meditation and Multi-Dimensional Consciousness* [p. 101]

What is especially appealing and significant, it seems to me, about the nondualistic perspective is that it can *conciliate and embrace all differences*—and do so *by affirming rather than eliminating multiplicity, variety and distinctions.* For nondualism validates multiplicity and diversity by virtue of its conception of ultimate Reality as an infinite continuum of potentiality. All forms are fundamentally precious, as Lama Govinda points out, because they are vehicles for the expression of universal Life.

The Unity of Opposites

By the same token, nondualism unites all contraries. Whereas modern theoretical philosophy sees dualities as fundamentally irreconcilable, nondualism sees the pairs of opposites as inseparable polarities. Because this insight into the nature of opposites is so significant in terms of self- and world-understanding, we need to consider it carefully.

Numerous pairs of opposites are a fact of existence; life is full of them. Think of joy and sorrow, good and evil, male and female, positive and negative, dark and light, above and below, within and without, subject and object, fact and theory, permanence and change, universal and particular, order and disorder, birth and death, freedom and necessity, the one and the many, God and the world.

Now the kind of logic espoused by Western theoretical philosophy is Aristotelian. It asserts that *A* cannot be *B* and *not B* at the same time. Dualities are irreconcilable if we stop at this logic; it has its place in analysis but not in synthesis. If we are to comprehend the fact that life is not a state of eternal conflict stemming from unresolvable differences, we must advance in our thinking from analysis (which takes things apart) to synthesis (which puts things together).

Seen from a nondualist perspective, opposites are inseparable polarities, mutually necessary and mutually defining. For example, the concept "light" has no meaning except in its contrast to "dark." We grasp the meaning of "up" against the meaning of "down." "Universal" attains meaning as the opposite of "particular." The concept of "freedom" is meaningless without the concept of "necessity" or "law." (In going to the moon, we achieved a new freedom but only because we discovered and applied the relevant natural laws. The laws, far from being an impediment to space travel, make such travel possible.)

To get a fuller idea of the nature and significance of polarities, recall the following facts. A magnetic field has both a positive and a negative pole; individual plants, animals and human beings issue from the conjoining of male and female sexual poles; a new ideology issues through the interaction of two older ideologies.

We see from these facts that the pairs of opposites are interactive and through their interaction *creative*, indeed *indispensable* for procreative and creative processes in nature and in man. And what they create by their union is a third term or entity which embraces both poles and which in turn creates its own opposing face.

All this is understandable intellectually. But of course the trick is to reconcile the polarities we experience in our life.

For example, is it possible for me to reconcile my particularity with my universality? The paradoxical position of perennial philos-

It is . . . necessary to develop a new kind of thinking, free from the dogmatism of our self-created laws which—though being useful and justified in a world of concrete objects and concepts—are not compatible with the laws of a universe that goes far beyond our sense-experience and thought-forms. [It is necessary] . . . to accommodate our thinking to the facts of the universe by trying to create a more all-inclusive basis for our thinking. . . . This can only be achieved by overcoming our one-dimensional logic which—while proceeding in a straight line towards any given object—cuts the world apart with the knife of its "Either-Or," in order to build from the lifeless pieces of a dissected world a merely conceptual and totally abstract universe.

> Lama Anagarika Govinda, *Creative Meditation and Multi- Dimensional Consciousness* [p. 230]

The complete human being, the man who has become whole (and therefore "holy"), is he who unites the universal with the individual, the uniqueness of the moment with the eternity of the cyclic recurrence of constellations and existential situations.

> Lama Anagarika Govinda, *Creative Meditation and Multi-Dimensional Consciousness* [p. 100]

ophy is that the more I, as a particular, unique being, can identify myself with other particular beings, the greater will be my personal fulfillment and self-realization. And I identify with others because we share something—that which is universal in us. Perennial philosophy holds that one feels unity with others when one feels harmonious within oneself, and vice versa. Therefore, the answer is yes! Unity within myself is achieved by integrating my particularity and my universality.

Thus I would be a human being first and foremost, not only a woman; the category of human transcends and embraces the male/female polarity. I would similarly transcend my other particularities. For example, I would perceive that the religion into which I was born is an interdependent part of the larger religious life of humanity, which itself points to the transcendent, indescribable Truth. (Part 3 will consider the proposition of the inner or transcendent unity of world religions.)

It will be obvious that this perspective has far-reaching implications for world understanding and world peace, at a time when we see a global society emerging on this planet.

On Consciousness

For mechanists, life and consciousness are epiphenomena (that is, derivatives) of matter. But for the perennial philosopher, consciousness is a primary datum. We shall see in Part 2 that many scientists are coming to the latter view. Some biologists, for instance, recognize and incorporate in their theories the ability of organisms as such to respond to change. Some neuroscientists have come to believe that the mind is the programmer of the brain. Some physicists, as we have mentioned, speak of the substance of the cosmos as "mind stuff."

When it comes to considering consciousness at the human level, the significantly unique feature is that a human being is not only conscious, but *self-conscious*. That is to say, the human mind can reflect upon its own thought, feelings and memories. These are the human attributes which go beyond the capacity of animals and whose advent made history and civilization possible. The very nature of evolution underwent a change as a concomitant of man's self-reflective mind: it is no longer biological but rather psycho-social and cultural. In man, as it has been said, evolution has produced an instrument whereby it became conscious of itself.

Consciousness cognizes objects but is itself no-thing. In Buddhistic terms it is *Sunyata,* Emptiness. In existentialist terms, it is Nothingness. In Vedanta it is indeterminable Being. Consciousness is something ultimate and indefinable. It is, like the Absolute, both intimate and a deep mystery.

On the Human Constitution

What a piece of work is man! How noble in reason! how infinite in faculty! . . . in apprehension how like a god!
                                        Shakespeare, *Hamlet*

The simple fact is that consciousness gives us no physical signals. . . . We have no way of identifying either the presence or the absence of consciousness. . . . [But further] the mind—consciousness—[cannot] be located. . . . [It] is not only not locatable, *it has no location.* It is not a *thing* in space and time, not measurable; hence . . . not assimilable as science. And yet it is not to be dismissed as an epiphenomenon: It is the foundation, the condition that makes science possible. The entire point of science is to bring ever deeper and subtler aspects of reality to recognition in our consciousness. That recognition is itself virtually an act of creation. What would it mean to assert that something exists for which we have no "evidence"? We encounter here the deep ambiguity between being and *being known.* Our consciousnesss is not alone the precondition for science, but for reality: What exists is what has become manifest to our consciousness.

George Wald, "The Cosmology of Life
and Mind," *Noetic Sciences,*
Spring 1989

[According to the materialistic image of man], consciousness is like an actively running program in the biocomputer; altered states are simply different programs. Various aspects of consciousness are merely subprograms of the larger program which is nothing but the totality of my biological, material self. The programs and subprograms may produce all sorts of outputs and experiences. Many of them are very useful to our pleasure and biological survival, but many of them are quite arbitrary or even nonsensical. To put it simply, the materialistic equation is: Mind equals Brain, and this is considered to be the complete story.

Charles T. Tart, Symposium on Consciousness and Survival,
Washington, D.C., October 1985.

There exist two vastly different conceptions of the human constitution. According to one, man is a being with infinite potential, a veritable god-in-the making. According to the other, man is merely an automaton with a bio-computer brain; no explanation is given as to who or what, if anything, programs the bio-computer.

We must ask ourselves: does our brain command our self or does our self command our brain?

In their book *The Self and Its Brain,* Sir K. R. Popper, eminent philosopher of science, and Sir John Eccles, one of the foremost brain specialists of this century,[5] propose that the self owns the brain and not the other way around. Eccles' conclusion is that man's mind is the executant and the brain is the instrument of the mind. He has elsewhere written that the activity of "selves" is the only genuine activity we know; that the psycho-physical self is the programmer of the brain, which is the computer. The self observes and takes action at the same time. It feels and suffers, recalls the past and plans and programs the future. It has a vivid consciousness of being a center of action (in Sloan, ed., 1984).

The idea that a human being is a computer is certainly at variance with self observation. For I in fact experience different states of consciousness at different times, including the sensory, emotional, mental, intuitive and the spiritual.

Imagine, for example, that on a particular day I undergo the following different experiences.[6] While at my desk at the office where I work, I experience my ordinary or everyday practical state of consciousness, as I methodically tick off the tasks of that day. On returning home from work, I find that my child appears suddenly to have taken very ill. I am seized with fear. I begin praying. This is a very different state of consciousness from the one that prevailed during the day. It then turns out that this was a false alarm—the child is perfectly all right. I am flooded with relief and with a feeling that life is very good—yet another state of consciousness. That evening my husband and I go dancing. At first this is nothing special—just dancing in our usual way. But suddenly, the two of us are dancing with extraordinary unity; in fact everything is melded into a unity— the music, the floor, the other people. It is a timeless interval when my whole being is focussed in the dancing in such a way that not only my husband and I but all things flow together. Later that evening, as my husband and I sit listening to music, I experience still another state of consciousness: I and the music become one; I am intensely *being* the music.

---

5. Adjectival phrases such as this may be a little tiresome but they are intended to reassure skeptical readers that holistic philosophy is not a crank school of thought but, on the contrary, includes scientists and others eminent in their field.

6. I here paraphrase an anecdote found in LeShan & Margenau (1982), pp. 9-11.

This anecdote, far from being unusual, is duplicated constantly; it shows that the proposition that man is nothing but his physico-chemical processes is an absurd aberration in human thought.

The world's different traditions are at one in regarding man as a multi-levelled or composite being. St. Paul spoke of man as consisting of body, soul and spirit. In Hindu thought, five different levels in man are distinguished. Other schools, notably theosophy, analyze human nature in terms of seven states of being, or of ten. Like any other subject of analysis, this one can be broken down into as much detail as one wishes.

Irrespective of the number of levels employed, all these systems, including psychology and psychosomatic medicine, understand that these different dimensions are interactive and that a person suffers when there is disharmony among them; that man, in other words, is a multi-levelled unity whose being needs wholeness.

It is clear to me that I cannot feel without thinking, that I cannot think without at least a modicum of feeling, and that when I experience a flash of intuition it occasions both thinking and feeling. It is also a matter of personal observation that I experience conflict when my heart and my mind pull me in two different directions, and that such a conflict impacts adversely on my physical body.

I also observe that my inner serenity often depends on my relations with others, and that inner balance and harmony affect those relations and vice versa. These personal observations in fact accord both with religious teachings and with the findings of psychology. One may even say that a person is *largely defined by his or her relationships,* including those with nature and with God or Reality.

Of course both religion and psychology deal with the laws or principles governing a person's relationships. Both in Eastern and Western thought, the fundamental psycho-spiritual principle here invoked is encapsulated in the phrase "we reap as we sow," or the principle called "karma" in Eastern parlance. Karma is however more than the basic law of *personal* morality: it is also the *cosmic principle* of balance and harmony. Thus karma *inter alia* correlates the cosmic with the human order, personal with societal morality, and morality with planetary affairs in all their dimensions. We shall discuss this most basic of laws at some length in chapter 15, and again in the final chapter.

According to the Bible, man is made in the image of God. According to the Qur'an, God breathed into man His Spirit. Again, the *Tao*

[Human] . . . relations enter into the essential structure of the individual self. Apart from relations to the social environment, the individual self is a mere abstraction. . . . He exists in close interdependence and interrelationship with his fellow beings. He grows through constant social intercourse with others. He belongs inseparably to a community and a country. He belongs in a larger perspective to the international human family. From a still broader standpoint, he belongs to the cosmic whole, to the entire universe. . . . Properly understood, it is not without purpose that individuals become differentiated from the creative universal and enter into all manner of relationships with one another. Part of that purpose is obviously the infinite diversification of the One. It is the self-imaging or self-representation of the One in the individualized Many. It is the growing manifestation of the creative joy of self-differentiation that throbs in the heart of reality. Individuals are increasingly differentiated in order to function as channels of expression of the unlimited glory of the infinite.

Haridas Chaudhuri, *Mastering the Problems of Living* [pp. 120-121]

Te Ching urges us to realize our Original Nature, while the ancient Delphic injunction was "Man, know Thyself."

Here, then, is another recurring or universal idea. We saw it earlier in Huxley's definition of perennial philosophy, in which he alluded to "the metaphysic . . . that finds in the soul something similar to, or even identical with, divine Reality; the ethic that places man's final end in the knowledge of the immanent and transcendent Ground of all being."

Another way this idea has often been formulated is that man is a microcosm of the macrocosm. That is to say, man and universe reflect each other; they are similarly constructed or embody the same principles; they are organically connected. Just as the universe is composed of a hierarchy of levels of being, so is man. Man is essentially one with the universe. In a still more subtle sense, the universe is man writ large. This oneness, as Lama Govinda (1976, p. 48) explains, "is not sameness or unqualified identity, but an organic relationship, in which differentiation and uniqueness of function are as important as that ultimate or basic unity."

From all this we may understand the import of the injunction, "Man, know Thyself." If human beings were but mechanically driven, reactive physical entities, this ancient injunction would hardly make sense. For that matter, neither would education nor civil and criminal law (that is, personal responsibility before the law), nor freedom, nor creativity. A machine, even one as sophisticated as a computer, has no responsbility for its actions.

Since we are a microcosm of the world, by understanding ourselves we may understand the world. Moreover, it is just our microcosmic nature that *permits or makes possible* such understanding. Thus, St. Thomas Aquinas said that it is because the objects we know are within us that we are able to know them. Conversely, and as

---

I have breathed into him [man] of My Spirit.

—Qur'ân, XV, 29

If you possess true knowledge [gnosis], O Soul, you will understand that you are akin to your Creator.

Hermes

Realize thy Simple Self,
Embrace thy Original Nature.
Tao Te Ching, XIX

[Self-consciousness reveals to man] the realm of boundless possibilities and makes him the master of his destiny. It bestows upon him the creative ability to refashion life and society into an image of his inner vision of truth and beauty and righteousness.

Haridas Chaudhuri, *Evolution of Integral Consciousness* [p. 42]

Ouspensky put it, in studying the world and its laws, a man studies himself. (In chapter 2, we shall enlarge on man's powers to know.)

Summary

In this chapter we have introduced some of the basic ideas of perennial philosophy—together with several corresponding scientific theories and facts. All of these suggest the wholeness of existence. The chapter is indeed intended to propose that wholeness pervades existence; that it is *the* key to self and world understanding.

The ideas and facts so far specifically introduced or implied may be summarized:

● Concerning ultimate Reality: All existence is rooted in, pervaded and transcended by the boundless, ineffable Oneness or Godhead or Reality or the Absolute.

● Concerning the universe: It issues from and is both pervaded and transcended by the ineffable Oneness. Thus the universe must be a unity. But it is also multi-dimensional, and so organized that each dimension or level of being produces the next, less inclusive level, from the most unitive to the most particular. The universe is thus a dynamic, living whole of which consciousness is the primary datum, and form but secondary.

● Concerning the physical cosmos studied by empirical science: Science does not claim to know what matter/energy ultimately is. But the relations among such ingredients of matter/energy as science has defined have proved amenable to accurate statement by advanced mathematics. Since matter/energy is thus open to reason, it must be fundamentally so ordered as to be compatible with mind and mental processes. Scientific observations have revealed facts that imply that all matter is basically the same in nature, independent of its position relative to the earth. Thus the universe is both consistent and lawful.

● Concerning man: Man is divine in his innermost nature.[7] He is a composite being embodying in potential the same levels of being and states of energy as the cosmos. It is this correspondence which enables man to understand the universe. By the same token, man's potentialities are limitless.

---

7. In case the use of the word "divine" in connection with humankind seems arrogant and irreligious, I should reiterate that the divine element in human nature is that spark which permits insight or response to the idea of the Good, the True, and the Beautiful within an imperfect world.

● Man is endowed with the power of choice and thus with responsibility and creativity. He reaps as he sows. Therefore, he can be the master of his own destiny. Individually and collectively we act both upon our correct and our incorrect or incomplete understanding of things, and our understanding and actions are, in turn, reflected in the world we ourselves thus create. In effect, we create our societal conditions and indeed our own reality.

● Concerning terrestrial life: Life is incipient in so-called inanimate matter and appeared when conditions were ripe. It is in fact difficult to draw a line between inanimate and living matter. Indeed, if the universe be understood as a living entity, there is no such thing as "dead" matter, and consciousness in some form is all-pervasive. Or, differently stated, matter, on the one hand, and consciousness or intelligence or responsiveness, on the other, are inseparable from one another. It is the presence of consciousness which permitted the successive emergence of qualities and powers in the course of evolution. The terrestrial continuum, spanning minerals, plants, animals, and humans, is a vast spectrum of consciousness. All life is interdependent and interpenetrating. Self-organization depends on relationships.

● Concerning order in the universe: The universe as a whole, terrestrial life, and man, in particular, are homologous in their hierarchical structure, wherein each dimension or state of being includes but transcends all "lower" or less inclusive levels or dimensions. Higher levels can explain lower levels but not vice versa.

● Concerning the individual and society: The two are dynamically linked together by and subject to one and the same cosmic law, the law of balance and harmony, which is also the law of morality whereby we reap as we sow.

● Concerning humanity: Rooted as we are in one source/cause, humanity is essentially a unity. By the same token, it shares one ineffable truth and the eternal values flowing from it. An esoteric wisdom tradition has immemorially leavened different civilizations and religions. It is notably evident in sacred scriptures. We need to tap it in the form of a philosophy of wholeness, one that integrates both spiritual and scientific principles, one that is both a way of thought and a way of life.

● Concerning the countless dualities of existence: The numerous pairs of opposites that abound are mutually defining polarities. They point beyond themselves to the all-embracing unity. They and all

> If we accept the idea of unity, not as an ideal but as a fact in
> nature, this obviously affects our entire life, and will determine
> our behavior for a long time to come. We have to ask ourselves:
> Is this a truth for me? Is it the highest truth? If so, what are the
> implications for my own life?
>
> Emily B. Sellon

other variations and differentiations are inseparably and dynamically
interwoven. At the same time, the different forms of being are each
significant in themselves, as varied expressions of the Absolute.

● Concerning avenues to understanding: In principle, religion,
science, and the humanities are harmonious and complementary and
point beyond themselves toward Reality, which is ineffable.

2

Our Powers of Knowing

Truth . . . is not the agreement of our apprehension of an external object with the object itself. It is the agreement of the mind with itself. Consciousness is therefore the whole basis of certainty. The mind is its own witness.

Plotinus

The nature of reality is congenial to powers which we possess.
William James

We can understand only as much of the world as we have developed and realized within ourselves.
Lama Anagarika Govinda

Some General Remarks

In this chapter we shall explore the capacity of a human being *to know,* given our composite nature as above described, that is to say, one comprising dimensions of consciousness grading from the most inclusive to the least inclusive; and a nature which corresponds to or parallels the structure of the cosmos or the macrocosm itself. Accordingly, we shall consider the modes of knowing, spanning the spectrum from the physical senses, through reason, to intuition and beyond.

The first thing to be said is that all knowing is, in the last analysis, *internal* or *subjective*—it takes place *interiorly.* In their downgrading of all "merely" subjective perceptions, materialist-mechanists do not realize what they are saying!

Secondly, knowing is *never passive.* Our mind is not just a mirror reflecting what is out there in the external world. Rather, knowing is an *act* and as such it is neither passive nor neutral nor "purely objective." Empirical science long claimed the ideal of pure objectivity. But, as we will see in Part II, there can be no such thing as *pure*

41

objectivity. Science has come upon the realization that it is not *possible* for observers to completely disengage themselves from the phenomena they are investigating or measuring. A figurative and creative element inevitably enters, to a smaller or greater degree, into our acts of observation.

What we know is not the thing-in-itself but our own experience of it. We see through a glass darkly, as it is said in the Bible. The glass is our set of beliefs, our personal prejudices, our culture, the prevailing scientific theories. And the image of reality we form is a self-fulfilling prophecy. Individually and collectively, we *create* our reality after our image of it. This is an old religio-philosophical insight which is gaining new currency today among philosophers of science.

While there is no such thing as *pure* objectivity or complete detachment, what we generally call knowledge is not merely fanciful or invented but meets criteria of validity, including tests by experiment or by such means as the matching of perceptions against each other for consistency, comparing our perceptions with those of others, establishing shared experiences and consensual findings.

As David Bohm points out, knowledge is comprised of disparate elements and is not static: it is a process. *Abstract knowledge* stored up in memory, in books, records, computers and so forth, is but one element of the total. There is also what Polanyi calls *tacit knowledge,* the knowledge of all sorts of skills, such as riding a bicycle. Other important ingredients of knowledge are our beliefs that can strongly motivate us, and the presuppositions beneath these beliefs, of which we are often unaware. Bohm draws a distinction between concrete and abstract knowledge, but stresses that the two cannot be separated in any permanent way: "Rather, there is a constant interplay of both, in which any particular content passes from one to the other and back. It is this interplay that gives effect to knowledge, and in it knowledge has its concrete existence as an actual living process. . . . In its actual concrete existence, knowledge is *an undivided whole in flowing movement,* an ongoing process, an inseparable part of our overall reality" (in Sloan, ed., 1984, p. 9).

Clearly, no consensual system or paradigm or model or image of reality can ever represent the last word of truth. Different individuals and communities and cultures hold different sets of beliefs and practices in terms of which they experience the universe. Sooner or later such a set of beliefs may be thrown into question by new data. We have experienced in our time a notable example: physics has had to

> Most of the time we have no idea that we are using "mental templates" to limit our experience and to cut it to fit our already entrenched views. . . . We ourselves have invested in these templates by our own action, committing our psychic energy to them, thus molding our personal substance to the given forms. Scientific theories, social relationships, basic notions of human nature, all seem to be subject to skepticism now that we know there are alternatives. . . . We never receive the totality of the universe but only that selection of (nevertheless genuine) communications which have been admitted by our particular psychic grid [the set of beliefs and practices in our culture in terms of which we experience the universe].
>
> Beatrice Bruteau, *The Psychic Grid:*
> *How we create the world we know*
> [pp. 48-49]

relinquish its Newtonian model of reality. As we shall see, physics has not up to now arrived at a consensus about a new model of physical reality; at present physics does not claim to know what physical reality is. Even so, physics must in fact be contacting reality in some way, since it is quite accurate in its predictions.

It is important to understand that to be in contact with reality is not the same thing as knowing what reality is. As we have already noted, Truth is infinite and therefore no model or picture or statement can be equated with it; there is no final truth. Yet human beings in their intense desire to be in contact with reality have always proposed philosophies, theories, and models of reality "whose function," in the phrase of Beatrice Bruteau (1979, p. 153), "is to organize and give intellectually and emotionally satisfying significance to our experience."

The Mode of the Five Senses

Even ordinary, everyday sense perception is necessarily relative or subjective, for a number of reasons. One is that the ranges of response of the human senses are peculiar to the human being. Humans are not visually sensitive to X-rays, for instance. If we were, a razor would look like a saw, and many objects which seem solid would appear porous. In point of fact, the human eye responds only to a very limited portion of the vast electromagnetic spectrum. Some other creatures' eyes can respond to a different or broader range than that open to humans. Again, our hearing is restricted to a relatively small portion of the broad range of acoustic waves. Obviously, the sharpness of a person's vision and other senses is also relative to the person's physical condition, a function in turn of other factors, notably of age.

In addition to the *physiological* variants, there are the variants of *interpretation* of sense data. For our mind not only registers the impressions of our senses (and, incidentally, we still do not understand the how's of this registration process) but also *interprets* what it registers, a process which is dependent upon the individual's memories, previous knowledge, selectivity in attending to the data registered, and so forth.

Given these variants, we cannot wonder that so-called factual accounts of one and the same event by different observers often diverge considerably.

The Rational Mode

Man is distinguished from other animals by his power of reason. (The word "man" is derived from the Sanskrit verbal root *man,* to think, to cogitate, to reflect.) Indeed, the advent of the power of reason was surely a watershed in the process of evolution. For, by virtue of reason, man can imagine beyond his experience, and conceive ethical, social, psychological, political and religious ideas and ideals as yet unrealized. Civilization becomes possible. The evolutionary process becomes psycho-social rather than biological.

Now, we may well conceive our thinking principle as being twofold in that it acts in a dual capacity—as synthetic or abstract mind, and as analytical or concrete mind. When directed "outward" it examines nature and accomplishes practical tasks, while when directed "inward" it is able to ponder intangibles such as infinity, as well as goodness, truth and beauty.

Humanity seems to have been developing the analytical mind for many millennia. Most people are relatively adept at its use in everyday or practical concerns, ranging from securing shelter and food to handling household gadgets, automobiles, and one's bill-paying (except that today whole populations of human beings are in an unprecedented situation wherein they are bereft of all *possibility* of providing themselves with shelter and food, let alone gadgets). On the other hand, because of faulty education far fewer people are today adept at philosophical thought or the use of abstractions.

Now, the powers of reason and logic are marvellous indeed, and confer on us the capacity for developing philosophy and science. Yet the powers of reason are not without limit.

When it comes to ontological questions such as truth, goodness, beauty, love, and compassion, reason has a limited if essential role. It can show us what these qualities are not, put them in context, discuss their attributes and effects, but it cannot make them realities in our lives. We do not love someone—for example, our child—because it is *reasonable* to do so. Love and compassion are *trans-rational*. So is beauty; it eludes and transcends all forms. *All* the higher values of existence are trans-rational. Then again, reason cannot conquer the irrational, which is impervious to logic. As the philosopher/scientist Raynor C. Johnson has written (1953, p. 24), reason "cannot fathom or understand the sources of inspiration or tell us how to produce a great statue, a poem, a concerto or a painting." He maintained that things such as goodness, unselfishness and self-sacrifice appear to have their source and find their justification at a level of our being deeper than reason.

Similarly, our ability to accept differences and to intuit/experience our unity with others beyond differences of race, creed, ideology, color and sex entails an awakening of a unitive faculty which lies beyond reason.

Trans-Rational Knowing

Let us then explore these higher levels—the trans-rational knowing exercised by a Beethoven or an Einstein, and more generally by the world's inventors, poets, artists and mystics. Some readers may be startled by the inclusion of such a figure as Einstein in a category labeled "trans-rational." On the other hand, in view of the just-discussed limitations of the power of reason, this may *not* seem surprising. We are not proposing, in any case, that reason could ever be dispensed with in the creative process. What *is* being asserted is

that higher faculties than reason necessarily *also* here come into play. These higher faculties have traditionally been identified as aesthetic intuition and spiritual perception.

Intuition is characterized by spontaneity and immediacy; in contrast with logical thought that builds up its argument step by step, each based on prior knowledge, the intuitive leap carries its creator directly into the unknown. Only after the leap do its links with past experience become clear. Thus it is a mode of knowing based upon unmediated, direct insight, and its consequences illumine personal knowledge and understanding. Thus many of the great scientific breakthroughs have come about through a sudden flash of intuition. Spiritual insight, on the other hand, is entirely impersonal, since it opens the human mind and heart to that which transcends personal being, and opens us to the One or the All—the Self of everything. "It is this principle which gives the illumined mind an identity as a spiritual consciousness, manifesting as understanding, judgement, and discrimination" (Slater, in Leslie-Smith, ed., 1975, p. 54).

Lama Govinda (1976, p. 233) says of trans-rational or intuitive knowledge, "It is the vision of a world-synthesis, the experience of cosmic consciousness where the Infinite is realized not only conceptually but actually." Thus it has *practical* consequences.

Mystics down the ages have testified to their spiritual experiences, in terms that are convincing and consistent.[1] They speak of becoming aware of an illumination or radiance which infuses everything "without" though it comes from "within." There comes a sense of belonging to a new and greater unity; the visible world is seen as part of a larger whole. The experience includes a pulsing light, livingness, joy, peace, happy wonder. "Through . . . [such feelings], and interwoven, is an enormously enhanced sense of the supreme values, and the most adequate description usually seems to the experiencer to be a 'revelation of God'. The mystic finds that words are inadequate to express the experience, and the terms used seem no more than symbols and analogies" (Johnson, 1954, pp. 324-325).

The experiences of unity apparently vary in depth, ranging from an intimacy to a complete identification of knower and known. The latter is the "mystical union," the ultimate state of consciousness

---

1. Incidentally, the term "mystical" is not a synonym of "mysterious." Nor should mysticism be confused, as it often is, with psychism, mediumship and out-of-body experiences.

alluded to in all the world traditions, East and West, and variously designated as Liberation, *turiya, bodhi, moksha, satori, sunyata, nirvana*, etc. In alluding to this state of consciousness, Jesus put it thus: "I and My Father are one," and, again, "Ye shall know that I am in my Father, and ye in me, and I in you." Analogous Hindu expressions are "That art Thou," and "Atman [Spirit] is Brahman."

In the Mandukya Upanishad of the Hindu scriptures, it is stated concerning *turiya* that it is a fourth state of consciousness beyond those we know: "It is not the knowledge of the senses, nor is it relative knowledge, nor yet inferential knowledge. Beyond the senses, beyond the understanding, beyond all expression is *turiya* (the fourth state of consciousness)" (Ravindra, 1984, p. 63).

How extraordinarily sophisticated is this ancient statement! The writer obviously had a knowledge spanning what we would today call epistemology (the science of knowing) and ontology (the science of being). Is such a statement not a potent reminder that the perennial philosophy is indeed *immemorial?* Whence did it issue? But, then, whence did the whole marvellous, terrestrial schematic process issue? The scheme/process obviously antedated its inception!

The experience of mystical union transcends all "normal" categories of thought—categories such as substance and attribute, knower and known, cause and effect, one and many. It can apparently only be described by such words as "ineffable," "unutterable," "nameless," "the Void," "the Abyss," "the unknowing." The Buddha maintained "a noble silence" concerning *Nirvana*. Lao-Tzu declared only that the *Tao* (the ultimate Principle of everything) one speaks about is not the real *Tao*. St. John of the Cross referred to the state of "unknowing" as follows (in Barnstone, tr., 1972, poem entitled "I Came into the Unknown"):

> I came into the unknown
> and stayed there unknowing,
> rising beyond all science.
>
> I was so far inside
> so dazed and far away
> my senses were released
> from feelings of my own.
> My mind had found a surer way:
> a knowledge by unknowing
> rising beyond all science.

This knowledge by unknowing
is such a soaring force
that scholars argue long
but never leave the ground.
Their knowledge always fails the source:
to understand unknowing,
rising beyond all science.

Mystical Experience as the Raw Material of Religion, Philosophy and Art

Mystical perception, to repeat, is direct, unmediated. The mystic experiences God or Goodness or Love both in their essence and in their fullness. These are ineffable intimations, beyond time and space, space-time that "authenticate themselves only in direct experience." They are not, "so far as we can see, symbols or shadows of a reality lying behind themselves on a still higher level of significance. They mediate to us directly, not indirectly, the nature of Reality" (Johnson, 1954, p. 345). But of course to express or to communicate these insights the mystic must of necessity recur to some medium of communication, whether it be poetic image or the symbolic language of art.

A mystical *theologian* will translate such experiences into religious dogma. As F. C. Happold (1970, p. 345) wrote,

> The dogmas of religion are the translation into the terms of the intellect, or into evocative symbols, or into a combination of both, of insights which have their origin in mystical intuition. Without such insights there would be nothing to dogmatize about.

Again, a mystical philosopher such as Plotinus will communicate mystical insights through discourses upon beauty, love, compassion and wisdom. Or the expression will be poetic, as when William Blake wrote of seeing the world in a grain of sand.

The point is that mystical insight is the raw "stuff" of which the great religious traditions are made, and intuition is, so to speak, its handmaiden: offering man the possibility of seeing more deeply into the truth of the more profound strands of religious, philosophical and artistic expression than reason may allow.

Concerning the nature of knowledge, Plotinus, the Alexandrian philosopher of the third century of our era, wrote in his letters to Flaccus:

> Knowledge has three degrees—opinion, science, illumination. The means or instrument of the first is sense; of the second, dialectic; of the third, intuition. To the last I subordinate reason. It is absolute knowledge founded on the identity of the mind knowing with the object known.

The Nature of Statements about Reality

Trying to share their perceptions with others, mystics have struggled to compress their vision of the whole or the Good into some kind of verbal statement. Such statements, however, have to conform to the nature of language, which is limited by its logic, i.e., its *form*. They cannot be equated, as already pointed out, with the *formless* perception itself. No matter how profound or evocative or affecting, their words are only statements *about* Reality, not Reality itself. When Meister Eckhart reputedly exclaimed, "Whatever thou sayest of God is untrue," he was not demeaning theological statements. He meant that no statement could comprehend the unfathomable truth of Reality Itself.·

Chaudhuri has well written, ". . . after everything has been said about the universe, after the entire world has been transformed on the basis of scientific knowledge into a hierarchical structure of ever-widening systems, we are still left with a profound sense of mystery" (1974, p. 195).

At each step in the evolution of our consciousness, our understanding widens and deepens, yet this very widening and deepening causes the horizon to recede. Knowledge is always open-ended, never final.

On the Interrelationship of the Modes of Knowing

The different levels of knowledge, such as the physical, the rational, and the mystical, are intimately interrelated. Today, given the neglect of the higher values, this intimate interrelationship tends to be lost from view. We witness instead the shallowness of most contemporary thought, and the lack of communication between the sciences and the humanities, which would fructify both.

In place of "tunnel vision," in place of relativism, it would be well for our society to reclaim the higher values, for it would be tanta-mount to reclaiming ourselves. In fact they properly have a place in every domain of thought, including science, religion, the humanities, and world affairs. In fact, in doing science, scientists, especially the more creative ones, often draw upon their intuition and even their aesthetic sensibilities, a point to which we will return in Part II.

Close is the relationship between the higher reason, as exemplified by philosophical thought, and intuitive and mystical perception. Just what is this relationship? St. Thomas Aquinas defined its nature thus: Intuition and reason "are not two powers, but distinct as the perfect from the imperfect. . . . The [intuition] means an intimate penetra-tion of truth; the reason, inquiry and discourse" (in Huxley, 1970, p. 133). Reason formulates inspiration and insight in language, so that they may be put to use, but the inspirations themselves come from higher levels than reason—from spiritual perception, via the intuition.

Jacob Needleman (1982) suggests that authentic philosophy (and also myth and religious ideals and certain kinds of art) influences and supports the inner morality. But while supporting this condition, philosophy, he believes, cannot itself directly create it. Instead, the direct cause of inner morality is *the desire for truth and being.* Philosophy speaks directly to this yearning and supports it. Where the yearning is absent or buried under egoistic habits and thoughts, philosophy or ideas are of no avail. "Ideas do not have energy. People do. The heart of philosophy is in myself" (pp. 232-4).

Haridas Chaudhuri (1974) stresses that the meaning of an impor-tant philosophical truth cannot be fully grasped at once. "After hear-ing it, your attempt will be just to understand it in whatever measure that you can . . . the more you meditate on it, the more the inner significance will come out for you. . . . As you meditate on it, the idea which was more or less clearly understood on the mental level becomes transformed into a living, flaming experience of the truth, a direct vision of the truth . . . born of your personal experience" (p. 92).

In sum, reason and intuition are mutually supportive and work hand in hand. Reason can help activate intuition. Intuition completes, perfects, or fulfills reason. Moreover, intuition comprehends reason but is not reducible to it: intuition transcends reason.

A similar relationship obtains between the physical senses and reason. The two are interactive. Sensory percepts need reason to

Although there is in every one of the lower states of consciousness something present which leads or points towards the next stage, it is impossible to solve problems belonging to a higher dimension of consciousness from the point of view of a lower level of consciousness. This is why scientific problems cannot be solved from an egocentrically conditioned emotional point of view, or metaphysical problems or those of modern atomic or astro-physics lying beyond the realm of the finite by using the laws of the world of three-dimensional experience or by a limited logic derived from it. . . . In this way each plane has its own laws and its own problems, and the methods helpful toward a solution in one case become a hindrance in another.

Lama Anagarika Govinda, *Creative Meditation and Multi-Dimensional Consciousness* [pp. 233-234]

In A.D. 535, the Christian monk Cosmas wrote a book called *Christian Topography.* Based entirely upon a literal reading of the Bible, Cosmas demonstrated once and for all that the earth had neither North nor South Pole, but was a flat parallelogram whose length is double its width. Dogmatic theology abounds with that type of howling error—and that is true of both Eastern and Western religions. The Hindus and Buddhists . . . believed that the earth, because it must be supported, was sitting on an elephant which, because it must also be supported, was sitting on a turtle (and to the question, "Upon what, then, rests the turtle," the answer was given, "Let us now change the subject."

Ken Wilber, *Eye to Eye* [p. 11]

furnish the context by means of which they can be understood. Thus reason comprehends but transcends the physical consciousness. In other words, these three faculties, sense perception, reason and intuition—the "three eyes of the soul," as one Western mystic called them—bear a hierarchical relationship to one another. Each has its proper role which cannot be fulfilled by either of the other two faculties. We must go further and say that when one eye tries to fulfill the role of another, it "commits a fallacy," to use Ken Wilber's phrase.

In philosophy, this fallacy is called a "category error." When fundamentalists read the Six Days of Creation to mean six literal days instead of six different phases in the evolution of the universe, they mistake a metaphor for a fact. Conversely, empirical science is wholly inadequate to the task of defining ultimate questions such as the origin of existence, of life and of consciousness.

Many category errors have been committed in religion, philosophy and science alike, with consequent conflicts among these domains which, in principle, are mutually compatible and complementary.

Now, it was earlier remarked that the average Western human being has developed more skill in the use of the concrete analytic mind than in the use of the abstract mind and the intuitions. At the same time, I would suggest that all the different levels, physical through spiritual, come into play, in *some* degree, in most of us. We are all in some sense scientists, philosophers and mystics.

We are scientists when we try to discover how something works—for example, some gadget, or our body, or the tax system. As the physicist/philosopher Henry Margenau remarked, "Common sense, if it has any meaning at all, is the method of science applied to everyday life." We are philosophical when we ponder, as we all do at times, some personal or societal problem of existence. We are mystical whenever we suddenly experience the transcendent unity—whether it be with others or with nature (or with beauty or truth met in any form).

We must not suppose for a moment that the powers of ordinary knowing are of minor importance. On the contrary, at the present stage of human development, it is essential to think clearly, logically and analytically. We need to improve our problem-solving abilities, seeking solutions based on knowledge and experience. But even more do we need creative innovation and creative imagination to deal with the intractable problems we ourselves have made.

To awaken or to develop one's higher faculties is inevitably to contact deeper or truer or more comprehensive levels of reality. Paradoxically, by going deeper into the particular well of self, a person reaches the universal, subterranean stream (to borrow Ira Progoff's metaphor). Again, a person flowers as an individual the more he or she transcends narrow egotism. In short, in being ourselves, we are more than ourselves!

Let us go one step further and affirm that *being and becoming are one.* As Huston Smith has written, "Knowing and doing, wisdom and method, work together; they walk hand in hand. Close from the start, they draw increasingly so, to the point where it becomes difficult to tell them apart" (1984, p. 56).

II
Science

Instead of being a product, mind may be the creator of the physical world.

Erich Jantsch, *The Self-Organizing Universe*

We have good reason to believe that we find ourselves in a universe permeated with life.

George Wald, Nobel Laureate

3

Modern Science:
The First Four Hundred Years

The Rise of Modern Science

The rise of modern science, as everyone agrees, was a great watershed in history. In *Science and the Modern World*, published originally in 1925, Alfred North Whitehead (1967) adjudged the event "the most intimate change of outlook which the human race had yet encountered," an occurrence which "recoloured our mentality so that modes of thought which in former times were exceptional are now broadly spread throughout the educated world (p. 2).

Today, only seventy-odd years later, even this strong claim for science seems an understatement. For it becomes ever clearer that science, directly and indirectly, impacts upon every department of our existence, that it is indeed an incalculably far-reaching force.

Physics originated the mechanistic model of reality and, some four centuries later, refuted it. But mechanism had meanwhile been embraced by all the other sciences. Entrenched ideas die hard, as we know; and although proven invalid, mechanism—or "rational" materialism— still holds sway in mainstream thought. This is unfortunate because, as we earlier argued, it is a very harmful outlook. But science itself promises to remedy this state of affairs. For, at the leading edges of many sciences—from biology to economics, from neuroscience to evolutionary theory—a radically different orientation is rapidly evolving.

Science, through the technology it made possible, has meanwhile radically transformed the material, social, environmental and other basic conditions of life on earth, in beneficial and adverse ways. A major—indeed, the overarching—consequence of this is the unprecedented global interdependence of nations and peoples.

We shall argue that this potent new factor, on the one hand, and science's revelations concerning the cosmos, terrestrial life and human nature, on the other, interact dynamically, and are together bound to deepen and expand human consciousness.

Science arose in Europe in the sixteenth century. It was a time, as Whitehead remarks, which also saw the disruption of Western Christianity, "an age of ferment, a time when nothing was settled, though much opened—new worlds and new ideas" (Whitehead, 1961, p. 1). The rise of science was, in retrospect, part of the historical revolt of the later Renaissance against the inflexibility of medieval thought.

Nature had hitherto been studied in theological terms. That is to say, the emphasis was on theological reasons *why* things happen. (The inefficacy of this approach, one may interject, became particularly and tragically evident when the Black Plague broke out and annihilated a large portion of Europe's population. Here, by the way, is a classical example of dire category error!) In contrast, the new focus was on observed facts as opposed to reasoned opinion.

Whitehead defines the new mentality as "a vehement and passionate interest in the relation of general principles to irreducible and stubborn facts" (p. 3). Until then, there had at all times been individuals absorbed in facts and individuals interested in the weaving of general principles, but never before the union of these two interests.

Another unique feature of the scientific movement was its universality; modern science was born in Europe, but the whole world became its home. In some ways, its impact on Asian civilization was tangential, yet overall it was a gift of the West to the East.

At the same time, the scientific movement built on certain legacies of medievalism and earlier thought—notably Greek and Roman. It benefitted, for example, by the medievalists' sense of order—something they had inherited from Roman Law, in turn traceable back to the Greek Stoics—and by their long-inculcated habit, emulating Aristotle, of orderly or logical thought.

Furthermore, notwithstanding its own anti-rationalism, the scientific movement retained the long-ingrained belief in the rationality of God. Whitehead considered this to be the greatest contribution of medievalism to the scientific movement: since God supervised and ordered every detail of life, the search into nature could only result in the vindication of the faith in rationality. In other words, the faith in

> Geniuses such as Aristotle, or Archimedes, or Roger Bacon must have been endowed with the full scientific mentality, which instinctively holds that all things great and small are conceivable as exemplifications of general principles which reign throughout the natural order. But until the close of the Middle Ages the general educated public did not feel that intimate conviction, and that detailed interest, in such an idea. . . . Why did the pace suddenly quicken in the sixteenth and seventeenth centuries? At the close of the Middle Ages a new mentality discloses itself. Invention stimulated thought, thought quickened physical speculation, Greek manuscripts disclosed what the ancients had discovered. Finally although in the year 1500 Europe knew less than Archimedes who died in the year 212 B.C., yet in the year 1700, Newton's *Principia* had been written and the world was well started on the modern epoch.
>
> Alfred North Whitehead, *Science and the Modern World [pp. 5-6]*

the *possibility* of modern science was an unconscious derivative from medieval theology.

There were also some weaknesses in the scientific movement right from its inception. In focusing on empirical facts and events, science tended to ignore their context. While an event "is a matter of fact which by reason of its limitation is a value for itself," it nevertheless "by reason of its very nature . . . also requires the whole universe in order to be itself" (Whitehead, 1967, p. 194). But Whitehead stressed that the historical revolt was "fully justified." "It was wanted. It was more than wanted: it was an absolute necessity for healthy progress. The world required centuries of contemplation of irreducible and stubborn facts" (p. 16). (As we shall soon see, the situation *now* is such that facts and theories in science are difficult if not impossible to separate from each other).

Scholasticism had reigned supreme from the twelfth to the fifteenth centuries, but now nature began to be studied not in *theological terms* nor by deduction from theological dogma, but in *mathematical terms*. It was a change that would spell the end of Scholastic dogma.

Whitehead goes on to describe the extraordinary development of

> It . . . [is] clear that although Roger Bacon's suggestion of experience and experiment as a means of criticizing ideas that appear to be reasonable was an important contribution to making modern science possible, it was not enough to prevent the block inherent in the active functioning of common knowledge from imprisoning us in fixed beliefs and false presuppositions. These are generally unyielding, even in the face of a great deal of experimental evidence. . . . What is needed further is the energy of insight, which dissolves such blocks. This has to be emphasized very strongly, as there is now little realization of the ultimate inability of the scientific approach to avoid the tendency to self-deception inherent in the active functioning of knowledge, if this is not penetrated by insight.
>
> David Bohm, "Insight, Knowledge,
> Science, and Human Values" [in
> Sloan, ed., 1954, p. 15]

mathematics that went hand in hand with this turn of events. (He himself, as we know, was one of the great mathematicians of his time.) Thus algebraic analysis arose concurrently with Descartes' discovery of analytical geometry and with the invention of the infinitesimal calculus by Newton and Leibnitz. "Apart from this progress of mathematics, the seventeenth century developments of science would have been impossible. Mathematics supplied the background of imaginative thought with which the men of science approached the observation of nature. Galileo produced formulae, Descartes produced formulae, Huyghens produced formulae, Newton produced formulae" (p. 31).

The dependence of science upon abstract mathematics was for instance illustrated in the notion of periodicity. "In the sixteenth and seventeenth centuries, the theory of periodicity took a fundamental place in science. Kepler divined a law connecting the major axes of the planetary orbits with the periods in which the planets respectively described their orbits; Galileo observed the periodic vibrations of pendulums; Newton explained sound as being due to the disturbance of air by the passage through it of periodic waves of condensation and rarefaction; Huyghens explained light as being due to the transverse waves of vibration of subtle ether. . . . The birth of modern physics depended upon the application of the abstract idea of periodicity to a variety of concrete instances. But this would have been impossible, unless mathematicians had already worked out in the abstract the various abstract ideas [concerned]" (Whitehead, 1967, p. 31).

Arthur Koestler, in *The Sleepwalkers* (1978), describes how the fathers of the scientific revolution, all devout men, managed the ticklish transition from reliance upon God to reliance upon mathematics. Koestler profiles this group of men. There was Johannes Kepler (1571-1630), the German astronomer and mathematician, who was the father of modern astronomy—"a mind to whom all ultimate reality, the essence of religion, of truth and beauty, was contained in the language of numbers" (p. 225). Secondly, there was Galileo Galilei (1564-1642), Italian astronomer, mathematician and physicist, founder of the modern science of dynamics, which complemented Kepler's laws of astronomy and provided the basis for Isaac Newton's monumental synthesis of seemingly disparate scientific findings. And thirdly, there was René Descartes (1596-1650), French philosopher, brilliant mathematician and scientist, a bold thinker "who promised to reconstruct the whole universe from matter and extension alone, [and] who invented the most beautiful tool of mathematical reasoning, analytical geometry" (p. 501). (Descartes was the initiator of what came to be called Cartesian dualism—the incommensurability of mind and matter, of body and mind, and of the observer and the observed, which has dominated—and bedevilled— philosophical and scientific thought up to our time.)

As already indicated, these men, the fathers of the scientific revolution, were all devout. Yet together they managed gradually to liberate science from reliance on God. They went further: they eliminated all qualitative values, and successfully concentrated scientific attention on measurement and quantitative analysis. Koestler recounts the progressive steps whereby this feat was accomplished.

First Kepler began to impute to geometry the role of model for the Creator and to regard "quantities" as the "archetypes" of the world. Next Galileo suggested that "the book of nature is written in the mathematical language," a language which was indispensable for the comprehension of even a single word of this book. Moreover, Galileo's chief mathematician is called Nature, not God, "and his references to the latter sound like lip-service." Koestler continues: "Galileo takes the hyperstatization of mathematics a decisive step further by reducing all nature to size, figure, number and slow and rapid motion, and by relegating into the limbo of 'subjective' and 'secondary' qualities everything that cannot be reduced to these elements" (Koestler, 1978, p. 525).

René Descartes took the next step by further reducing primary qualities to "extension" and "motion," which for him formed the material realm—the realm he termed *res extensa.* Descartes held that not only plants and animals but the human body itself were machines. But since he was a religious man, he had to find place for the rational soul. Thus he called it *res cogitans* and housed it in the pineal gland in the center of the brain. For Descartes *res extensa* (body) and *res cogitans* (mind) both came from God, but otherwise had no connection or interaction with each other. They were two entirely separate realities. [1]

Last but far from least came the input of Isaac Newton, the English mathematician, natural philosopher and founder of pre-twentieth-century physics. Newton, one of the greatest scientific geniuses history has ever known, completely changed the scientific picture of the world. Up to the seventeenth century its vision was Aristotelian, after that Newtonian.

In the 1660s when Newton began his work as a young man, he was confronted by a "scattered cosmological jigsaw puzzle" wherein key pieces provided by Kepler and Galileo did not fit together at all. And the pieces provided by Descartes made the confusion even worse.

> There was . . . complete disagreement (a) on the nature of the force which drives the planets around and keeps them in their orbits, and (b) on the question what a body in the vastness of space would do with itself if it were left alone, that is, without external agents acting on it. These questions were inextricably mixed up with the problem of what "weight" really meant, with the mysterious phenomenon of magnetism, and with the perplexities of the emergent concepts of physical "forces" and "energies" (Koestler, 1978, p. 498).

Newton marvelously succeeded in putting the bits and pieces together.

---

1. While Descartes did initiate the mind-matter dichotomy which has plagued us ever since, the error is often made of designating him as the originator of radical materialism—of the view that mind is reducible to matter. Descartes held no such view.

> What he achieved was rather like an explosion in reverse. . . . New-
> ton found fragments and made them fly together into a simple, seam-
> less, compact body, so simple that it appears as self-evident, so com-
> pact that any grammar-schoolboy can handle it (p. 497).

Newton grasped the underlying analogies between sets of utterly
diverse physical phenomena and, with the aid of mathematics, a tool
partly created by himself, he succeeded in analyzing these phenomena *and relating them to each other.* His extraordinary ability to see
into the order of nature explains, in retrospect, the tremendous impact
Newtonian science has had upon the world.

Newton's *Philosophiae Naturalis Principia Mathematica* was published in 1687 and remains in print to this day. In it he introduced the
method on which natural science has been based ever since, a method
which utilizes both induction from facts and deduction from principles, since he emphasized that neither experiments without systematic interpretation nor deduction without experimentation could produce reliable theory. Both were indispensable (Capra, 1983, p. 64).

Mechanism in the Eighteenth and Nineteenth Centuries

To continue our historical sketch,[2] Newtonian mechanical theory
achieved tremendous successes in the eighteenth and nineteenth centuries. It was able to explain the motion of the planets, moons, and
comets, the flow of the tides and various other phenomena related to
gravity. It was also applied to the study of gases and to the atomic
theory of chemistry, which paved the way to the conceptual unification of physics and chemistry in the twentieth century.

In the eighteenth century the mechanistic worldview had become
so well established that physics began to influence other sciences,
including those of human nature and human society.

During the nineteenth century the mechanistic orientation took
further root—in physics, chemistry, biology, psychology, and the
social sciences. "As a result, the Newtonian world machine became a
much more complex and subtle structure. At the same time, new
discoveries and new ways of thinking made the limitations of the
Newtonian model apparent and prepared the way for the scientific
revolutions of the twentieth century" (Capra, 1983, p. 70).

The medievalists had perceived a living world, a world bespeaking

---

2. We can thank Fritjof Capra, *The Turning Point,* 1983, and other accounts.

purposive harmony. Now, in contrast, nature came to be viewed, in the phrase of Whitehead (Whitehead, 1967, p. 17), as irreducible, brute matter, in itself senseless, valueless, purposeless material which "just does what it does do, following a fixed routine imposed by external relations which do not spring from the nature of its being." The universe came to be seen as a dead machine, a wound-up clockwork ticking away in a predictable manner. Human beings were cogs in this immense machine, and equally predetermined.

The machine model of the physical universe was eventually (early in the twentieth century) refuted by physics itself. But meanwhile the mechanistic worldview had permeated the other sciences, and colored the public outlook on every human concern. Though scientifically untenable, it is still deeply ingrained. Even today, when so many scientific findings support the suggestion that the physical world is more like an organism or, alternatively, like a thought, than like a machine, mechanism is still entrenched, especially in the life sciences, which by and large look upon organisms as molecular machines.

Yet machines cannot change, grow or evolve. If human beings are so conceived, their case is hopeless. For their fate in a universe destined to run down and extinguish itself leaves them no options.

This worldview and its concomitant image of ourselves, then, is unwholesome to say the very least. It fosters, among other things, an alienation from self, from others, and from nature.

Mechanist reductionism, by its nature, cannot communicate with the humanities and religion. As long as it continues to reign, the noncommunication between "the two cultures" will continue and so will the decline in our societal/planetary affairs.

From its inception, the reductionist view of man was vehemently repudiated as grossly untrue and offensive by poets, artists and the like, as well as by many philosophers, and it gave rise to the famous determinism/free-will controversy in theoretical philosophy, a controversy which remains unresolved to this day. Nor, I believe, could theoretical or dualist philosophy ever resolve it. It could only be resolved, as I have argued elsewhere, in a nondualist context wherein it is understood that it is up to individuals progressively to win a measure of inner freedom by obeying inner or moral law—the understanding, to put it otherwise, that freedom and necessity are a mutually-defining polarity.

The first cracks appeared in the mechanistic edifice of physics during the latter part of the nineteenth century. These were at first discounted as very minor. The prevailing mood was one of great optimism and confidence that physics already knew most of what there was to know about the universe—that only a few details remained to be worked out. Soon, however, the anomalies became more numerous, not only in physics but also in biology and other disciplines.

An early snag was the discovery by Faraday and Maxwell, in course of their investigation of electric and magnetic phenomena, of a new type of force which could not appropriately be described by the mechanistic model. They were in the end compelled to replace the concept of a force with the much subtler concept of a force field, a solution which in fact exceeded the Newtonian framework.

One of the anomalies which put the machine theory of organic life in question was Darwin's evolutionary theory. Although the principle of natural selection was mechanistic in that it posited development through small random changes, evolution introduced so many controversial ideas about organic life that it opened up thousands of problematic areas still under investigation. For the important questions raised by evolution are far from answered. Subsequently, the contradiction was compounded when physics formulated the concept of entropy and the second law of thermodynamics. Whereas evolutionary theory said that organic development was in the direction of increasing *order* and *complexity,* thermodynamics proposed that the world was running toward increasing *disorder* and an ultimate grinding halt. Thus the second law of thermodynamics began to come into question.

Physics Reluctantly Refutes Mechanism

What had at first appeared as "small clouds" on physics' horizon quickly turned into a maelstrom, as one disorienting development came upon the heels of another. Within less than thirty years after the turn of the century, the most authentic and most emulated of modern exact sciences had unravelled the basic fabric of its conceptions and found itself forced to relinquish all of its certainties about physical reality. Here in brief are the dramatic events.

One of the "small clouds" was the inexplicable way in which hot bodies behaved: they glowed and changed color. Max Planck was investigating this problem when, to his dismay, he discovered that energy is emitted and absorbed not continuously, as hitherto assumed, and as the mechanical model required, but in chunks or packets—later to be called "quanta" (from which the name "quantum physics" derives) and still later specifically termed "photons."

Then one after another of the several brilliant investigators figuring in this drama—scientists who were continuously aware of each other's findings and built on each other's work—got results that were fundamentally at odds with classical physics. The scientists concerned at one or another time over the period at issue were Einstein, Planck, Bohr, de Broglie, Schroedinger, Pauli, Heisenberg, and Dirac. In thirty short years they involuntarily disproved the whole conceptual framework of the Cartesian-Newtonian model of reality: namely, absolute space and absolute time, the basic building blocks of matter, radical or determinist causality, and the notion of strict separability of observer and observed.

They could find no way of interpreting their findings in a manner which permitted them to save the mechanical model. In the end, they bowed to their own incontrovertible equations and experiments. The story bears remarkable witness to the disinterested yet passionate character of pure science. In retrospect, as we shall see, this unexpected upheaval in physics brought it into far greater harmony with other branches of knowledge, notably depth psychology, mystical and religio-philosophical insights, and the humanities in general.

4

Modern Physics

Introduction

Physics today comprises the Newtonian-Cartesian or "classical physics"—which is still valid for its own range of phenomena, the normal scale of observation, but is inapplicable in the realm of the very large or the very small or very fast-moving phenomena—and in addition two new branches, namely, quantum theory and relativity theory. The foundations of these two branches were in place by 1927.

Quantum theory probes the universe in its smallest dimension, that is, at the atomic and subatomic levels. Relativity theory, on the other hand, is concerned with the universe in large, as studied in the sciences of astrophysics and cosmology. The two branches overlap in respect of high velocities, and accordingly take into account each other's relevant findings. Newtonian physics is thus a subset of the new physics, which although broadened, has not as yet been able to achieve an overall or unified theory, notwithstanding the much-felt need for it.

Our purpose here continues to be a philosophical one. What we want to understand is the nature of exact science, and also how it makes contact with the world of experience and ideas.

Quantum Physics

Let us first take a look at quantum physics or quantum mechanics, as it is also called.

For science at the turn of the century, the basis of the physical world was solid matter—indestructible units or building blocks called atoms. It was then suddenly and unexpectedly discovered that atoms

[For the past three centuries there has persisted the scientific cosmology] which presupposes the ultimate fact of an irreducible brute matter, or material, spread throughout space in a flux of configurations. In itself such a material is senseless, valueless, purposeless. It just does what it does do, following a fixed routine imposed by external relations which do not spring from the nature of its being. It is this assumption that I call 'scientific materialism.' . . . It is not wrong, if properly construed. If we confine ourselves to certain types of facts, abstracted from the complete circumstances in which they occur, the materialistic assumption expresses these facts to perfection. But when we pass beyond the abstraction, either by more subtle employment of our senses, or by the request for meanings and for coherence of thoughts, the scheme breaks down at once. The narrow efficiency of the scheme was the very cause of its supreme methodological success. For it directed attention to just those groups of facts which, in the state of knowledge then existing, required investigation. . . . [But the necessary historical revolt against scholasticism] has . . . been exaggerated into the exclusion of philosophy from its proper role of harmonising the various abstractions of methodological thought.

Alfred North Whitehead, *Science and the Modern World* [p. 17]

were *not* solid but composed of sub-entities (electrons, protons and neutrons) which were so minute compared with the size of the tiny atom that an atom was mostly empty space. Then came the further discovery that the minute components or particles of the atom are not ultimate either. They have been dubbed "elementary particles," but this is a misnomer because many different particles have been discovered and new ones continue to be found, and also because these particles often transform themselves into each other. Many physicists are still trying to find the ultimate particle, but others consider this to be a misguided effort and are persuaded that there is no such thing in nature as basic material building blocks.

Subatomic particles are baffling because their behavior and appearance depend on how the physicist sets up the experiment. Looked at one way, a subatomic entity may appear as a particle, as one may expect—an entity confined to a very small volume; looked at another way, it is a wave. Whereas a particle is localized in space, cannot be split apart, and retains its identity when it collides with other particles, a wave spreads over vast regions of space, is divisible in an infinity of ways, and merges completely with other waves it happens to meet (Herbert, 1985, p. 64). And yet the wave and the particle are the same entity seen from two different points of view.

Adding to this mystery, subatomic particles can jump from one orbit of an atom to another without touching the intervening space. Furthermore, it is possible to establish either the position of a particle or its velocity and momentum, but not both.

Finally, when two particles in a certain state of relationship drift apart from one another in space—no matter how distantly apart (one may be on Earth and the other on the moon)— they are found to display a non-local connection; i.e., they have a relationship which cannot be explained or accounted for in terms of any force of interaction between them.

What have physicists made of the strange behavior of the subatomic, microscopic world—the world that underlies our own ordinary world of "macroscopic" phenomena? What sort of theory have they formulated?

In order to explain the paradoxical wave-particle duality, Niels Bohr developed the concept known as complementarity which states that these two conflicting behaviors are not so much properties of the particles themselves as *of the physicist's interaction with these phenomena*. In other words, the properties of the entities result from the scientist's act of measurement. Many questions arose from this complementarity theory, and a clear answer to them is lacking to this day. For example, what is a wave/particle's nature *before* it is measured? Does it pre-exist its measurement, and if so, how is it related to the macroscopic world? The complementarity principle contents itself with stating that the two aspects (wave-particle) are both needed for an adequate account of atomic reality. It regards them as partial aspects of some broader matrix whose nature is yet unknown.

Notice that physics has here come upon a phenomenon for which it has been forced by circumstances to accept what we might call a nondualist solution, namely, that *seemingly-contradictory manifestations are but two aspects of a more basic unity*.

Fritjof Capra (1983, p. 79) elucidates the wave-particle phenomenon as follows:

The situation seemed hopelessly paradoxical until it was realized that the terms "particle" and "wave" refer to classical concepts which are not fully adequate to describe atomic phenomena. An electron is neither a particle nor a wave, but it may show particle-like aspects in some situations and wave-like aspects in others. While it acts like a particle, it is capable of developing its wave nature at the expense of its particle nature, and vice versa, thus undergoing continual transformations from particle to wave from wave to particle. This means that neither the electron nor any other atomic "object" has any intrinsic properties independent of its environment. The properties it shows— particle-like or wave-like—will depend on the experimental situation, that is, on the apparatus it is forced to interact with.

And here, for good measure, is an explanatory remark of David Bohm's, "Under different experimental conditions, matter behaves more like a wave or more like a particle, but always, in certain ways, like both together" (1983, p. 128). At any rate, complementarity is accepted as an essential concept in quantum physics.

This brings us to the closely related uncertainty principle, which was formulated by Werner Heisenberg (in 1927) in a further effort to deal with the dual nature of matter and light. In defining the mathematical limits of relationship of particle and wave, it states that although as a particle a given entity is localized, its wave nature makes its location within a particular atom impossible to ascertain with certainty; it remains a probability only.

Bohr, after reflecting on this situation, concluded that matter does not exist at definite places *with certainty,* but that it has a *tendency* to exist at certain places, and that these tendencies are expressed as probabilities and are associated with mathematical quantities which take the form of waves. "This is why," Capra (1977, p. 56) explains, "particles can be waves at the same time. . . . They are 'probability waves, abstract quantities with all the characteristic properties of waves.' "

Thus, at the subatomic level the solid material world of classical physics dissolves away into wave-like patterns of probabilities. The world of quantum physics does not consist of isolated things or objects but rather of a web of dynamic interconnections, or correlations, between various processes.

Thus the abundant evidence which supports quantum theory implies that ours is a dynamic world wherein all objects, including those identified with ordinary perception, are interconnected, inasmuch as the molecules and atoms of which they are composed are in turn made of particles which are defined by their relations and connections with other "objects" (events), both local and *non-local.*

The term "non-local" refers to yet another extraordinary concept related to quantum physics—one that is perhaps the most far-reaching in its significance. The phenomenon of nonlocality first arose unexpectedly in the famous experiment known as the Einstein, Podolsky and Rosen Experiment. For our purposes, we need not discuss how it there arose. What is more important is that it has since been repeatedly corroborated, most notably by John S. Bell's mathematical proof, known as Bell's Theorem.

According to David Bohm (1983), Bell's Theorem shows that when a physicist probes a particular atom, it is disturbed not only by the probe but by a vast array of distant events—events that are occurring right now elsewhere on the globe or in other galaxies. Nonlocality is a fundamentally different kind of relationship which may be described as a non-causal connection of elements that are distant from each other. Whereas local variables are represented by connections between spatially separated events through *signals* (particles and networks of particles) that cannot be transmitted faster than the speed of light, nonlocal connections involve *no* signals but are instead *instantaneous* (they cannot be predicted, at present, in a precise mathematical way.) Nonlocality implies "that the analysis of a total system into a set of independently existent but interacting particles breaks down in a radically new way. One discovers, instead, both from consideration of the meaning of the mathematical equations and from the results of the actual experiments, that the various particles have to be taken literally as projections of a higher-dimensional reality which cannot be accounted for in terms of any force of interaction between them" (pp. 186-187).

The importance of what nonlocality signifies is not yet fully grasped. Yet one thing is clear: The "higher-dimensional reality" (or unifying ground) of which Bohm speaks *has primacy over all separate parts, not the other way around.*

What does quantum physics tell us about physical reality? Leading physicists have put forward varying interpretations, and as of now there is no consensus. We may, however, compare the type of order quantum physics suggests with the order premised in mechanism.

Two Types of Order: Mechanism and Quantum Physics

The principal feature of the mechanistic order according to David
Bohm (1983, p. 173) is

> . . . that the world is regarded as constituted of entities which are
> *outside of each other* [italics his] in the sense that they exist indepen-
> dently in different regions of space (and time) and interact through
> forces that do not bring about any changes in their essential natures.
> The machine gives a typical illustration of such a system of order.
> Each part is [manufactured] . . . independently of the others, and
> interacts with the other parts only through some kind of external
> contact. By contrast, in a living organism, for example, each part
> grows in the context of the whole, so that it does not exist indepen-
> dently, nor can it be said that it merely "interacts" with the others,
> without itself being essentially affected in this relationship.

To recapitulate the previous section, Bohm enumerates the key
features of quantum theory which challenge mechanism as follows
(p. 175): "1. Movement is in general *discontinuous,* in the sense that
action is constituted of *indivisible quanta* [italics his] (implying also
that an electron, for example, can go from one state to another,
without passing through any states in between, 2. Entities, such as
electrons, can show different properties (e.g., particle-like, wave-
like, or something in between), depending on the environmental
context within which they exist and are subject to observation, and
3. Two entities, such as electrons, which initially combine to form a
molecule and then separate, show a peculiar non-local relationship,
which can best be described as a non-causal connection of elements
that are far apart."

Bohm names one other feature, namely, that the laws of quantum physics are statistical and do not determine future events uniquely and precisely. (Also see Weber, 1986, p. 89.) Bohm has remarked
that every new moment could in principle be entirely unrelated to the
previous one—that it could be totally creative. This contrasts with
classical laws, which *do* in principle determine such events, but the
indeterminism does not in itself, unlike the other three features,
affect the question of whether the fundamental order is mechanistic
or not. (Rules of chance come into play, for instance, in a pinball
machine.)

Bohm explains why the three above-mentioned features show that
the entire universe has to be thought of as an unbroken whole (1983,
pp. 175-176):

. . . if all actions are in the form of discrete quanta, the interactions between different entities (e.g., electrons) constitute a single structure of indivisible links, so that the entire universe has to be thought of as an unbroken whole. In this whole, each element that we can abstract in thought shows basic properties (wave or particle, etc.) that depend on its overall environment, in a way that is much more reminiscent of how the organs constituting living beings are related than it is of how parts of a machine interact. Further, the non-local, non-causal nature of the relationship of elements distant from each other evidently violates the requirement of separateness and independence of fundamental constituents that is basic to any mechanistic approach.

The Theory of Relativity

Let us now move on to the other branch of twentieth-century physics, namely, the theory of relativity.

As everyone knows, Einstein published three very fundamental papers in 1905: one on the quantum of light (photoelectric effects), one on Brownian motion, and one propounding his special theory of relativity, which deals with phenomena involving large distances and/or high velocities. The first two were to prove fundamental to the development of quantum theory, which was carried to completion some two decades later, through the collaboration of a whole team of physicists. The special theory of relativity and its extension, ten years later, into the general theory were the achievement almost entirely of Einstein himself.

Late nineteenth-century physics firmly held that interstellar and interplanetary spaces, far from being empty, were occupied by a material substance they called ether. It was presumed that ether was the medium by means of which light waves were propagated, and therefore research into the mechanical properties of the ether was receiving top priority. But in 1887, two Americans, Albert Abraham Michelson and Edward Williams Morley, completed an experiment whose aim was to determine the velocity of the Earth through this ever-present vibrating medium. The results were bewildering: the experiment failed to detect any movement whatsoever of the ether past the Earth. The velocity of light was found to be constant under all circumstances.

This was the scene onto which Einstein, then an unknown clerk in the Zurich patent office, broke like a bolt from the blue—through the publication of his three famous papers. The one which proposed what came to be known as the special theory of relativity originated out of Einstein's interest in two problems, namely, the Newtonian notion of absolute motion, which was undemonstrable, and the problem of the velocity of light.

Einstein based his hypothesis on three bold assumptions: he discarded absolute motion, he discarded ether, and he assumed that the constancy of the velocity of light was not just a co-incidental accident in the Michelson/Morley experiment, but a physical principle. Thus, contradicting common sense, he stated that the measured speed of light is constant for all observers regardless of the motion of the observer, thereby formulating his famous equation, $E = mc^2$, which has been substantiated in many ways—not least, the development of the atomic bomb.

Among the assertions and consequences of this theory are the following: the maximum velocity attainable in the universe is that of light; mass increases with velocity; mass and energy are equivalent; objects contract in the direction of motion; the rate of a moving clock decreases as the velocity of movement increases; events that appear simultaneous to an observer in one system may not appear as simultaneous to an observer in another system.

Einstein's relativity theory is of course a physical, not a psychological theory. The stretching out and contraction of phenomena moving at high speeds relative to each other are well established. It is the motion that affects the clocks and measuring rods; more accurately, it is the atoms of which these are made and the electrical forces holding the atoms together which are affected, and which thus cause the contraction and the dilation. These effects are too infinitesimal in ordinary circumstances to be noticed.

But while relativity is a physical theory, it is one which complements psychological and philosophical insights into time and space. We shall return to this point.

The special theory of relativity provided a common framework for the hitherto unrelated fields of electrodynamics and mechanics. But while thus unifying and completing the structure of classical physics, relativity undermined its very foundations by introducing radical changes in its basic assumptions about space and time, which were further extended by Einstein in his general theory.

In ordinary experience, we are not accustomed to thinking of time and space as being intimately related to one another. For relativity, however, the connection between the two is essential. It emphasizes

Those who knew Einstein will agree that his work was permeated with great passion. It was perception growing out of such passion that made possible the dissolution of mental barriers, contained in the previously existent state of knowledge. In the case of special relativity, one of the principle barriers was the notion that because it had worked so well for several centuries, the entire structure of Newton's thought on the subject constituted an absolute truth. . . . Few scientists had the energy of mind needed to question ideas with such great prestige, and yet Einstein did not mean to disparage Newton in doing so. Rather, he said that if he saw further than Newton, it was because he stood on Newton's shoulders. Newton himself revealed a similar humility when he said that he felt like one walking on the shores of a vast ocean of truth, who had picked up a few pebbles that seemed particularly interesting.

David Bohm, "Insight, Knowledge,
Science and Human Values"
[in Sloan, ed., 1984, pp. 14-15]

that space and time, though distinct, are interwoven inextricably: a thing cannot exist at some place without existing at some time, nor can it exist at some time without existing at some place. Einstein's theory expresses this relationship as a "space-time continuum" in which time becomes the "fourth dimension" of space.

By showing that time depends on the speed of the observer, relativity called into question the idea that time flows uniformly across the whole universe. In David Bohm's words (1987, p. 108), "No longer could a single time order span the entire universe; indeed past, present, and future could not be maintained in the same absolute sense as for Newton."

In the space-time continuum, events do not develop, they just *are*. Compare this with a similar perception, though arrived at differently, of mystics.

The most famous finding of the special theory of relativity is that mass is a form of energy, and vice versa, an insight which (together with the quantum theory) has completely changed our view of nature. The physical world has dissolved into a spectrum of energetic states which is completely open-ended, thus leaving the possibility of its extension to life, mind and even higher states—all part of one vast system.

The special theory proved successful, but Einstein felt it was incomplete in that it applied only to co-ordinate systems moving uniformly relative to each other. He asked himself whether it might be possible to describe events in such a way that they were meaningful to observers in systems which were not moving uniformly. Or, in other words, could a unified physics be created that was valid for observers in different frames of reference? That in fact was the aim and achievement of Einstein's general theory of relativity.

In the course of this further work, Einstein saw that Euclidean geometry (which assumes a flat, not a spherical earth) is valid only in limited regions of space—not for the entire expanse of the universe. "This freed him [Einstein] to behold the universe in a way that no person had seen it before," remarks Gary Zukov (1979).

The thought experiments which Einstein performed involving imaginary elevators, the observations of their riders and the observations of people outside the elevators, are famous and have often been described (see for example Zukov, 1979). They show the fascinating way Einstein developed a physical theory into a revolutionary geometry which illustrated the fact that the observations of space and time are not independent of the observer's own situation.

The general theory of relativity in fact expands the special theory to include acceleration, which Einstein found to be the same thing as gravity. The general theory states that space-time is curved and that this phenomenon is the result of gravity—or rather the gravitational fields of massive bodies. Wherever there is a massive object, such as a star or planet, the space around it is curved to a degree which depends on the mass of the object. "And as space can never be separated from time in relativity theory, time as well is affected by the presence of matter, flowing at different rates in different parts of the universe" (Capra, 1977, pp. 52-53). Even though we all accept the statements of physicists regarding four-dimensional and curved space-time of relativity theory, it is impossible for us to picture, since it is beyond our sensory experience and ordinary language, and can only be expressed mathematically.

The general theory of relativity accomplished an awesome synthesis: that of space, time, gravity and inertia or matter, which, as we have said, has completely altered our world picture.

Capra (1983) remarks that in showing that space, time and matter are interdependent, Einstein revealed the dynamic nature of matter even more fully than does quantum theory. Particles can no longer be regarded as "stuff" or objects but rather as dynamic bundles of energy or as patterns of activity which have both a space aspect and a time aspect—their space aspect making them appear as objects, and their time aspect making them appear as processes. The implications for unitary theory are immense, as Capra states: "The being of matter and its activity cannot be separated; they are but different aspects of the same space-time reality" (p. 91).

The new physics shows that neither time nor space are physical entities. As Roger S. Jones (1982) remarks, space, time, matter and number—the four fundamental pillars of physics—are *all* metaphysical; none has a purely objective status. They are rather creations of the human mind. Jones calls them "metaphors" which disclose otherwise unapparent qualities of reality.

From the foregoing discussion, it will be clear that among the basic concepts of physics that underwent radical change as a result of quantum physics and relativity theory were those of time and causality. Up to then, time in Western thought had been regarded as linear, and classical physics was deterministic. Now strict determinism and absolute time were disproved, and it became apparent that causality was much more complex than had been thought.

Actually, these radical changes in physics' conception of time and causality brought it into much more harmony with other areas of thought, notably those of parapsychology, metaphysics, and mysticism. (See, for example, Chapters 9, 10 and 14.)

5

The Nature of Exact Science

Any theory of wider scope implies a world view . . . any major development in science changes the world outlook and is "natural philosophy."
Ludwig von Bertalanffy, *Robots, Men and Minds*

Physics Has Given Up Its Certainties

What kind of statement does the new physics make about physical reality? The surprising fact is that physics no longer purports to say what physical reality is. Physics is in fact experiencing "a reality crisis."

As we earlier saw, modern science has revolved around the aim of discovering and measuring "irreducible and stubborn facts." The fathers of the scientific revolution were impelled to liberate themselves from theology and to explore the physical world for themselves—by observation, experimentation and measurement. In light of René Descartes' dictum to the effect that matter and mind, the knower and the known, subject and object are strictly separable from one another, science adopted the ideal of "pure objectivity." Nor, in retrospect, was it anything but natural for scientists to adopt the stance of neutrality vis-a-vis the universal clockwork. For, how should one feel empathy for, how should one feel a relation with, a cold, dead, clockwork? Furthermore, was it not logical, once the idea was accepted that mind and matter are completely separable, to believe that the scientist could stand totally outside the machine and dispassionately to take its measure?[1]

The rigor and prestige of science led many people to believe that

---

1. Although Descartes' belief that mind and matter were separate is not valid, it proved useful for the time being, enabling scientists to focus totally on matter. However, as pointed out in an earlier footnote, the further erroneous idea, that mind is only an epiphenomenon of matter, cannot be laid at Descartes' door. By the same token, Descartes never contradicted himself, as do the materialists, by assigning to a mere automaton the ability to observe and to measure.

what science does not discover is not true, and to equate the findings of science with reality itself. This is known as scientism, a perversion of science (Cf. Huston Smith, 1977 and 1984).

In the twentieth century, as we have shown, physics has given up its certainties and even its ideal of "pure" objectivity. As a result of quantum physics and relativity theory, modern physics has revealed that no such thing as "pure" objectivity exists or could exist.

What the Physicist Observes

That the scientist's mind is involved in his observations should have been obvious from the fact, if nothing else, that mathematics, the very language of physics, is a product of the mind.

As Werner Heisenberg, one of the giants of twentieth-century physics, once remarked, what the scientist observes is not nature itself but nature exposed to the scientist's method of questioning. And as Thomas Kuhn later showed, in his influential work, *The Structure of Scientific Revolutions*, first published in 1962, the scientist's method of questioning is usually shaped by the prevailing world image or paradigm or scientific theory. Kuhn, a historian of science, likens the paradigm to a pair of spectacles worn by the scientist. He proposes that the observer, his or her theory, and the apparatus used are all essentially expressions of a point of view. Every now and then, a paradigm shift occurs, the spectacles get smashed and scientists begin to look at things from a different angle.

David Bohm (1983) declares that in science there is a wholeness of three elements—mode of observation, instrumentation and theoretical understanding. He is persuaded that consideration of this relationship "is essential for an adequate understanding of science itself, because the content of the observed fact cannot coherently be regarded as separate from modes of observation and instrumentation and modes of theoretical understanding" (p. 144).

To illustrate the close interrelationship between instrumentation and theory, Bohm compares the use of the photographic lens and that of the type of photograph known as the hologram. The former arose in the context of classical physics; it fosters and facilitates analysis into parts; it attests the one-to-one type of order implied in classical physics. The hologram, in contrast, is an instrument that suits the new type of order that is emerging: in the holographic photograph, the whole is found in every part (we will return to Bohm's idea later).

The physicist/philosopher Henry Margenau has remarked that when a researcher is looking for facts, he is usually guided by accepted concepts. These provide the matrix in which the facts to be found will be embedded. Similarly, Ludwig Von Bertalanffy, originator of the seminal General Systems Theory, has emphasized that facts have meaning only within a pre-existing conceptual system—that, indeed, *no ultimate data exist.*

Here, as the reader may notice, we have come full circle to something discussed in the first chapter: the perennial perception that ultimate reality cannot be defined, that knowledge is never final and ultimate but only partial, relative and open-ended.

The Limitations of Physics

Over and above the fact that all knowledge is intrinsically incomplete, exact science has its special limitations.

The chief tool of the scientific method, quantification or mathematics, is, as mentioned before, inapplicable to inquiry into many aspects of our multi-faceted experience—for example, suffering, love and compassion. It is thus unable to pronounce on reality as a whole, and even on physical reality, which cannot be separated from its "inward" or indeterminate aspects. By omitting consciousness *per se* from its·accepted province, it indeed omits that from which the world takes its rise.

Admittedly, consciousness *has* crept into physics, in the problem of measurement, but only through the back door, so to speak. Small wonder that it should have crept in, for, as we earlier stressed, knowing takes place *within* us, and of course that does not exclude appraisal of external objects.

The fact is that physics neither directly pronounces upon reality nor has it purported to do so, since the demise of the clockwork universe. In reconceptualizing its basic premises about space, time, matter and the observer-observed relationship, physics paradoxically lost its certainties. But inasmuch as the certainties were erroneous, that was unquestionably a maturing development.

The picture of the world physics gives us is in fact very incomplete. It "tells us nothing about the things that really matter to us." It is in fact silent about all the qualitative, non-measurable, aspects of the world—the colors, tastes, sounds and beauty which are most meaningful to human life. Interestingly enough, Isaac Newton himself eventually abandoned physics for religious pursuits, declaring that science was too narrow.

Science as an Art Form

Now, we think of scientific methodology as being a clear-cut, step-by-step procedure starting with induction from empirical "facts," followed by the formulation of a hypothesis, which is then put to experimental testing. But this is not always or perhaps even mostly the case. What actually occurs in the doing of exact science is that scientists experience *hunches* or intuitions which they then try out experimentally or mathematically. As Michael Polanyi, Owen Barfield, Arthur Koestler, Roger S. Jones and others have shown, doing exact science is a *creative, not just an automatic process*. It often proceeds "by pure speculation guided by criteria of internal rationality," in Polanyi's words.

David Bohm has pointed out that the customary belief that physics is exact, and that all its statements have exact meaning, is erroneous. He believes that science is really closer to art in that it deals with things that are ambiguous, scientific theories being "art forms" which indeed reflect actual experience but which give no final answers.

By all accounts, the sudden, spontaneous revelations that come to the great scientist are moments of intense concentration—passionate moments. When Archimedes, for example, perceived one day, as he was getting into the bath, that the volume of water displaced is independent of the shape of the object, the sudden insight was such a tremendous one that he reputedly shouted, "Eureka!"

The physicist's recognition of nature's inner harmonies, symmetries and proportions is an artistic pursuit. What is more, the physicist, no less than the poet, expresses his perceptions *symbolically*—except that, unlike the poet's, his symbolic language is shared only by mathematicians. No less than the poet's protagonists, the denizens of the quantum world, such as electrons, protons, neutrons, etc., are not actualities but metaphors, standing for other realities. In emphasizing their metaphoric nature, Roger S. Jones (1982) remarks that they are in the nature of characters in a fairy tale in that they are wonderfully evocative of the excitement, wonder and mystery of existence, but yet are creatures of the imagination, projections of the human mind in its search for meaning and order.

In short, the gifted scientist is also a veritable artist. (One could

The scientific picture of the real world around me is very deficient. It gives a lot of factual information, puts all our experience in a magnificently consistent order, but it is ghastly silent about all and sundry that is really near to our heart, that really matters to us. It cannot tell us a word about red or blue, bitter and sweet, physical pain and physical delight; it knows nothing of beautiful and ugly, good or bad, God and eternity. . . . So, in brief, we do not belong to this material world that science constructs for us. We are not in it; we are outside. We are only spectators. . . . [Only] our bodies are in the picture. . . . I am not needed as an author. . . . [The great changes that go on in this material world, of which I feel myself partly the author] take care of themselves—they are amply accounted for by direct energetic interplay. . . . The scientific world-picture vouchsafes a very complete understanding of all that happens— it makes it just a little too understandable. It allows you to imagine the total display as that of a mechanical clockwork which, for all that science knows, could go on just the same as it does, without there being consciousness, will, endeavor, pain and delight and responsibility connected with it—though they actually are. And the reason for this disconcerting situation is just this: that, for the purpose of constructing the picture of the external world, we have used the greatly simplifying device of cutting our own personality out, removing; hence it is gone, it has evaporated, it is ostensibly not needed.

In particular, and most importantly, this is the reason why the scientific worldview contains of itself no ethical values, no aesthetical values, not a word about our own ultimate scope or destination, and no God, if you please. Whence came I, whither go I?

Erwin Schroedinger, *Nature and the Greeks*, pp. 93-96

add that art, conversely, is in some sense a science!) And, even as an artist is moved by the subject he addresses, so may a scientist be moved by the marvels of nature and of cosmic order. One recalls Einstein's famous remark about the awe and reverence he felt before the "superior intelligence" which he saw as pervading the universe.

We may see that in principle there is no boundary, no incompatibil-

It is a travesty of the scientific method to conceive of it as an automatic process depending on the speed of piling up evidence for hypotheses chosen at random. . . . [Also unfounded are the claims of specific rules of empirical inference] to show how to verify, or at the very least . . . how to falsify, an empirical proposition according to some such rules. . . . [The reason is that] all such formal rules of scientific procedure must prove ambiguous, for they will be interpreted quite differently, according to the particular conceptions about the nature of things by which the scientist is guided. And his chances for reaching true and important conclusions will depend decisively on the correctness and penetration of these conceptions . . . there is a type of empirical discovery that is achieved without any process of induction. De Broglie's wave theory, the Copernican system and the theory of Relativity, were all found *by pure speculation guided by criteria of internal rationality* [italics ours].

Michael Polanyi, *Personal Knowledge*
[p. 167]

ity, between science and the humanities. As Jones remarks, "There may be a culture gap between the sciences and the humanities, but there is no existential gap. Physics is relevant not only because it surrounds us with television and computers and sends us to the moon, but because it is rooted in the same human soil that nourishes all meaningful human endeavor" (p. 211).

Physics and Truth

In the twentieth century, physics, as we saw, underwent a fundamental reconceptualization. Scientific knowledge is always dynamic and changeable, and therefore physics' present accuracy pertains only to presently entertained problems. Undoubtedly, many new problems will arise in the future, as they did in the past. They will occasion the formulation of new approximations, new theories. If Thomas Kuhn is right, these, in turn, will only bring us fragmentarily closer to the truth, since each theory is the outcome of a particular perspective or angle of vision. New theories do not so much build on what has been learned already as look in a different direction. By attending to one aspect or direction, we tend to lose sight of or forget something known earlier.

Yet does not history show that themes and views recur repeatedly but with different emphases? Whitehead wrote something apposite (1967, pp. 184-185): "Even when the same assertion is made today as was made a thousand, or fifteen hundred years ago, it is made subject to limitations or expansions of meaning, which were not contemplated at the earlier epoch. . . . we may know that a proposition expresses an important truth but that it is subject to limitations and qualifications which at present remain undiscovered." If we return in our time, as now seems likely, to an image of the world as a living entity rather than an inanimate machine, the new image will

---

It is mind that we see reflected in matter. Physical science is a metaphor with which the scientist, like the poet, creates and extends meaning and value in the quest for understanding and purpose. . . .

The things about science that make it useful to us and that make us appreciate it—predictability, objectivity, self-consistency, generality—do not exist in some external, independent reality. They are part of our experience and interpretation of the world, of our consciousness and values, of our game of meaning. I see Newton's monumental achievement as a mental creation, a humanly conceived world system, incorporating self-consistency and causal order, which pleases the human mind and helps to allay our fears of a chaotic universe. His is as much a work of art as it is of science.

To protest that Newton's conception is supported by countless observations of the physical universe is no argument, for my point is that the conception or theory and the observed quantities are created in parallel so as to corroborate each other (not necessarily without a struggle, and not in any overtly conscious way). Furthermore, the quantities themselves are based on a definition and procedures of measurement that are fundamentally subjective.

Roger S. Jones, *Physics as Metaphor,*
[pp. ix-42]

not be the same as the old one, for it will incorporate details of knowledge gained in the interim.

Interpreting Quantum Reality

Quantum physics treats only of relationships between entities that are invisible, non-picturable, insubstantial and perhaps nonexistent. Since the demise of the clockwork universe, physics has not come up with a substitute metaphor to describe the universe. Physicists do not claim even to know what they are measuring. It may not be anything physical at all. At the same time, quantum physics is extremely suggestive, evocative, even provocative. Quantum "facts" seem to point insistently to some metaphysical reality.

In his book *Quantum Reality,* Nick Herbert examines eight major interpretations of quantum reality by as many leading physicists. He finds that the eight interpretations differ, some radically, some contradicting each other, some compatible with each other. He comments that inasmuch as these differing interpretations all predict exactly the same observable phenomena, each of them is possibly true. At the same time, all may be wrong.

The most widely held explanation, known as the Copenhagen interpretation, was developed primarily by Niels Bohr and Werner Heisenberg. Essentially it states that "in a certain sense the unmeasured atom is not real: its attributes are created or realized in the act of measurement"; that "there is no deep reality"; that, in the words of Bohr, "There is no quantum world. There is only an abstract quantum description."

According to another interpretation, reality is an undivided wholeness notwithstanding its apparent partitions and boundaries. This is the view presently held by David Bohm, Walter Heitler, Fritjof Capra and some others. Fritjof Capra developed his view in the *Tao of Physics,* wherein he drew some striking parallels between notions of the universe of modern physics and those of Eastern mystical thought.

Wholeness and the Implicate Order

One of the most impressive physical-philosophical theories to have been proposed in recent times is that of the distinguished physicist, David Bohm, set forth in his *Wholeness and the Implicate Order,* a work which has been widely quoted and which we have already mentioned more than once. Bohm infers from modern physics that it implies a new order—the order of "undivided wholeness." In order to defend this statement, the meaning of *order* itself must be probed, especially since different notions of order have presented themselves in the past.   Whereas Aristotle compared the universe to a living organism in which each part had its proper place and function so that all worked together to make a single whole, there eventually arose a new spirit in scientific research, which led to the questioning of the *relevance* of the old order—a movement started notably by Copernicus, Kepler and Galileo. The notions they conceived were incompatible with the idea of the universe as a single living organism.

> Rather, in a fundamental description, the universe now had to be regarded as analysable into separately existing parts or objects (e.g., planets, atoms, etc.) each moving in a void or vacuum. These parts could work together in interaction more or less as do the parts of a machine, but could not grow, develop, and function in response to ends determined by an "organism as a whole." The basic order for description of movement of the parts of this "machine" was taken to be that of successive positions of each constituent object at successive moments of time. Thus, a new order became relevant, and a new usage of language had to be developed for the description of this new order" (Bohm, 1983, p. 113).

The change entailed the discrimination of new relevant differences along with new similarities, since in general one way of perceiving order is to give attention to similar differences and different similarities.

Bohm probes the meaning of order, measure, structure and creativity. For instance, the kinds of structure that are possible are limited by their underlying order and measure. "A simple example of this can be taken from music. Here, the structures that can be worked with will depend on the order of the notes and on certain measures (scale, rhythm, time, etc.). New orders and measures evidently make possible the creation of new structures in music" (p. 120).

Moreover, very significant change of language is involved in the expression of the new order and measure of time entailed in relativistic theory. The speed of light is taken not as a possible speed of an *object*, but rather as the maximum speed of propagation of a *signal*, a communication.

The new order and measure introduced in relativity theory imply new notions of structure in which the idea of a rigid body can no longer play a key role. It is evident that the classical idea of the separability of the world into distinct but interacting parts is no longer valid or relevant. Rather, we have to regard the universe as an undivided and unbroken whole.

All these developments indicate a new order to Bohm, which he describes as *undivided wholeness*. Neither relativity nor quantum theory is compatible with analysis of the world into separate components. However, both theories contain certain elements that contradict the order they otherwise imply. In relativity theory, the signal—its basic role—is such an element. In quantum theory, "the quantum state of the system," or the wave function, is such an element. Bohm concludes: "To give up both the basic role of signal and that of quantum state, is, however, no small thing. To find a new theory that goes on without these will evidently require radically new notions of order, measure and structure" (Bohm, 1983, p. 138).

Before we can perceive the new order that Bohm proposes is emerging, we will have to free ourselves further from long-ingrained ways of thinking, using language, and observing.

By way of "preliminary steps" toward understanding the present situation in physics in a new way, Bohm presents his own tentative theory of what he calls the implicate and explicate order—as it would apply in physical law and in relation to life and consciousness.

As we have already noted, Bohm infers directly from physics that the world is an unbroken wholeness in flowing movement. While there is a great diversity of manifest forms (which are wholes in themselves), these are derived from the larger whole. Bohm likens the forms to vortexes thrown up by a stream, an analogy in which the vortexes are "the explicate order" and the stream is the "implicate order." While the vortexes are distinct and intricate configurations, there is yet no sharp division between any of them and the stream. Each manifested form, whether it be an undersea current, a stone or a subatomic particle, is a separate whole, but each is only a relatively separate or autonomous "subtotality" whose stability derives not from its separateness but from the movement of the whole, from the "holonomy" as Bohm calls it.

A significant feature of Bohm's theory is its inclusion of consciousness. For Bohm's "implicate order" is a more comprehensive, deeper and more inward order; it is the common ground which enfolds the "explicate order"—enfolds all the subtotalities, including the human being and his or her mind and body. For Bohm, the

A great deal of work has been done showing the inadequacy of old ideas . . . but we have not yet freed ourselves thoroughly from the old order of thinking, using language and observing. We have thus yet to perceive a new order. As with Galileo, this must involve seeing new differences so that much of what has been thought to be basic . . . will be perceived to be more or less correct, but not of primary relevance. . . . [Then] we will be able to perceive a new universal ratio or reason relating and unifying all the differences. This may ultimately carry us as far beyond quantum theory and relativity as Newton's ideas went beyond those of Copernicus.

> David Bohm, *Wholeness and the Implicate Order* [pp. 138-139]

. . . there is a broad spectrum of order . . . [containing] whole ranges of subtle and complex orders, some of infinite degree, which contain embedded within them many orders of lower degree. . . . Language, for example, may be considered as having an infinite order, because its potential for meaning is unlimited. . . . Within the infinite order of language of a novel, for example, is contained the order of the sentence; the orders of tense, action, and the subject of the paragraph; the orders of character and plot. . . . Each of these suborders . . . is not independent, for it is conditioned by the overall flow of the novel. . . . The infinite order of language in the novel therefore contains a richness which is not predictable and cannot be fully pinned down within any finite series of differences and similarities. . . . Only within the context of a human being, with his or her capacities, knowledge, and experience can an order of meaning in what is read . . . emerge. . . . A similar dependence of meaning on a broad context is found in music. . . . [The context, in turn] depends on the tacit infrastructure of ideas, knowledge, and skills that are available in a given community and subculture. . . . Obviously it is of key importance that such an infrastructure should not be maintained in a rigid and inflexible way . . . [something that holds equally] for language and music and indeed for every area of life, as it does for science.

> David Bohm and F. David Peat, *Science, Order and Creativity* [pp. 128-130]

> . . . in the implicate order the totality of existence is enfolded in each region of space (and time). So, whatever part, element, or aspect we may abstract in thought, this still enfolds the whole and is therefore intrinsically related to the totality from which it has been abstracted. Thus, wholeness permeates all that is being discussed."
>
> David Bohm, *Wholeness and the*
> *Implicate Order* [p. 172]
>
> To see a World in a Grain of Sand,
> And Heaven in a Wild Flower,
> Hold Infinity in the palm of your hand,
> And Eternity in an hour.
>
> William Blake

movements of mind and body are "the outcome of related projections of a common higher-dimensional ground" (Bohm, 1983, p. 209).

By way of analogy, to help us understand the nature of the new order that is trying to emerge, Bohm employs the hologram. The hologram has been widely described in popular scientific literature, but for easy reference, we can reiterate that it is a process which makes a photographic record of the interference patterns of light waves reflected from an object. Whereas the usual photograph displays a point-to-point correspondence between the image and the object photographed, the hologram displays no such correspondence, but rather *enfolds* the form and structure of the entire object within each region of the photographic record. Thus every portion of the hologram yields the image of the whole object, or in other words, the part contains information about the whole.

Bohm does not wish to push this analogy too far, because the hologram produces only a static record whereas reality is dynamic— characterized by a constant unfoldment and enfoldment, a movement that goes immensely beyond what has revealed itself to science's observation so far.

For Bohm, the emergent order will demand that science reverse its procedure. Up to now, it has started with parts and proceeded to derive the wholes through abstraction, explaining them as the results of interaction of the parts. But the implicate order requires that one begin from the undivided wholeness of the universe, and derive the parts by abstraction from the whole, "explaining them as approximately separable, stable and recurrent, but extremely related elements making up relatively autonomous sub-totalities, which are to be described in terms of an explicate order" (Bohm, 1983, p. 179).

It will be evident that Bohm's idea of the implicate and explicate order accords in many striking ways with the nondualist perspective which was presented in Chapter 1. It is exciting that a scientist should have come, by the empirical route, to an approach to reality which parallels that of the perennial philosophy, one which emphasizes wholeness, multi-dimensionality, dynamism and the primacy of consciousness.

How is Bohm's thought accepted among physicists? As a physicist, he is much respected, but his theory of the implicate and explicate order is not yet widely accepted, compelling as it may be to the few. For example, it has been remarked of Bohm's ideas of the implicate and explicate order: "One can't help but be astonished at the degree to which he [Bohm] has been able to break out of the tight molds of scientific conditioning and stand alone with a completely new and literally vast idea, one which has both internal consistency and the logical power to explain widely diverging phenomena of physical experience from an entirely unexpected point of view. At the same time, the theory remains provocative, creative, and open— extending off into mists and depths still to be explored" (Briggs and Peat, 1984, p. 152).

Physics and Holism

As we saw, in the twentieth century physics was forced to give up some former certainties. Though its predictions are now stated in terms of probabilities, they are still impressively accurate. It has as of now not succeeded in reaching an overall or unified theory uniting quantum mechanics and relativity, although two of the four force fields, the electromagnetic and the weak field, have been united. In fact, uncertainty and controversy beset physics (although the average physicist is happy that science works excellently, and just wants to leave well enough alone!).

In the broad context we are invoking, it appears but natural that physics should not have arrived at finalities. Nor does this detract from the fact that it conducts a marvellous, impassioned yet highly disciplined quest. If it encounters and wrestles with ambiguities, these are surely a sign of its continued vitality, growth and creativity.

As early in this remarkable century as 1931, Sir James Jeans, the mathematician, physicist, astronomer and philosopher of science, described in *The Mysterious Universe* the accomplishments of twentieth-century physics in a way which largely still applies. He listed the following achievements: the theory of relativity with its welding of space and time; the theory of quanta with its apparent negation of the laws of causation; the dissection of the atom with the resultant discovery that things are not what they seem; *and, the discovery that physics is not yet in touch with ultimate reality,* an achievement which he considered greater than all the rest!

If one adds to Jeans's list the the discovery of the inseparability of the observer from the observed, and the revelation of nonlocality, it becomes amply evident that physics has achieved some sublime unifications and integrations in the twentieth century; that indeed physics, remarkably and insistently (if unintentionally), corroborates in its own way the fundamental holism and impartibility of the cosmos. It has been suggested, notably by the cultural historian Thomas Berry, that the revelations of science are comparable, in spiritual and philosophical import, to those of religion. At any rate, one is not surprised to discover that most of the grand theorists of physics have also engaged in the pursuit of philosophical ideas (see Chapter 14).

The Far-Reaching Significance of Science

For the philosophical and mystical mind, science's twentieth-century revelations cannot but be profoundly significant. But scientific progress has had and will have still other far-reaching consequences.

It is obvious, for example, that physical science was a *sine qua non* for the transformation, for better and worse, of the conditions of life on this planet. For, through its consequent technology, science has impacted upon not only the material but also the political, social, environmental and moral dimensions of life, and it has indirectly contributed in a major way to the present unprecedented condition of global societal interdependence.

We cannot yet foresee the consequences of the new technologies of information, communication and automation that are now triggering the second industrial revolution, but that they will be extremely far-reaching is clear. They are of an entirely different nature from the industrial technologies spawned by classical science, and will call for radically new mind-sets in individuals, as well as new forms of social, economic and political organization. (Cf. Lazlo, 1987; and Castells in Mendlovitz and Walker, eds., 1987.)

Physical science has permitted the proliferation of weapons of mass destruction, and, equally, science has put within our reach the means for solving a whole range of problems which lie at the root of conflict and war. There is, in fact, no end to the ramifications of the planetary convergence made possible under the impact of science and technology.

Take for instance the new zest for comparative study of religious, mystical, mythological, therapeutic and other traditions. This trend is clearly not unrelated to the planet-wide communication network, which has both stimulated and facilitated such studies. In turn, the studies concerned are a potent universalizing and broadening force whose impact is reinforced by the same mass facilities (discussed below).

Although we have not yet considered the life and social sciences, I believe we may safely, in sum, say this: in the absence of modern science, humanity could not and would not have reached the present unprecedented juncture wherein (1) it is imperative, as a practical matter of survival, to learn greater tolerance, sharing and cooperation; and (2) a set of conditions exists which, on the one hand, holds practical solutions to problems impeding peace, and, on the other hand, conduces to the development of a sense of the wholeness or unity of the cosmos, the planet and humanity itself.

All this should become more evident as we further examine science, and as we then go on to explore the spiritual domain.

6

The Biological Domain

Is there nothing common in the sciences—from physics to biology to the social sciences to history—so that the scientific enterprise must remain a bundle of isolated specialities, without connecting link and progressively leading to the type of learned idiot who is perfect in his small field but is ignorant and unaware of the basic problems we call philosophical, and which are of primary concern to man in one of the greatest crises of his history?

Ludwig von Bertalanffy

It is mind that has composed a physical universe that breeds life, and so eventually evolves creatures that know and create. . . . In them, the universe begins to know itself.

George Wald

We are members of one another.
St. Paul

A living body . . . is a work of art. Its beauty resides in its internal teleology.

T. Dobzhansky

Introduction

Let us now turn to the domain of nature investigated by biology, that of plants and animals.

Biology has developed into a large range of specializations—whose massive output is far beyond the possibility of an individual's study. At the same time, and notwithstanding the spectacular achievements of molecular biology in the twentieth century—such as the discovery of the structure of DNA, the cracking of the genetic code, and the discovery of the mechanism of protein synthesis—biology is considered to be still in its infancy. This is so because its conceptual framework is a matter of controversy and is constantly

95

undergoing change in order to accommodate the stream of current findings.

Mainstream biologists are mechanists or neo-Darwinists; that is to say, they study plants and animals as molecular machines. This mechanistic/reductionistic orientation has yielded the mentioned successes, but it increasingly poses problems. Some biologists do not believe that molecular biology alone can hope to resolve biology's still unsolved major problems, and in fact, various alternative or additional approaches are being proposed.

We shall briefly glance at mechanistic biology, as well as at some of the newer developments, especially as the latter bear on biology's central theory, that of evolution. It will become apparent that evolutionary theory is itself evolving.

We previously underscored the vital and dynamic links of exact science with religion and the humanities. If *exact* science makes contact with these other domains, one should all the more expect the *life* sciences to share this common ground. For they lie at the very intersection of different avenues of knowledge. But as yet there is little recognition of this fact.

Insofar as biology has based itself on physical concepts, it has given rise to such overlapping fields as biophysics, biochemistry, neurophysiology and neuropsychiatry. Neurophysiology (the study of the brain and nervous system) and neuropsychiatry (which is concerned with both the psychic and organic aspects of mental disorder) are branches of medicine, but the other two fields, together with genetics (the study of heredity, currently pursued mainly in molecular terms) and ecology (the study of the relations of a group of organisms to its environment), have become in the present century separate biological disciplines.

Biology itself grew out of both medicine and agriculture. In a sense, the roles have been reversed in the twentieth century, since basic research in biology is now contributing to major advances in medicine and agriculture.

In addition, paleontology (the study of fossils), which is part of evolutionary science, is closely interrelated with geology or earth science. The technique of radiocarbon dating, which was developed by chemists to determine the age of biological remains, has also been of great use in the fields of archaeology and anthropology. A new scientific discipline, space biology, has arisen through the activities of scientists and engineers concerned with space exploration. Thus the field of the biological or life sciences spills over into physics and chemistry, and vice versa; there are no longer clear-cut distinctions, but everywhere an overlapping of domains.

As for the non-sciences, biology shares with religion, philosophy and the humanities concern with the question of life's origin and development, including man's place in the evolutionary scheme—questions that biology cannot alone determine or arbitrate.

Consider the issue of the origin of life. Just as astrophysicists seek clues to the origin of the physical universe, so biologists speculate about the origin of life. Cosmological theory traces events back to the Big Bang and speculates even on the moments that preceded it, but it does not undertake to pronounce upon the significance of that event or what its antecedents might have been.

Mainstream biology assumes that life developed by means of a physico-chemical process. But this assumption, we assert, is extremely implausible. Undeniably, life cannot be divorced from its physical forms. But it does not follow that chance development of primitive forms caused the appearance of life *merely* from a chemical combination. If this were so, human skill and knowledge of the chemistry should have been able to replicate the process.

Most biologists today hold that life, consciousness and mind are epiphenomena—derivatives—of matter. But what *is* matter? It has rightly been pointed out that the mechanistic argument about life is in fact circular, for it starts and ends with the mystery of matter. Dissenters from mainstream biology, as we shall show, perceive life to be implicit in matter, ready to appear spontaneously wherever conditions are ripe for it, where vehicles for its use exist. Perennial philosophy, for its part, holds that life and consciousness are concomitants of matter, both being implicit in the cosmos.

In studying organisms as molecular machines, biologists assume that given enough knowledge it will be possible fully to explain organisms in terms of physico-chemical processes; that the ultimate reduction of the phenomena of life to the molecular properties of DNA and related substances will permit finding the secret of life itself. But as microbiology continues its probe into living matter, it finds only endless, intricate order opening out like a hall of mirrors; it does not find life within the living. The mystery only deepens.

What this suggests is that intelligence and life are *not* epiphenomenal and a by-product; that they were not created *de novo* out of chemical substances; but that, conversely, *the mechanisms* of nature

Cosmologists are now beginning to think seriously of our universe, with all its oceanic immensities and shoals of suns, as after all just our own particular hometown, only one of many—perhaps an infinite number—of other universes. They sparkle throughout a superspace which is, . . . [in] the words of Helena Blavatsky, "the playground of numberless Universes incessantly manifesting and disappearing," like "sparks of Eternity."

But why do these universes appear? Why does the Unknown Root set aside its anonymity sufficiently to come veiled as stars and worlds? Neither cosmology nor theosophy can do more than hint at an answer, so far above the normal range of human thought is a question like this. Theosophy can supplement science, though, when it postulates consciousness as present right from the beginning along with matter.

Robert Ellwood, *Theosophy: A*
Modern Expression of the Wisdom of
the Ages [pp. 55-56]

To assert that there is only matter and no mind is the most illogical of propositions, quite apart from the findings of modern physics, which show that there is no matter in the traditional meaning of the term. For if we had no consciousness we could have no knowledge—of matter, or of our own existence, or of anything. . . . The existence of our own mind is the primary datum of all experience; the rest is inference.

W. A. Firsoff, *At the Crossroads of*
Knowledge [p. 5]

A man's general attitude toward organic life reflects his general attitude toward that which surpasses his ordinary thinking. The science of biology therefore has an extremely crucial role to play in the evolution of human consciousness. . . . To understand that nature is *like* a teaching is to be better prepared for the ideas and psychological forms of an actual sacred teaching.

Jacob Needleman, *A Sense of the*
Cosmos [p. 85]

cannot be fully understood without taking into consideration what they do in terms of the living, functioning creature.

As we shall see, there are in fact today a good many dissenters from mechanism among biologists and neuroscientists, including some particularly distinguished individuals (for example, biologist and Nobel laureate George Wald, biologist and Nobel laureate Barbara McClintock, and neuroscientist and Nobel laureate Roger Sperry, to mention but a few), who are convinced about the primacy of the mind and consciousness in nature, or are impressed with nature's simplicity, beauty and purposiveness.

It is interesting that mechanistic biology seems to be developing in a parallel way to the denouement, earlier described, of pre-quantum physics. That is to say, it has proved extremely fruitful for a certain range of investigations but eventually is making discoveries which are incompatible with its basic conceptual system.

The Science of Biology Is Still in Its Infancy

Biology, unlike physics, is mainly a descriptive science. Also, physics is at a more advanced stage of development in that it is already a cosmological science, whereas biology as yet addresses terrestrial life only.

A cosmological biology would undertake the study of life throughout the cosmos, not only on planet Earth. It would of necessity harmonize and merge with other domains of thought, including relevant philosophical insights, somewhat analogously to the way David Bohm's tentative physical theory of the implicate and explicate order extends beyond physics to merge with metaphysics.

I say "would" of a cosmological biology, but in fact over a century ago a work was written that actually presents a cosmological biological theory—although admittedly by a non-scientist. I speak of H.P. Blavatsky's *The Secret Doctrine,* first published in 1888. We will discuss this remarkable work when we come to biology's central theory of evolution. For Blavatsky put forward some ideas that are strangely akin to some theories now emerging at the leading edge of evolutionary theory.

Ludwig von Bertalanffy has pointed out that organisms are organized entities both in structure and function, exhibiting hierarchical order, differentiation, interaction of innumerable processes, goal-directed behavior, negentropic trends, and related criteria. Molecular

I believe there is a radical difference between biology and the so-called exact or inorganic sciences, particularly physics. In the latter, we postulate elementary particles which are necessary to the structure of the universe and the laws controlling their movements are intrinsically necessary, and in general, hold over the whole universe. Biology on the other hand deals with descriptions and orderings of very special parts of the universe, which we call life. . . .It is primarily a descriptive science more like geography, dealing with the structure and working of a number of peculiarly organized entities, at a particular moment in time, on a particular planet. Undoubtedly, there should be a real and general biology but we can only just begin to glimpse it. *A true biology in the full sense would be the study of the nature and activity of all organized objects wherever they were to be found on this planet and others in the solar system, in other galaxies and at all times future and past* [italics ours].

J.D. Bernal [in Morowitz, 1975, [p. 60]

In the 1950's, the advent of molecular biology opened up the possibility of creating the basis for a theoretical biology. But molecular biology became hampered by a reductionist attitude and failed to connect with the phenomena of macroscopic order. The structure of DNA and the genes does not contain the life of the organism which develops by using this information.

Erich Jantsch, *The Self-Organizing Universe* [pp. 5-6]

biology and its adjuncts generally say nothing about any of these features. Many doubt that it *could* say much about any of them. Bertalanffy in fact considers that biology is still in its "pre-Copernican" stage. Yet even now biology's revelations are tremendously significant. For instance, it has established (albeit unintentionally), in its own unprecedented way, the dynamic interdependence and unity of terrestrial life. Heretofore this was an insight confined to the world's sages and mystics.

Biology Reveals the Impartibility of Life

Physics, as we saw, unexpectedly found that matter/energy is impartible within the whole cosmos. Biological data, which pertain to the earth alone, show, for their part, that terrestrial living matter—the biosphere—is essentially a unity whose myriad facets are *interdependent* and interact continually with one another. In Harold Morowitz's words (1975, p. 64):

> Individuals *per se* cannot exist, that is, an individual of one species can only *be* in so far as he is part of the food chain. Plants themselves cannot exist except by the process whereby they are eaten by animals, returning carbon-dioxide to the small molecule reservoir in the atmosphere. Animals cannot exist apart from the food chain. The nitrogen supply that we use comes to us by courtesy of hundreds of other organisms which are chemically processing nitrogen in a wide variety of ways.

In the probings of biology that show the unity of *life*, biology parallels physics' revelation of the unity of the *physical* cosmos. Read the words of the paleontologist-philosopher-mystic, Teilhard de Chardin (1965, pp. 43-44):

> The arrangement of the parts of the universe has always been a source of amazement to men. But this disposition proves itself more and more astonishing. . . . The farther and more deeply we penetrate into matter, by means of increasingly powerful methods, the more we are confounded by the interdependence of its parts. Each element of the cosmos is positively woven from all the others. . . . It is impossible to cut into this network to isolate a portion without it becoming frayed and unravelled at all its edges.

Biological Data: Pervasive Holism

The fact is that the biosphere consists of nothing but wholes that are both partly autonomous and partly dependent upon or subsidiary to greater wholes. Jan Christian Smuts, the South African philosopher/scientist and statesman, pointed this out more than six decades ago in his book *Holism and Evolution*. Today, biology substantiates the truth of this statement through its description of the organization and dynamics of "inanimate" and "animate" matter on earth.

Thus, in an elementary biology textbook (Weisz and Keogh, 1977), one finds the chart reproduced below. The caption, as you may see, reads: "Hierarchy of levels in the organization of matter. The biosphere represents the sum total of all living things on earth." The text explains that the smallest structural units of matter, including living forms, are *subatomic particles.* The next larger units are *atoms,* each of which consists of subatomic particles. Atoms in turn form still more complex combinations called *chemical compounds,* and the latter are variously conjoined into *complexes of compounds.*

It is further explained that these units can be regarded as representing successively higher *levels of organization* of matter. "Such levels form a pyramid, or hierarchy, in which any given level contains all lower levels as components and is itself a component of all higher levels. For example, atoms, contain subatomic particles as components, and are themselves components of chemical compounds."

The chart draws the line between nonliving and living units (a moot point now, in the opinion of some respected scientists, as we shall see) after organelles and before cells. "A cell is a specific combination of organelles, a usually microscopic bit of matter organized just complexly enough to contain all the necessary apparatus for the performance of metabolism and self-perpetuation."

A living organism, the text states, must consist of at least one cell. "Indeed, *unicellular* organisms probably constitute the majority of living creatures on earth. All other organisms are multicellular, each composed of up to hundreds of trillions of joined cells."

Proceeding from the bottom of the pyramid upwards, succeeding levels contain progressively fewer units. "There are fewer communities than species, fewer cells than organelles; and there is only one living world, but there are uncountable numbers of subatomic particles." Furthermore, succeeding levels are structurally more complex than lower ones, inasmuch as a given level combines the complexities of all lower levels and has an additional complexity of its own. For instance, "social complexity results from the characteristics of each member organism as well as from numerous special characteristics arising out of the ways in which the members are organized as a society."

The text states more generally that as we proceed from the bottom of the pyramid upward, all of the following features increase: structural complexity, size of units, energy requirements, order, and instability. It is further stated that this hierarchy of levels provides a rough outline of the past history of matter.

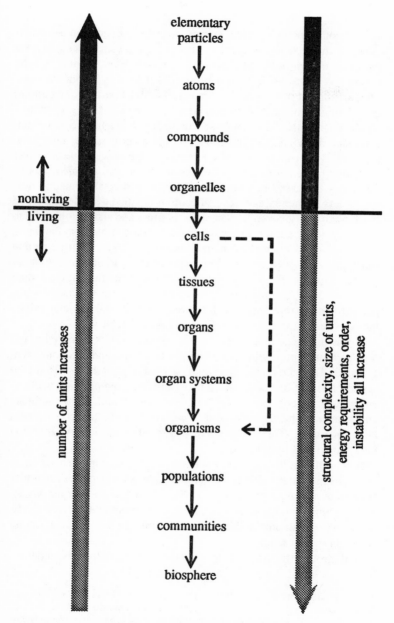

Hierarchy of levels in the organization of matter. The biosphere represents the sum total of all living things on earth.

Yet another point is made: energy must be expended in the emergence of the next higher level. "Such energy expenditures represent
the price that must be paid for the new properties obtained at the
higher level. One of these new properties is united, integrated function, arising out of cooperation among functional parts. For example,
once atoms unite and form compounds, they function jointly as a
single 'cooperative' unit. Similarly, cells forming a multicellular unit
surrender their independence and become a cooperative, integrated
system." By virtue of greater cooperation, the new whole, the new
level that has emerged, has "increased operational efficiency" (we
might say increased functions and powers or increased autonomy).

The text further explains that an atom is small and stable compared
to a human entity, and a human entity is small and stable compared to
a community of human entities. Similarly, the complexity of an atom
is very simple compared to the incredible complexity of structure and
functioning of even miniscule components of molecules, such as
genes. In turn, the structure and functioning of the human individual
is enormously complex, yet it is relatively simple and stable compared to the complexity and functioning of human society, which
includes the complexity of individuals plus that of society.

In this organizational picture,[1] the myriad entities comprising nature are living entities that are both interdependent and autonomous to
a degree. They are both wholes and parts of larger wholes. That is to
say, each is self-assertive and self-organizing—maintaining itself by
engaging in a continuous exchange of energy and matter with its
environment. The "environment" for each entity in turn consists of a
larger organism. Thus entities live within other entities. All lives are
intertwined and interdependent.

In its self-assertive autonomous role, each entity is intent upon its
self-consummation, whereas in its role as subsidiary part, each entity
is capable of transcending itself in the interest of the greater whole.
There is apparently a dynamic balance to be maintained between self-
assertion or autonomy and submission to the needs of the next higher
whole in the hierarchy.

And through the sacrifice, the cooperation, the self-transcendence,

---

1. This is admittedly oversimplified, and the hierarchical picture here sketched must
be understood as a schema representing a much more complicated real-life situation.
The inhabitants of even the lowest rungs exhibit the most complex behavior, and give
evidence of such attributes as like and dislike, choice, etc.

something new occurs at the next higher level. The latter does not represent merely an aggregate of units of the lower level. Rather, it represents a new *integration*, a new *form*, a new *whole*, a new *unity* which is greater than the sum of its parts. If we take the level of chemical compounds, for example, one such compound is water. Water, as we know, is not merely the aggregate of two substances, hydrogen and oxygen, but a totally new substance. Were these two gases merely mixed together, the mixture would be highly explosive, whereas their combination as water puts out fire.

Two or more substances may have identical chemical compositions but different arrangement of parts. It is the *arrangement* or *structure* which determines the physical and chemical properties. For example, two different substances have the molecular formula $C_2H_6O_6$. One is ethyl alcohol, the familiar intoxicant, which is a liquid. The other is dimethyl ether, a poisonous gas. Each calls for its own specific arrangement of the atoms within the molecules. The structure or form is primarily responsible for a substance's identity, not the material components (Augros and Stanciu, 1987, p. 60).

As already noted, something new happens at a supervening level of organization, and this event is *not explainable in terms of the lower level*. A tissue, for instance, is more than the sum of its cells. There is thus a leap between levels. Dobzhansky has spoken of such fissures or gaps in the evolutionary process (which D'Arcy Thompson noted much earlier) as "transcendences," a term which is also applicable to the transition to higher levels of organization. There is no purely logical explanation of this situation; with present understanding the relation between the levels could not be predicted.

There is another way of stating this case: it is a dual process of alternating differentiation and integration. Earlier (in Chapter 1) we suggested that all creative processes depend on interaction between two opposing poles: here we have a case in point. As Arthur Koestler has put it, nature exhibits two opposing tendencies—one a self-assertive, and the other an integrative tendency. It has a propensity to build up more complex forms through a dynamic process of differentiation followed by integration at a higher point on the spiral of existence. And he pointed out that the dual tendencies are ubiquitous. Throughout nature there are both competition and cooperation. On the one hand, plants compete for light and space, animal species compete for ecological niches, and within each species there is competition for territory, dominance, mates and food. On the other hand,

> The independent unities of hydrogen and oxygen are sacrificed
> and absorbed into the higher level of water's form. . . . [These]
> elements . . . are not actual parts of water. They are there only
> potentially . . . and can be recovered actually only by breaking
> down, that is by destroying, the water. . . . The same holds for
> any other chemical compound as opposed to a mixture. In
> sodium chloride both the sodium and the chlorine give up their
> characteristic properties in forming a new unity. The physical
> properties of $NaCl$ differ from those of sodium and chlorine.
>   Robert Augros and George Stanciu,
>   *The New Biology* [p. 34]

nature manifests an integrative tendency ranging from symbiosis and colonialism, to the cohesive forces in flocks and herds, to the sexual ties and social hierarchies of primates and humans.

There is another significant implication of the way life is organized. The interconnections or transactions or flows of information within and between the levels of organization are intricate; they include numerous multi-linear connections and a flow both from the bottom up and from the top down. While higher levels *co-ordinate* lower levels, *all levels affect each other.* This is not a control hierarchy in the manner of a top-down business organization; for, as said, each entity has a degree of autonomy, and its place in the hierarchy is determined interiorly, not merely through external pressures. Its status is an outcome of the evolutionary process as a whole, which is *within* the entity, not outside of it.

While one direction of evolution is toward increasing autonomy and capacity, these properties are won at the cost of greater vulnerability. Just think of the vulernability of a human being as compared to that of an amoeba!

A significant implication of the chart on p. 000 that we have used for reference is the interdependence of the physical, biological, and social (including, where man is concerned, the psychological/cultural/spiritual) levels of existence. In this respect, the scheme coheres with religio-philosophical-psychological tenets concerning the interdependence and interaction of states of existence.

Finally, in implying the mutual interpenetration of all life on the

In the growing embryo, successive generations of cells branch out into diversified tissues, which eventually become integrated into organs. Every organ has the dual character of being a subordinate part and at the same time an autonomous whole. . . . The individual self is an organic whole, but at the same time a part of his family or tribe. Each social group has again the characteristics of a coherent whole but also of a dependent part within the community or nation. Parts and wholes in the absolute sense do not exist anywhere. . . . Each holon [Koestler created this word meaning entities that are both parts and wholes] . . . must preserve and assert its autonomy . . . but at the same time . . . [it] must remain . . . subordinate to the demands of . . . the whole. . . . Thus the self-assertive tendency . . . has its counterpart in its integrative tendency to function as part of the larger whole. . . . Janus also reigns in inanimate nature. . . . The Principle of Complementarity ascribes to subatomic entities a dual nature. . . . In the universe at large, stability is maintained by the equilibration of opposite forces: inertial, centrifugal tendencies . . . [as against] . . . the cohesive forces: electromagnetic or gravitation.

Arthur Koestler, *The Roots of Coincidence* [p. 111]

The benefit of evolutionary . . . [progression] toward high organizational levels is the dynamism and autonomy available to hierarchically organized systems . . . [the cost] is increasing vulnerability. For example, the body temperature of mammals is close to the upper threshold of permissible termperatures for most living protoplasm. Also, the survival range becomes dramatically reduced: while a cold-blooded organism can tolerate a wide range of temperature conditions . . . warm-blooded animals must be able to maintain their body temperature within a few degrees from the norm, or succumb. . . . The arrow of time in biological evolution points toward increasingly dynamic and autonomous species. At the same time it points toward species that are highly complex and vulnerable, forced to rely on delicate survival functions that include, in higher species, not merely genetically coded and inherited behavior, but also learning acquired in the lifetime of the individual.

Ervin Laszlo, *Evolution: The Grand Synthesis* [pp. 82-83]

planet (while expressing it in a new way), the scheme coheres with the immemorial mystical perception that All is in each and each is in All.

The Earth as a Living Entity

We saw that the arrangement of inanimate and animate matter on earth is through and through holistic in nature, an arrangement of wholes within larger wholes—wholes thus interpenetrating each other. Is earth itself an organic, impartible whole?

Conventional biology does not yet accept such an idea, but it has been advanced persuasively by the chemist James Lovelock (1979 and 1988), to whom it came first from space research, and by his collaborator, microbiologist Lyn Margulis. Lovelock calls his theory the *Gaia Hypothesis,* after Gaia, the earth goddess of ancient Greece.

That the earth is a living being was an intuition of older civilizations and is in fact a tenet of perennial philosophy, extensively expounded in Blavatsky's *The Secret Doctrine,* where earth is presented as a living entity in its own right which has evolved over billions of years and continues to evolve.

For a brief summary of the Gaia hypothesis, we may borrow the statement found in Fritjof Capra's book *The Turning Point* (1983, pp. 284-85): "The planet is not only teeming with life but seems to be a living being in its own right. All the living matter on earth, together with the atmosphere, oceans, and soil, forms a complex system that has all the characteristic patterns of self-organization. It persists in a remarkable state of chemical and thermodynamic nonequilibrium and is able, through a huge variety of processes, to regulate the planetary environment so that optimal conditions for the evolution of life are maintained. . . . The earth, then, is a living system; it functions not just *like* an organism but actually seems to *be* an organism, a living planetary being."

The conceptualization of the earth as a living being has now become a matter of practical urgency. Thomas Berry, a historian of religion, points this out: "Concern for the well-being of the planet is the one concern that hopefully will bring the nations of the world into an inter-nation community. Since the earth functions as an absolute unity, any dysfunctioning of the planet imperils every nation on the planet" (Zonneveld, ed., 1985, p. 55).

Viewed from the distance of the moon, the astonishing thing about the earth, catching the breath, is that it is alive. . . . If you could look long enough, you would see the swirling of the great drifts of white cloud, covering and uncovering the half-hidden masses of land. If you had been looking for a very long, geologic time, you could have seen the continents themselves in motion, drifting apart on their crustal plates, held afloat by the fire beneath. It has the organized, self-contained look of a live creature, full of information, marvelously skilled in handling the sun.

Lewis Thomas, *The Lives of a Cell*
[p. 170]

The earth *is* us, it is not ours. We are earthlings. Physically and spiritually we are woven into the living processes of the planet itself. Together with the sea, air, sunlight, and other life forms, we take part in what appears to be a planet-sized living system, the Gaia. This system is so unified that biologist Lewis Thomas tells us that the closest analogy to the biosphere of the earth is that of a single cell. We are an integral part of this living cell, sustained by its currents of energy and patterns of organization. And it is not only our bodies that share this life; the human spirit itself depends, for its vitality, on the exuberant health of the natural world.

Elias V. Amidon and Elizabeth J.
Roberts, "Gaian Consciousness,"
ReVision, vol. 9, 2 (1987)

The Systems View: A New Perspective

Ludwig von Bertalanffy, in his search for an explanation of how organisms are able to sustain themselves in their environment, proposed a powerful new approach which has come to be known as General Systems Theory, although it is not so much a theory as a different way of looking at the world. According to the systems approach, the world is not a fortuitous concurrence of atoms but a great organization in which nothing can be understood in isolation but must be seen as part of a dynamic process. The model of the organism which Bertalanffy proposed is the open system, as contrasted with the machine model, which is a closed system that runs down unless it is fueled by outside energy.

Ervin Laszlo, who extended the systems approach to philosophy and the social sciences, explains this new orientation (1972, p. 6): "Instead of looking at one thing at a time, and noting its behavior when exposed to one other thing, science now looks at a number of different and interacting things and notes their behavior *as a whole* under diverse influences. . . . This is what we do in everyday life, too, when we think of it. . . . We do the same thing . . . in thinking of business enterprises as companies rather than as individual workers and administrators. In fact, we do it with nations as well, and with classes and groups of people within nations. . . . We [similarly] . . . speak of international blocs."

In a paper Bertalanffy gave some years ago, he epitomized the systems approach as follows:

> The modern reorientation of thought, the new models, appear to be centered in the "concept of system." . . . In a very aphoristic characterization: the procedure of classical science was to resolve observed phenomena into isolable elements; these, then, can be put together, practically or conceptually, to represent the observed phenomenon. Experience has shown that this isolation of parts and causal chains, and their summation and superposition, works widely, but that now we are presented, in all sciences, with problems of a more difficult sort. We are confronted with wholes, organizations, mutual interactions of many elements and processes, systems—whichever expression you choose. They are essentially non-additive, and therefore cannot adequately be dealt with by analytical methods. You cannot split them into isolable elements and causal trains. Compared with the approach of classical science, they require new concepts, models, methods—whether the problem is that of an atomic nucleus, a living system or a business organization. Mutual interaction instead of linear causality; organized complexity instead of summation of undirected and statistical events—these, somewhat loosely, define the new problems. (Breck and Yourgrau, eds., 1983, p. 102)

Thus it will be seen that system theory elaborates and extends the hierarchical principle by showing that the complex interactions between different levels of organization serve the greater whole which they comprise.

> In a true system . . . not all macroscopic properties follow from the properties of components and their combinations. Macroscopic properties often do not result from static structures, but from dynamic interactions playing both within the system and between the system and its environment. . . . A human being falling in love—perhaps only once in a lifetime—changes the life of the community of which he or she is a part. Such considerations already hint at the fact that a systemic view of necessity leads to a dynamic perspective. Quite generally, a system becomes observable and definable as a system through its interactions.
>
> Erich Jantsch, *The Self-Organizing Universe* [p. 24]

In the same paper, Bertalanffy discusses his concept of an open system. He begins by posing the question: what is the difference between a normal living organism and a sick or dead organism? His answer is that from the point of view of physics and chemistry there is none:

> For from the viewpoint of "ordinary" physics and chemistry, a living organism is an aggregate of an enormous number of processes which, sufficient work and knowledge presupposed, can be defined by means of chemical formulas, equations of physics and the laws of nature in general. Obviously, these processes are different in a living, sick or dead dog; but the laws of physics don't tell us a difference; they are not interested in whether dogs are dead or alive. This remains unchanged even if we take into consideration the last results of molecular biology. One DNA- molecule is as good as another . . . none is better, healthier or more normal than another. (Breck and Yourgrau, eds., 1983, p. 19)

Bertalanffy defines an open system by the fact that it exchanges matter with its environment, that it persists in import and export, building up and breaking down its material components. The state of an open system is one of being *far-from-equilibrium,* in the parlance of thermodynamics, whereas a closed system is either in the state of *near-equilibrium* or in *equilibrium.* [The term "equilibrium" denotes the state wherein useful energy has degraded and dissipated away to the state of maximum entropy or complete disintegration.] Examples of a closed system are a steam engine or a rock or a cup of cold soup.

Now, the chart we discussed showing the hierarchical scheme of organisms may just as well be described as a scheme of natural or open *systems*. In other words, cells, plants, animals, humans, nations are all open systems. As we saw from the chart, these are wholes within greater wholes, and we may describe them equally as open systems within greater open systems.

The systems approach reverses that of reductionism. That is to say, it focuses on wholes as primary, and parts as secondary—as subtotals of wholes. That is because the scientists concerned realize that the parts—whether they be cells or genes or elementary particles—can only be adequately understood in the context of the system of which they are an integral part. To investigate them in isolation from their context means losing the ability to understand the coordinating activities of the whole system (Capra, 1983, pp. 102-114).

The Sciences of Complexity

General systems theory and cybernetics have led, since the 1960s, to the development of a whole new group of specialities called the sciences of complexity. Cybernetics is the general analysis of control and communication systems both in living organisms and in machines. Its chief founder was the mathematician Norbert Weiner.

The sciences of complexity deal with the appearance, development, and functioning of complex systems regardless of the domain of investigation to which they belong. They include nonequilibrium thermodynamics (developed by Aharon Katchalsky, Ilya Prigogine and their followers), cellular automata theory (pioneered by John von Newmann and further developed in the autopoietic system theory of Humberto Maturana and Francisco Varela), as well as catastrophe theory and dynamic systems theory (developed by René Thom, Christopher Zeeman, Robert Shaw and Ralph Abraham, among others). Within dynamic systems theory, an important new branch has arisen: chaos science, which will be discussed separately below.

The sciences of complexity are useful in many different fields, including ecology, urban planning, communal and institutional development, socio-economic planning. Their wide applicability reflects the fundamental homology (true relatedness) of the self-organizing dynamics at many levels. In Erich Jantsch's words, "This homology makes it possible to view evolution as a holistic phenomenon dynamically linking many levels" (Jantsch, 1980, p. 11).

Since the sciences of complexity have so many implications in terms of our thesis of wholeness, we will spend a little time discussing the work of Ilya Prigogine, one of the originators of the concepts that underlie the field.

Order Through Fluctuation

Prigogine, a Russian-born Belgian, had long been studying the theory of thermodynamics, which embraces both physics and chemistry, when he set himself to investigating a problem that had remained unresolved since the time of Charles Darwin. The question was: How do we reconcile the fact of the evolution of natural species (which is a fact) with the second law of thermodynamics (another fact) which states that the "universe is running down" (known as the law of increasing entropy)? In other words, evolution proves that species develop ever more complex forms, which seems to contradict the second law's conclusion that everything must degrade eventually into a dead homogeneity. The usual explanation of this has been that local decreases in entrophy are purchased at the cost of a general increase. Prigogine, aided by several others, eventually succeeded in resolving this contradiction. (A major breakthrough came in 1967.)

In brief, it was found that whereas in closed systems, entropy and therefore disorder must increase owing to irreversible processes, in open systems "there is not only entropy production due to irreversible processes but also entropy transport due to the import of matter as potential carrier of free energy or negative entropy" (Breck and Yourgrau, 1974, p. 23). In this way, organismic systems display a negentropic trend; indeed they "feed on negative entropy" and thus may even advance toward increasing differentiation and organization, as is the case in the biological phenomena of development and evolution.

Thus the apparent contradiction between the inorganic and organic domains is resolved. As Bertalanffy put it, "According to the second principle of thermodynamics, the general direction of physical events is toward increasing entropy, that is, toward states of increasing probability and decreasing differentiation. Organisms can evolve toward decreasing probability and increasing differentiation, because they represent open systems, exchanging matter with their environment" (Breck and Yourgrau, p. 23).

The fact that far-from-equilibrium structures can occur in a chemical environment had been discovered by two Russian researchers in 1958 (in what is called the Belousov-Zhabotinsky reaction). This discovery offered new insights into the dynamics of these spontaneous forms—forms that are quite different from "regular" reactions. As Prigogine began his investigations, he realized that life and nonlife both appear in nonequilibrium situations and that such situations are everywhere (Briggs and Peat, 1984, p. 167).

Prigogine called the far-from-equilibrium forms *"dissipative structures,"* reflecting the fact that to keep their shape, they must constantly dissipate entropy to preclude going into the state of equilibrium (which "kills" them). And he named the dynamics of such structures *"order through fluctuation."*

In essence, Prigogine's theory states that the movement of energy through a dissipative structure results in fluctuations. If these are minor, they do not alter the structural integrity of the system. But if the system is subjected to intense perturbation it may, in Prigogine's words, "escape into a higher order." (It is suggestive that this theory coheres with the psychological insight to the effect that stress can have creative consequences.)

Ken Wilber has remarked that Prigogine's work falls into the category of endeavors which indicate that reductionistic science is on the wane, all of which show that physics and other fields are opening up to the notion of an unending novelty and creativity within natural processes. Dissipative structures are not actual *explanations* of life or mind, as is sometimes said, but are rather *descriptions* of what has to happen to matter in order for higher orders to unfold. Prigogine's equations furnish the mathematics which permits the evolution of higher, more organized states from less complex structures. Or, as Wilber puts it (1982, pp. 280-81), Prigogine describes "the complexities of material perturbations that allow life or *prana* to emerge through—but not from—matter. In other words, he built a bridge between living and nonliving systems, whereas heretofore there had been a great gulf between the two."

Prigogine's theory is in fact currently being applied in a wide variety of fields, ranging from the prediction of traffic flow patterns to the study of cellular fluctuations as they relate to the cause of cancer. "The behavioural modes deduced from [dissipative structures] theory are recently finding their empirical confirmation in numerous non-linear oscillation phenomena of physical, chemical, biochemical, electrochemical and biological nature" (Jantsch, 1980, p. 40).

Prigogine was the recipient in 1977 of the Nobel Prize in chemistry, awarded him mainly for his theory of dissipative structures. In making the award, the Nobel Committee stated: "Prigogine has fundamentally transformed and revised the science of irreversible thermodynamics. He has given it new relevance and created theories to bridge the gap that exists between the biological and social scientific fields of inquiry" (quoted in Weber, 1986, p. 182). As Renée Weber writes, "[Prigogine] hopes to show that even subatomic particles are subject to his law of dissipative structures, just as macro-processes are, and hence that all matter in the universe is characterized by responsiveness, creativity and—in that sense—by dialogue" (Weber, 1986, p. 184).

Prigogine himself fully realizes the immense implications of his work, for he writes at the end of his book *Order Out of Chaos:* "We can no longer accept the old *a priori* distinction between scientific and ethical values. . . . Today we know that time is a construction and therefore carries an ethical responsibility. . . . As a result, individual activity is not doomed to insignificance."

Order, Chaos and Wholeness

Are all natural manifestations in fact of an orderly nature? Are even disorderly manifestations paradoxically subject to order? The new chaos science answers in the affirmative. But before discussing that science, it may be well to reflect briefly on the meaning of order and chaos themselves.

Clearly some notion of order is indispensable to all understanding and meaning. Order and meaning do in fact go hand in hand, and they always arise in some context, whether it be the cosmic, or the temporal, or the timeless, or the psychological, or the social, or the natural order.[2]

The word "chaos" is derived from the Greek word *Chaino,* which means the Void or the Great Deep or the Abyss. It would seem to refer to a pre-manifestation condition, the condition of which it is said in Genesis, "Darkness was on the face of the deep." Genesis also

---

2. For a stimulating essay on order, see *Science, Order and Creativity* (Bohm and Peat, 1987).

uses the term "Waters." Equivalent terms are found in other traditions as well. For example, the Sanskrit term *Akasa,* derived from the root *kas,* to shine, connotes Precosmic or Primordial Substance. According to Lama Govinda, *Akasa* implies an active, if not creative quality of space, something which is connected with movement, vibration or radiation. Blavatsky equated the Void with Universal Space. In these traditions, the Void is not an emptiness but a boundless plenum. As such it holds all the potentialities that are or may be unfolded in a manifested universe; it is the fullness which makes possible the dynamic world process. Obviously, these are not the common usages of the word "chaos"; ordinarily it simply denotes a state of disorder. In fact I argue below that in truth, existence, individually and collectively, notwithstanding the undeniable personal and societal disorder we face, is *not* a chaos, if by chaos is meant the absence of inner order; that, on the contrary, the imbalances and disharmonies we experience are themselves evidence of the operation of inner order (this paradoxical proposition is the gist of the cosmic-metaphysical-moral law called karma, the subject of Chapter 15).

Now science has based itself on the order and regularities it finds in nature. But what about the many irregularities in nature? The new science of chaos, which is an offshoot of dynamic systems theory (itself one of the sciences of complexity),[3] deals with just this category of phenomena: irregularities. Chaos science finds that irregularities, too, are not devoid of order, that even seemingly chaotic processes such as weather patterns and turbulence in fluids are found, on detailed analysis, to exhibit subtle strands of order. Chaos science, as James Gleick (1988) explains in his enthralling introduction to this new discipline, discovers universal laws governing chaos or disorder. It is a science which demands certain sensibilities such as an eye for pattern, an eye for the whole. Whereas classical science analyzes systems in terms of their constituent parts (whether they be quarks, chromosomes, neurons), chaos scientists look for the whole.

It has been said, Gleick reports, that the new chaos theory repre-

---

3. Dynamic systems science states that dynamic systems are destabilized by the appearance or disappearance of what are called "attractors." These are "complex and subtly ordered structures that constrain the behavior of seemingly random and unpredictable systems. Several kinds of chaotic attractors have been discovered so far. Even a chaotic attractor does not produce an entirely random chaotic phase, and the system concerned passes through the phase to a new steady state, one that is unpredictable but both orderly and creative (Laszlo, 1987).

sents the third great revolution in modern science after quantum mechanics and relativity. Since the particular notion of order in a given realm of understanding is most fundamental, we may well understand why chaos science, discovering as it does a new notion of order, should be of a revolutionary character. Recall, for example, the profound societal change earlier described that came about when modern science arose and introduced an idea of order that differed radically from that held by medieval society.

Nature is full of systems that never find a steady state—that *almost* repeat themselves but never *quite* do so—for example, the weather system, fluctuations in animal populations, aperiodic recurrences of epidemics. Chaos theory models the behavior of the systems concerned and provides the mathematics needed for linking aperiodicity with unpredictability. It employs for this purpose nonlinear mathematical equations—that is to say, equations that express relations that are not strictly proportional.

Chaos science is concerned with the dynamics of pattern formation. Although these change in space and time, chaos science discovers universal laws of pattern formation and it has created special techniques by which to study them.

A case in point is ice crystals. Gleick writes (p. 309): "Ice crystals form in the turbulent air with a famous blending of symmetry and chance, the special beauty of six-fold indeterminacy. . . . As water freezes, crystals send out tips [dendrites]; the tips grow, their boundaries becoming unstable, and new tips shoot out from the sides." Gleick explains that a natural molecular symmetry in the case of ice gives a built-in preference for six directions of growth. One of the physical forces involved is the diffusion of the heat released when water freezes. But the physics of heat diffusion failed to completely explain the patterns of snowflakes when observed under microscopes. "Recently scientists worked out a way to incorporate another process: surface tension. *The heart of the new snowflake model is the essence of chaos: a delicate balance between forces of stability and forces of instability; a powerful interplay of forces on atomic scales and forces on everyday scales*" (p. 309, italics added). No two snowflakes are identical. "The final flake records the history of all the changing weather conditions it has experienced, and the combinations may as well be infinite" (p. 311).

A few statements about chaos theory such as these must excite any inquirer into holism. So much seems to come together—the notion of

Where chaos begins, classical science stops. For as long as the world has had physicists inquiring into the laws of nature, it has suffered a special ignorance about disorder in the atmosphere, in the turbulent sea, in the fluctuations of wildlife populations, in the oscillations of the heart and the brain. The irregular side of nature, the discontinuous and erratic side—these have been puzzles of science, or worse, monstrosities.

But in the 1970s a few scientists in the United States and Europe began to find a way through disorder. They were mathematicians, physicists, biologists, chemists, all seeking connections between different kinds of irregularity. Physiologists found a surprising order in the chaos that develops in the human heart, the prime cause of sudden, unexplained death. Ecologists explored the rise and fall of gypsy moth populations. Economists dug out old stock price data. . . . The insights that emerged led directly into the natural world—the shapes of clouds, the paths of lightning, the microscopic intertwining of blood vessels, the galactic clustering of stars.

James Gleick, *Chaos* [pp. 3-4]

Chaos has become a shorthand name for a fast-growing movement that is reshaping the fabric of the scientific establishment. . . . At every major university and every major corporate research center, some theorists ally themselves first with chaos and only second with their nominal specialities. . . . The new science has spawned its own language, an elegant shop talk of *fractals* and *bifurcations, intermittencies* and *periodicities, folded-towel diffeomorphisms* and *smooth noodle maps.* These are the new elements of motion, just as, in traditional physics, quarks and gluons are the new elements of matter. To some physicists chaos is a science of process rather than state, of becoming rather than being.

James Gleick, *Chaos* [pp. 4-5]

a gradation of scale and the interaction and interpenetration of these dimensions, the idea that dynamic process always obeys necessity or universal law even as it creates form and pattern, the uniqueness yet universality of each moment and each manifestation of nature. Thus it is clear that chaos science coheres with and supports in its own way the ancient notion of chaos as a state pregnant with infinite possibilities for order, beauty and meaning.

Chaos scientists, as they look at computer simulations of dendrite growth, suspect that they will soon be able to extend the use of their science to biology: they see algae, cell walls, organisms budding and dividing. Many new applications beckon or are already being found. "Scientists use the physics of dynamical systems to study the human immune system, with its billions of components and its capacity for learning, memory, and pattern recognition, and they simultaneously study evolution, hoping to find universal mechanisms of adaptation. Those who make such models quickly see structures that replicate themselves, compete, and evolve by natural selection" (Gleick, 1988, p. 314).

We are now ready to discuss the theory of evolution.

7

Evolutionary Theory and Its Evolvement

The theory of evolution is central to biology, but is also important to perennial philosophy, for evolutionary theory touches upon all realms of thought, including religion, philosophy and science. It implicates the two former because it raises basic philosophical questions. What is our origin as a species and as individuals? Are things put together meaningfully? Are they developing in some intelligible direction? If so, how, if at all, are we individually and collectively related to this process?

The notion of evolution goes back a long way, to the time of the ancient Greeks. But evolutionary thought remained purely speculative until the nineteenth century, when empirical evidence began to furnish the basis for a well developed theory of evolution. To this day, some speculative elements still remain. But even though much of the data is indirect and circumstantial, no scientist really doubts that evolution is a fact of history.

In 1809 the French biologist Chevalier Jean-Baptiste de Lamarck published a theory of evolution in which he proposed that all living beings have evolved from earlier, simpler forms under the pressure of their environment, and that the acquired characteristics were inherited by succeeding generations.

The year 1809 was also the year in which Charles Robert Darwin was born. In his youth, Darwin undertook a five-year voyage around the globe as biologist on the expeditionary ship the HMS Beagle, and he made innumerable observations and collected a large number of different plants and animals. He spent the next twenty years meticulously analyzing this information and developing some generalizations from it.

Meanwhile, another biologist, Alfred Russel Wallace, had independently come to substantially the same conclusions, which he communicated to Darwin, and in 1858 the two biologists jointly announced a new theory of evolution to supplant that of Lamarck. It proposed that the environment would gradually weed out organisms with unfavorable variations but preserve those with favorable variations. Over a long succession of generations, and under the continued process of natural selection, a group of organisms would eventually accumulate so many favorable variations that a new species would in effect arise from the ancestral stock (Weisz and Keogh, 1977).

Darwin's monumental book *On the Origin of Species by Means of Natural Selection* was published the following year, that is in 1859. Darwin supplemented this work and elaborated his theory in many later books, notably in *The Descent of Man,* published in 1871.

"Darwin's evidence for evolution rested on the data of comparative anatomy, especially the study of homologus structures in different species and of rudimentary (vestigial) organs; of the recapitulation of past racial history in individual embryonic development; of geographical distribution, extensively documented by Wallace; of the immense variety in forms of plants and animals (to the degree that one species is often not distinct from another); and, to a lesser degree, of paleontology" (*The Columbia Encyclopedia*).

Darwin's carefully documented observations led him to question the then current belief in special creation of each species. The fact that Wallace had come to conclusions similar to his own prompted Darwin to present his evidence for the descent of life from a common ancestral origin.

Many religious people saw Darwinism not primarily as a scientific hypothesis but as a formidable challenge to revealed religion, and indeed it had a profoundly unsettling effect upon men's and women's perception of themselves. To this day, as we well know, the conflict between evolutionists and creationists that Darwinism originated continues unabated.

Darwin's theory, moreover, came upon the scene at about the same time as another scientific finding which conflicted with church teachings, namely, the second law of thermodynamics or the law of entropy. The two theories were a double jolt to the collective psyche: not only were humans not a special creation, but also they were living in a universe destined to come to a grinding halt, seemingly in contravention to the divine will.

Neo-Darwinism—A Theory in Serious Difficulty

Today we can, of course, assess Darwin's theory in retrospect: it was both flawed (Darwin himself recognized many of its weaknesses) and was to prove one of the most powerfully explanatory, unifying and influential theories of all time—a milestone in human thought.

In the twentieth century, "a number of new breakthroughs in such areas as genetics, population biology, and paleontology were able to clear up many of the most glaring inconsistencies of Darwinism, in the process producing a 'Modern Synthesis' that seemed capable of unifying every area of biology" (Andrew P. Smith, 1984, p. 18). Notably, in the 1920s, 1930s and 1940s, genetic theory was incorporated into Darwinian theory, which has come to be known as neo-Darwinism.

Neo-Darwinism postulates that all the phenomena of life, including human behavior, can in principle be explained by physics and chemistry; that life began by pure accident and developed mainly by means of a mechanical, physico-chemical process. The theory attributes all evolutionary change to three factors: (1) genetic inheritance, that is, automatic chemical process; (2) chance mutations, which may be likened to typing errors in the reduplication of the genetic code; and (3) natural selection, that is to say, selection of random mutations that have a survival advantage—a somewhat circular argument.

Neo-Darwinist theory was extremely serviceable. Yet there remained objections on scientific and philosophical or simply logical grounds, and more and more questions arose in the course of time. Not a few scientists today consider the theory inadequate to explain all evolutionary change (for example, sudden changes and great gaps in the ladder of evolution, which Dobzhansky has called "transcendencies"), and many alternative theories have been proposed. We shall look at a few of these below, but first, we need to sketch in some of the problems with neo-Darwinism.

One of the major difficulties of the theory is that "there is no direct evidence for natural selection as an evolutionary process. No one has ever observed an organism evolve, under *natural* conditions, into another kind of organism" (Andrew P. Smith, 1984, p. 21).

Another major deficiency is that neo-Darwinism has great difficulty explaining major evolutionary changes of the kind that could not have entailed any intermediate forms. What conceivable intermediate forms could have led to the appearance of the eye? How could natural selection have brought about the advent of birds? A bird needs both a light bone structure and two wings. Neither wings in themselves nor a light bone structure alone would offer any survival advantage.

Again, neo-Darwinism has great difficulty explaining many forms of animal behavior, especially altruism. When an animal risks its life to save a fellow creature (as happens frequently in nature), its survival probability is scarcely increased, and such behavior should therefore have been selected out.

One of the challenges to neo-Darwinism today comes from the investigative tools that reveal the intrinsic design in even the simplest living systems. Consider, for instance, the fact that the apparatus that assembles protein, responsible for constructing every living thing on earth, is several thousand million million times smaller than the smallest piece of functional machinery ever constructed by human beings (Denton, 1986). Again, how can neo-Darwinism account statistically for the accidental emergence of the mammalian brain, given its connections of 10 to the 15th power? Even if only 1 percent of the connections in a single brain were specifically organized, this would represent a greater number of connections than in the entire communications network on earth (Denton, 1986). The complexity, the incredible ingenuity, the sheer brilliance in the execution of design that is so often manifest in living systems profoundly challenge the proposition that they could ever have been the result of chance.

Genetics itself has severely undermined neo-Darwinism, which relies on DNA as the major mechanism for evolutionary stability and transformation. Recent discoveries, however, show that genes themselves are of a flowing or changing nature. In bacteria, "DNA jumps on and off chromosomes, expanding and contracting so that . . . [the very concept of a gene now requires revision] . . . Nobel Laureate and Vitamin C discoverer Albert Szent-Gyorgi argues that the cell actually feeds information back to DNA and changes its instructions" (Briggs and Peat, 1984, pp. 187-188). In other words, DNA seems to be affected by some of the very things it is supposed to be controlling. This had led Waddington and other biologists to suggest that genes actually interact with the environment.

Augros and Stanciu (1987) quote Stephen Jay Gould of Harvard as saying that "the synthetic theory [i.e. neo-Darwinism] . . . as a general proposition, is effectively dead, despite its persistence as a textbook orthodoxy," but they also point out that since evolution is

To grasp . . . [what has been] revealed by molecular biology, we must magnify a cell a thousand million times until it is twenty kilometres in diameter and resembles a giant airship large enough to cover a great city like London or New York. What we would then see would be an object of unparalleled complexity and adaptive design. On the surface of the cell we would see millions of openings, like the port holes of a vast space ship, opening and closing to allow a continual stream of materials to flow in and out. If we were to enter one of these openings . . . we would see endless highly organized corridors and conduits branching in every direction . . . some leading to the central memory bank in the nucleus and others to assembly plants and processing units. The nucleus itself . . . [would resemble] a geodesic dome inside of which we would see, all neatly stacked together in ordered arrays, the miles of coiled chains of the DNA molecules. A huge range of products and raw materials would shuttle along all the manifold conduits in a highly ordered fashion to and from all the various assembly plants in outer regions of the cell. . . . We would see all around us . . . all sorts of robot-like machines. We would notice that the simplest of the functional components of the cell, the protein molecules, were astonishingly complex . . . each one consisting of about three thousand atoms arranged in highly organized 3-D spatial conformation.

Michael Denton, *Evolution: A Theory
in Crisis* [pp. 328-329]

Gaping holes exist in the fossil record, where one species is followed by another, totally different one. Remarkable new adaptations, such as the eye, appear out of the blue. They seem impossible to explain by any kind of gradual process. The course of evolution takes many strange twists and turns: similar adaptations appear in very different circumstances, while different adaptations appear in the same circumstances. An apparently well-adapted species suddenly becomes extinct; another regresses; still another remains, but fails to evolve. . . . And lurking below all of these oddities is the high degree of improbability of the entire affair: evolution, as Darwinists say it happened, depends on the random appearance and combination of hundreds or thousands of events, each of which, by itself, is an extremely rare occurrence.

Andrew P. Smith, "Mutiny on The
Beagle," *ReVision*, Spring 1984

the single theory that unifies all biology, any major revision in it will now require a readjustment in virtually every biological science and a reassessment of the whole framework of the life sciences.

On the Origin of Life on Earth

We can all recognize the living, but we cannot say what life is. It is certainly not the form—we cannot equate a particular plant or a particular creature with life itself. For the sake of clarity one must distinguish between a specific form and the life within that form. And then we come to at least two realizations: that life is protean, manifesting in multifarious and ever-changing ways, and that it is ultimately a mystery. Each living thing has its own inherent disposition, its own spontaneity, its own impulses, its own state of being. Each is self-unfolding. But to admit this is by the same token to imply that life is already present within the creature, enabling it to unfold—otherwise no unfoldment could be possible.

In the perennial philosophy, life or *Jiva* (as it is called in Sanskrit) is the Great Mystery. Blavatsky stated that it is an eternal energy, uncreated in that it is underived from other forms. It is that which impels every entity to struggle to express itself, by means of self-unfoldment, self-regulation, self-determination. Even if science were ever to succeed in producing life in a test tube (something once thought easily possible, but now seen as more complex), life itself would still remain a mystery.

How life originated on earth is still a matter of speculation, but as the event happened in the very distant past, it is improbable that it can ever be known for certain. Obviously, there is a plethora of speculations on the circumstances of the origin of life on earth. Among the differing suggestions are the terrestrial origin of life within a primaeval broth; the infection of the earth by micro-organisms deliberately sent on a spaceship by intelligent beings on a planet from outer space; and the evolution of life on comets containing organic materials derived from interstellar dust (Sheldrake, 1981).

According to neo-Darwinist theory, life originated by chance within a pre-biotic soup. But many scientists now consider this idea highly implausible, given the evidence that the smallest bacteria and algae, and even the still smaller viruses, are so complex that they could not have assembled themselves by accident. As one biologist,

Andrew Smith, puts it, the mainstream theory of the origin of life depends on the random appearance and combination of hundreds or thousands of events, each of which, by itself, is an extremely rare occurrence. Francis Crick, the co-discoverer of DNA, and a popular spokesman among molecular biologists for radical reductionism, has admitted that "an honest man, armed with the knowledge available to us now, could only state that in some sense the origin of life appears at the moment to be almost a miracle, so many are the conditions that would have had to be satisfied to get it going" (*Mind/Brain Bulletin,* 1985, vol. 9, 2).

A miracle—or a matter of purposeful design? Empirical science has up to now shunned the idea of purpose in nature. But today there are many scientists (Cf. for example, Harold J. Morowitz, 1987; Augros and Stanciu, 1987; Erich Jantsch, 1980; and Lovelock, 1979), who point to the evidence of *express purpose and fitness in design* within nature.

In the context of the perennial philosophy, as we have tried to make clear, the universe is both living and multi-levelled. Behind the visible cosmos are the invisible levels of the living hierarchy. At its cutting edge, science is coming to a similar view. For example, David Bohm postulates (as we earlier saw) what he calls the implicate and other generative orders behind the explicate or sequential orders. In their book *Science, Order, and Creativity,* Bohm and F. David Peat propose that instead of attempting to reduce life to the explicate order—to atoms, molecules, DNA, cells, and other structures—it is necessary, for the understanding of life, to perceive that the present theories of science are abstractions of "an infinity of generative and implicate orders." They propose that a deeper generative order is common to all life and to inanimate matter as well.

> Within this order there is room for new kinds of "pools of information" from which life could be generated. The wholeness of the living being, and even more of the conscious being, can then be understood in a natural way, rather as the wholeness of the molecule and the superconducting system is understood (although it must not be forgotten life is much subtler and more complex than molecules and superconducting systems). Life is no longer seen as the result of somewhat fortuitous factors, which perhaps happened only on an isolated planet, such as Earth. Rather it is seen to be enfolded universally, deep within the generative order (Bohm and Peat, 1987, pp. 200-201).

Evolution: The Perspective of the Perennial Philosophy

Helena P. Blavatsky's massive and unique work entitled *The Secret Doctrine* was first published in 1888. It consists of two large volumes, entitled, respectively, *Cosmogenesis* and *Anthropogenesis*. This work is too arcane to be characterized in a few short words. But what is of immediate relevancy for our present subject is that *The Secret Doctrine* is a monumental treatise on cosmic evolution or, more accurately, on a cyclic process which includes both involution and evolution.

Blavatsky saw evolution as the universal process by which all things are produced, undergo change, grow and develop. To suggest its nature, she used a few familiar illustrations. When a seed, a minute particle hardly distinguishable from any other kind of seed, is planted, it eventuates, via stages of development, in a fully grown tree or plant with flowers and fruit, unique to its kind. This is a kind of evolution; the tree has evolved from the seed. Again, a fertilized ovum in the womb passes through many embryonic stages until a fully formed human infant is produced, and the infant in turn develops into an adult. This, too, is a kind of evolution—a human being has evolved from a germ. Analogously, preceding the materialization of a building, such as a great cathedral, there must be a conception in the architect's mind, followed by plans, followed by the execution of those plans and working drawings, and this in turn followed by the actualization of the building from those plans, which involves many hands. Thus an edifice has "evolved" from an idea. In short, evolution is the realization of ideas. Or it may be defined as the coming into visibility of something that was invisible, or the bringing into activity of something that was until then only a latent potentiality.

The point is, whatever evolves must have some antecedent existence, whether mental and/or physical. The seed, according to Blavatsky, has within it an ideal design or plan (as Plato would have agreed), though each of its embodiments in nature is idiosyncratic and unique, since no tree or plant or leaf is identical to any other.

In short, evolution is an unfolding from an existing inner order. But since it is intelligent, rather than a mechanical process, there is room for creative variation and individual response to environmental circumstances.

One might say that *Blavatsky integrated the idea of evolution with the venerable idea of the universal hierarchy of being.* Thus stated, the hierarchical principle is no longer rigid; it has become the working principle of a dynamic *process* involving all levels of being, "a progressive development toward a higher life." In her emphasis on process, Blavatsky foreshadowed the present shift in science from static or structure-oriented to process-oriented thinking.

What Blavatsky delineates is a journey in consciousness, encompassing a hierarchy of levels of being of which terrestrial evolution is a small but integral part. It is a journey which begins with the involutionary arc of world formation, in which the emphasis is upon the geological development of material substances, followed by the evolutionary arc, wherein all beings, all life forms are co-participants, first developing individuality and the sense of self through proliferation of species, then gradually through conscious experience, realizing their unity and oneness with the source of being, which is divine and beyond experience.

More generally speaking, Blavatsky challenged the orthodoxies of both the science and theology of her day. Her assertions (such as her view of the dynamic nature of matter) seemed implausible and even preposterous at the time, but many of them have since been vindicated by science. A case in point here is her conception of evolution. An essentially similar view is now advanced by other exponents of the perennial philosophy, without crediting her as their source. (She herself always insisted that she was only reiterating the most ancient—and perennial—teaching.) More to the point, ideas essentially similar to hers have recently emerged among scientists at the cutting edge of evolutionary theory.

We must first recount the thrust of her critique of Darwinism. Blavatsky applauded Darwin's contribution as far as it went. She rejected the idea that evolution consists of a slow, mechanical accumulation through the ages of small increments of advantage. She saw it, on the contrary, as an unfolding in progressive stages of inner or inherent potentialities, which exist within the process itself. Furthermore, it was for her a dual process: the involution of a diffused and generalized consciousness into separate, specialized material forms, thereby developing the structure of the world with all its chemical and physical complexity, followed by the evolution of conscious life through the development of self-aware, self-determined and finally, self-transcendent forms. The two processes worked synchronously, every step in the evolution of responsive forms being likewise a step in the acquisition of knowledge or information, leading finally to conscious freedom, or spiritualization.

Furthermore, Blavatsky proposed that there are three separate but interwoven streams of evolution in the terrestrial scheme of things: the spiritual, the intellectual, and the physical, each with its own rules or inner laws. All three streams are represented in the constitution of man, the microcosm of the macrocosm (nature itself) and it is this which makes us the complex beings we are (Blavatsky, 1979, Vol. I, p. 181).

To my knowledge, Blavatsky was the first writer to regard matter not as dead, passive and inert, but as living, dynamic and energetic, and to speak of a cosmic evolutionary process which amalgamates, as mentioned, the traditional hierarchical order and the scientific theory of evolution.

One can recall a number of recent thinkers who have propounded views kindred to those of Blavatsky. More or less chronologically, they include the Hindu sage Sri Aurobindo; the philosopher Alfred North Whitehead, who in the 1920s pioneered the philosophy of process, in which organisms take the place of matter; and the philosopher-statesman-scientist Jan Christian Smuts, whose book *Holism and Evolution* was published in 1926. Still later came the paleontologist/mystic/philosopher Pierre Teilhard de Chardin, whose controversial writings are still anathema to many scientists, although he is proving to be one of the most influential minds of our age (Ferguson, 1987, and Morowitz, 1987).

In retrospect, so far as evolutionary theory is concerned, Blavatsky introduced several new ideas, including the concepts that evolution proceeds on three different levels, each with its own rules and *modus operandi*, and that evolution is a cosmic process to which the development of mind is critical. Among scientists, these particular ideas emerged only very recently, as we shall describe below.

Meanwhile, let us recall something stated earlier: perennial philosophy is an open-ended wisdom whose meaning is expanding during the course of time, and which in fact requires continuing reformulation in terms consonant with the growth of knowledge. I believe that *The Secret Doctrine* represents one such reformulation, and as such, a few more words about it are in order. It is a book far from easy to read, in part because of its subject matter, which treats the profound and inherently mystical themes of the birth of the cosmos and the birth of man largely in symbolic or mythic or poetic terms. At the same time, the style is to us old-fashioned and diffuse, drawing upon history, poetic narrative, myth and religious symbolism to support its thesis, and spending a great deal of effort to contradict nineteenth-century scientific theories now outmoded.

According to the esoteric doctrine, the formative thrust of a manifesting universe is toward the concretization of consciousness and its reciprocal, the spiritualization (that is, responsiveness to the quality of spirit) of matter. The involution/evolution spiral is, it is said, from unconscious perfection (undifferentiated oneness) to conscious imperfection (the struggle for selfhood and self-expression) to conscious perfection (a state of fully aware oneness, as exemplified by the Buddha or the Christ). Thus it is only through the experience of the limitation of finiteness, of embodied life, and the conquest of this limitation, that consciousness can free itself from the illusion of the separateness of self and world, mind and body, and thus win enlightenment.

Emily B. Sellon (private paper)

As we look at the evolutionary process . . . it's hard not to notice its most outstanding feature: its *holistic* growth. . . . Natural selection can account, at best, for the survival of present wholes, not their transcendence into higher-level wholes. . . . [The] orthodox scientific theory of evolution seems correct on the *what* of evolution, but it is profoundly reductionistic and/or contradictory on the *how* (and why) of evolution.

But if we look upon evolution as the reversal of involution, the whole process becomes intelligible. Where involution proceeded by successive separations and dismemberments, evolution proceeds by successive unifications and higher-order wholes. Where involution proceeded by successive forgetting or amnesis, evolution proceeds by successive remembering or anamnesis. . . . Further, anamnesis and holism are actually the same thing: to remember is really to re-member, or join again in higher unity. . . . Evolution *is* holistic.

Ken Wilber, *Up From Eden*
[pp. 304-305]

Blavatsky herself characterized her work as a re-presentation of the wisdom tradition in a version designed for the modern world, which was her own nineteenth century. Yet, although the twentieth century world picture is very different, many of her ideas are still unique, and growing steadily less improbable. Blavatsky's work contains many mistakes and self-contradictions, but many of the ideas she proposed are now matters of fact. So perhaps some of the still unknown theories she advanced may find corroboration in the course of time. If so, they would help to clarify some still unexplained problems of evolution.

In any case, the present obscuration of what is in fact a unique work on esotericism or the perennial philosophy seems ironic, especially when one considers how few such statements are available for study. (Many writers today allude to the perennial philosophy, but usually as context for this or that postulate, without attempting to treat the worldview as a whole.)[1]

The old conflict between science and religion over the idea of evolution is nullified when evolution is understood nondualistically, for so understood, evolution is seen as a transcendent, creative, even divine process, not a mechanical and hence ungodly affair. Everything is sacred. In the memorable words of William Blake, one may see the world in a grain of sand. All existents in both the visible and invisible worlds are together journeying toward divine perfection.

From this perspective, man is not only divine in his essential nature, but writ large, is one with the universe itself—the measure of all things. This ancient idea rings all the truer when one thinks about what the human species has already wrought, for good and evil, upon this planet. The main groups of plants and animals were established long ago, though species formation continues apace. We are now to witness a psycho-social and spiritual evolution whose rules (or types of order) are not those of biological evolution, but completely their own.

If there were an oracle today, the new injunction might be: *Oh, humanity: Evolution on Planet Earth is henceforth in your hands!*

That injunction would take its place beside the ancient Delphic one: *Man, Know Thyself!*

Co-Evolution—The Living, Creative Universe

As earlier noted, a number of biologists are now departing from habitual reductionistic traditions. One example is the late Erich

---

1. For those who want to acquaint themselves further with Blavatsky's thought, her chief works will be found in the bibliography. In addition, surveys of her works include ones by Barborka and Purucker, among many others. Two of the most recent books are those by Nicholson (1985) and Ellwood (1986).

> The Universe is worked and *guided*, from *within outwards*. As above, so it is below, as in heaven, so on earth; and man, the microcosm and miniature copy of the macrocosm, is the living witness to this Universal Law and to the mode of its action.
>
> H. P. Blavatsky, *The Secret Doctrine*,
> [Vol. I, p. 274]

> Man is the measure of all things, the Microcosm of the Macrocosm. . . . [From Man's act of understanding] both the Self of Man and the universal Self accumulate their store of experience. . . . Without the whirling array of atoms, suns, and planets, without the molecular cells of his physical form, without his inheritance of animal instincts, and his human intelligence, without the harshness of pain, the enticement of pleasure, and the fire of love, there would be no human evolution, and neither man nor God could unite heaven and earth in the actual and conscious experience of their unity both in essence and form.
>
> Sri Madhava Ashish, *Man, Son of Man*
> [pp. 36-37]

Jantsch, who wrote a complex, and truly remarkable work, *The Self-Organizing Universe*. Jantsch, who began his professional career in his native Vienna as an astrophysicist, had wide-ranging interests. He was an accomplished musicologist, businessman, engineer, and consultant to numerous national governments (Briggs and Peat, 1984).

In his opening chapter, Jantsch notes the self-renewal and far-reaching restructuring of science that is now under way. Areas which for a long time had only been open to speculation, notably cosmology and paleontology, now find empirical foundations. Micropaleontology's new laboratory methods have permitted the identification of microfossils in sedimentary rocks dating back 3500 million years. "The scope of space and time which is accessible to observation has widened immensely. . . . In this tremendously extended space-time-continuum, interconnections and patterns emerge which are primarily of a dynamic nature and which give for the first time a scientific basis to the idea of an overall, open evolution which is interconnected at many irreducible levels" (1980, pp. 4-5).

Jantsch continues: "In the realm [of direct human experience] we find the phenomena of biological, social and cultural life. . . . Biological and social systems need an understanding of phenomena such as self-organization and self-regulation, coherent behaviour over time with structural change, individuality, communication with the environment and symbiosis, morphogenesis and space- and time-binding in evolution" (pp. 5-6).

Jantsch's book, which builds on the work of Ilya Prigogine, is a synthesis of a number of process-oriented scientists, beginning as far back as Alfred North Whitehead and Jan Smuts. More particularly, Jantsch applies the dissipative-structure approach to the origin of species, following in the wake of the chemist Manfred Eigen and the biologists Conrad Waddington, Paul Weiss, Humberto Maturana, Francisco Varela and Ricardo Uribe.

The new process-oriented approach is in contrast to the emphasis on "solid" system components and structures. With it, structure and function become complementary and dynamically evolving. In dynamic systems, even being is an aspect of becoming.

> The notion of system itself is no longer tied to a specific spatial or spatio-temporal structure, nor to a changing configuration of particular components, nor to sets of internal or external relations. Rather, a system now appears as a set of coherent, evolving, interactive processes which temporarily manifest in globally stable structures that have nothing to do with the equilibrium and the solidity of technological structures. Caterpillar and butterfly, for example, are two temporarily stabilized structures in the coherent evolution of one and the same system. (p. 6)

In this new interpretation of the evolutionary process, evolution is no longer considered under the aspects of adaptation and survival, which have had such a "fateful influence" on the images we hold of ourselves and of human life in general. "Such a 'heroic pessimism' . . ." says Jantsch, has been further enhanced by "theories which view the origin of life as a mere accident, so unlikely that it perhaps occurred only once in the whole universe.

"But life is more than survival, and the environment to which it adapts, itself evolves and adapts. . . . The emergent paradigm of self-organization permits . . . a vision . . . of the interconnectedness of the human world with overall evolution . . . [and] a new sense of *meaning*" (p. xiii).

Emphasis on structure, adaptation and dynamic equilibrium (steady-state flow) characterized the earlier development of cybernetics and General System Theory. These interdependent fields of study, actively developed since the 1940's, arrived at a profound understanding of how given structures may be stabilized and maintained indefinitely. This is of primary concern in technology and it was in this area that cybernetics and a specialized system theory triumphed in the control of complex machinery. In biological and social systems, however, this type of control—also called negative feedback—is only one side of the coin. No living structure can be permanently stabilized. The other side of the coin concerns positive feedback, or destabilization and the development of new forms.

Erich Jantsch, *The Self-Organizing Universe* [p. 5]

Biological, sociobiological and sociocultural evolution now appear as linked by *homologous* principles (i.e., principles related through their common origins) and not just by analogous (formally similar) principles. This should not come as a surprise since the whole universe evolved from the same origin.

This new type of science which orients itself primarily at models of life, and not mechanical models, spurs change not only in science. . . . [Its themes] may be summarized by notions such as self-determination, self-organization and self-renewal; by the recognition of a systemic inter-connectedness over space and time of all natural dynamics; by the logical supremacy of processes over spatial structures; by the role of fluctuations which render the law of large numbers invalid and give a chance to the individual and its creative imagination; by the openness and creativity of an evolution which is neither in its emerging and decaying structures, nor in the end result, predetermined. Science is about to recognize these principles as general laws of the dynamics of nature. Applied to humans and their systems of life, they appear therefore as principles of a profoundly natural way of life. The dualistic split into nature and culture may now be overcome. In the reaching out, in the self-transcendence of natural processes, there is a joy which is the joy of life. . . . We are not the helpless subjects of evolution—we *are* evolution.

Erich Jantsch, *The Self-Organizing Universe* [p. 8]

Neo-Darwinism, with its emphasis on adaptation and the struggle for survival, is a limited picture of the way living forms change. The fact that some of the best adapted that also reproduce most rapidly—bacteria—are also both the oldest and the least complex of creatures shows that adaptation and survival cannot explain a central feature of evolution, namely, the fact of the complexification of living forms. Indeed, some of the most complex forms are not particularly well adapted. The human being is a prime case in point. Though extremely adaptable in some respects, the human being is also extremely delicate in other respects, and must go to great lengths in order to survive in inhospitable climates.

"It is not successful adaptation to a given environment which is the foremost formative factor in life, but the web of ecological processes in an environmental system which shape physiological and behavioural patterns which subsequently may become genetically anchored" (p. 145).

Jantsch writes, "The evolution of the universe is the history of an unfolding of differentiated order or complexity. Unfolding is not the same as building-up. The latter emphasizes structure and describes the emergence of hierarchical levels by the joining of systems 'from the bottom up.' Unfolding, in contrast, implies the interweaving of processes which lead simultaneously to phenomena of structuration at different hierarchical levels." There is a mutual or reciprocal development of organisms and environment, of microevolution and macroevolution. The two processes mirror each other. They coevolve. "Such an overall evolution is indeterminate, imperfect and prefers dynamic criteria in the choice of its strategies before morphological ones. It is self-consistent and creative" (p. 75).

Whereas neo-Darwinist theory postulates that life forms are created piece by piece in small changes, co-evolutionary theory sees forms as dissipative structures arising spontaneously and holistically out of the flux and flow of macro and micro processes. Evolution takes place not in response to the demands for survival, but as the creative play and cooperative necessity of an entire evolving universe. This play is open with respect to the products to which it gives rise and even to the rules of its own game which are also subject to change.

Jantsch, like Prigogine, sees the step between inanimate dissipative structures and animate or "self-organizing" organisms as a natural and inevitable one, not the "accident" or chance which orthodox biology assumes. "Life no longer appears as a thin superstructure over a lifeless physical reality, but as an inherent principle of the dynamics of the universe" (p. 19).

This statement is consistent with David Bohm's notion that life is everywhere implicit (which is also Blavatsky's position), although the two came to a similar view by different routes. Both point up the fact that science is not only becoming ever more harmonious with perennial philosophy, but positively reinforces some of its tenets in a new way.

Jantsch reconstructs the condition of the first years of earth; it was a bubbling cauldron of gases and chemical reactions in which dissipative structures abounded. He presents a fascinating account of how pre-biotic evolution and the subsequent emergence of life might have occurred, citing empirical observations that support a conclusion that life's appearance was not accidental, and that microscopic and macroscopic developments played a complementary role in bringing about the right conditions for its terrestrial appearance.

Whereas orthodox molecular biologists believe that the shape life forms take is controlled by the information in the genes, Jantsch holds the contrary view that organisms only *use* genetic information. An organism's self-creative regime expresses a particular individuality, a particular autonomy in terms of the environment. "Structure and function are realized the more characteristically the more degrees of freedom there are available to the system. The natural dynamics of simple dissipative structures teaches the optimistic principle of which we tend to despair in the human world: The more freedom in self-organization, the more order!" (p. 40).

The Systems View and the Perennial Philosophy

The first lesson taught in Esoteric philosophy is that the incognizable Cause does not put forth evolution, whether consciously or unconsciously, but only exhibits periodically *different aspects of itself* to the perception of *finite* Minds. Now the collective Mind—the Universal— . . . however infinite in manifested Time, is still finite when contrasted with the unborn and undecaying Space in its supreme essential aspect. That which is finite cannot be perfect.

H.P. Blavatsky, *The Secret Doctrine*
[Vol. II, Pt. II, XVIII, B, p. 487]

The systems orientation in science represents a long stride toward the reconciliation of science and holistic philosophy. As noted, Erich Jantsch's vision of a self-organizing universe is remarkably harmonious with Blavatsky's evolutionary theory. But one cautionary note is in order. We must never be misled into believing that any system, however large and comprehensive, is complete, or representative of reality itself. To do so would be just as egregious as taking reality to be a vast clockwork. For, as we have tried to show, reality is far more than the sum of the phenomena of the manifested cosmos. It is boundless and ineffable, and at the same time, it shines through everything and is present everywhere.

Haridas Chaudhuri superbly clarifies the point we wish to make (1974, pp. 195-196):

> After everything has been said about the universe, after the entire world has been transformed on the basis of scientific knowledge into a hierarchical structure of ever-widening systems, we are still invariably left with a profound sense of mystery. The unfathomable mystery which lies at the core of reality baffles both the analytical function of thought pointing to the infinitesimal as well as its synthetic function, building higher and higher systems toward the infinite. This luminous experience of the impenetrable mystery is common to all the scientists, philosophers and mystics of the highest rank. The scientist calls it the mystery of Nature. The philosopher calls it the mystery of Being. The mystic calls it the mystery of the Spirit. . . . *The universe in its essential structure has two inseparable dimensions: relational and nonrelational, spatio-temporal and nontemporal, rational and suprarational. In respect of the first dimension the universe can be envisaged as a hierarchy of systems within systems within systems. . . . It is an intelligible scheme of relations and relata explicable in terms of laws, theories and working hypotheses. In respect of the nontemporal depth dimension, the cosmic whole transcends all relations and distinctions . . . of the whole and part, of subject and object, of system and reason* [italics added]. Every system of existence and energy is . . . a product of interaction between the fullness of reality and rational consciousness, or between immediate existence and the mediating categories of thought. So *it is absurd to equate any system, however comprehensive, with the entire universe or ultimate reality* [italics added].

Self-Reference

Process oriented biologists look upon biological organisms not as machines but as self-created organic wholes with attributes such as consciousness, self-reference or identity, "autopoiesis," cognition, creativity, and purposiveness.

The concept of "autopoiesis," from the Greek, meaning "self-production," was originated in the 1970s by Humberto Maturana, a Chilean biologist. "Autopoietic" systems are contrasted with "allo-poietic" systems. The former are organic systems such as a plant or an animal; the latter are machines. Unlike a machine whose identity is given to it by its manufacturer and which contains virtually the same molecules from the time it is made until it is trashed, an autopoietic system has an inherent, self-sustained identity: it changes its molecules continuously and yet remains somehow "the same." Thus its identity is not a function of its components, but rather issues from its relationships with its environment. That is to say, an organism paradoxically derives its *autonomy* from its *interdependence* with its environment. Here is a description of this significant feature of organisms:

> Dissipative or autopoietic process structures are not like gears always going around the same way. Take as an example an individual wheat plant. A wheat plant's identity is defined by an intricate web of connections with sun, air, soil. These connections involve complex molecular reactions which convert matter and energy from one form to another to maintain the dynamic balance that is the plant . . . [a balance whereby] all the various processes . . . stay in the same relationship to one another but are constantly moving . . . even if a part is lost, identity will be retained. . . . What we call "parts" are really different expressions of a whole movement (Briggs and Peat, 1984, pp. 179-180).

The group of Chilean biologists known as the Santiago School, which includes Humberto Maturana, Francisco Varela and Ricardo Uribe, has extended the theory of autopoiesis to include such concepts as life, cognition and even meaning. Varela has emphasized that meaning is connected with life at a very elementary level, since all interactions of an autonomous, self-organizing system with its environment are cognitive or mental interactions (Capra, 1983).

What is perhaps most significant here from our standpoint is the recognition of the pervasiveness of consciousness and the principle of selfhood within even so-called primitive forms of life. Jantsch, for example, writes, "If consciousness is defined as the degree of autonomy a system gains in the dynamic relations with its environment, even the simplest autopoietic systems such as chemical dissipative structures have a primitive form of *consciousness*. . . . And a dissipative structure 'knows' indeed what it has to import and to export in order to maintain and renew itself. It needs nothing else but the reference to itself" (Jantsch, 1980, p. 40). Thus consciousness becomes a universal attribute of the cosmos.

Nature's Mentalist Activities

The word "cosmos" connotes order. The word "universe" connotes a unitary turning. These words of common usage are employed by mechanistic scientists, who thereby impute mental qualities to machines, perhaps without realizing their self-contradiction.

As scientists, they must *rely* on nature's order. It is after all the ubiquitous order that makes science possible in the first place.

In speaking of even the most minute organisms, biologists routinely talk of such characteristic behavioral processes as *specializing, regulating, controlling, communicating,* and *cooperating*—words which connote mental activities.

On occasion, mechanists go so far as to express wonder and awe before nature's "feats" or nature's "majesty," seemingly unaware of the fact that these are odd terms to use in talking about happenings that are supposed to be blindly mechanical.

It is ironical that, while physicists concede that matter is a category that it is difficult, perhaps impossible, ultimately to separate from mind, biologists still insist on looking at living creatures as nothing but machines, and, moreover, compound this nonsense by imputing to the machines many mental activities. (This notion is made culturally ubiquitous by the many science-fiction books and films that attribute all sorts of human feelings in order to personalize robots.)

The specialization of cells, especially in animals, is enormous, as we know. In the adult human there must be close on a thousand billion cells that perform countless different cooperative or integrative tasks. Instances of specialization or differentiation, integration, cooperation and co-ordination are found throughout the processes of animate nature. Perhaps the most amazing instances of co-ordination are found in the embryological process. Cells go to their appointed places at the right time and develop the right properties for carrying out the necessary organic functions. Cells that initially are all alike begin to differentiate, and in the end, although they originated in a single progenitor, some cells have become rigid bone, some the enamel of teeth, some fluid as water, some a system of transmitting electrical signals, and so forth.

"Why should the position in space within the foetus determine whether a cell shall manufacture adrenalin, thyroxin or play a humble role as muscle?" asks the British scientist Raynor Johnson. It is quite true, he continues, that chemical substances have been isolated from certain parts of the growing embryo which appear to stimulate and control growth, and that these are called "organizers." But what organizes the "organizers"? (Johnson, 1953, pp. 54-55).

Morphogenetic Fields

We have already discussed in some detail one of the integrative— as opposed to cellular or molecular or mechanistic—approaches to biology and to the concept of evolution: the relatively new systems approach which emerged from further research into thermodynamics combined with the model of the organism as open system that Ludwig von Bertalanffy had proposed some three decades earlier. This particular line of investigation, carried out especially by Ilya Prigogine and his collaborators, has yielded the unifying self-organization paradigm, one that, as Erich Jantsch has shown, sheds a good deal of light on the all-embracing phenomenon of evolution. (The systems view, as we made clear, concerns not only biological systems: the sciences of complexity to which it gave rise deal with the appearance, development, and functioning of complex systems regardless of the domain of investigation to which they belong.) This approach is however by no means the only integrative orientation in biology: various versions of an organicist paradigm have been advanced by many writers, including biologists, for many years.

Whereas in the dominant biological view, the focus is on the composition of the organism (genes and molecules), the emphasis in organismic biology is on the organism itself. Contemporary organicism holds that the way the constituents are *ordered* can explain the organism's *form;* that formulating a theory of the *organization* of organisms will be crucial in understanding the large questions of embryonic development and the evolutionary origins of the major classes of organisms. Parenthetically, there is in fact no correlation between the DNA content of species and their morphological or other complexity: for example, humans and chimpanzees are significantly different morphologically and behaviorally, yet their DNA content is extremely similar (Goodwin, 1989).

Instead of seeing the organism as an uncertain category that is a function of its genes plus its environment, organicism sees the organism itself as the mediator between these two factors, and as both selecting and altering its environment. In this way, the organism/ environment duality is replaced by an emphasis upon organisms as dynamic processes. (It will be evident that this view has a significant commonality with the systems view.) In addition to the element of form, classical organicism has been concerned to study such elements as symmetry, polarity and pattern, and also fields and particles. Our purpose here is to draw attention to the important concept of fields as applied in organismic biology.

In an essay entitled "Changing from an evolutionary to a generative paradigm in biology," noted biologist and mathematician Brian C. Goodwin remarks (in Pollard, ed., 1984) that Darwin elevated historical process to a primary explanatory principle in biology, but that in fact Darwin had nothing to say about how common ancestors themselves originate; he discussed only how their descendents may become different from one another in a historical process. Goodwin holds that questions relating to organization, to invariance and to transformation cannot be answered in terms of historical processes and inheritance. Instead, he proposes morphogenetic fields as the source of developmental and evolutionary potential. He terms these fields as domains of potential, capable of generating a great diversity of forms which belong to a general type or class of structures. Regenerative processes, in which whole structures are produced from parts, are also characterized by field behavior of this kind. Goodwin emphasizes that the biological domain is a primary realm of order and intelligibility such that it structures the effects of historial contingencies and randomness, and that this primary realm determines not only spatial order but all aspects of biological process, including temporal order and behavior.

Goodwin does not doubt that in developing organisms the relevant equations are field equations, but exactly what form these will take for an adequate description of morphogenetic processes is not yet known. For Goodwin, a major task for biology is to discover these equations that embody the organizing principles, the order and the regularity of this domain, and hence to define "a domain of constraint." He holds that this task is no less important than has been the derivation of equations of mechanics, of electromagnetism, of relativity, of quantum mechanics.

> We must stop thinking about movement as something that happens to things as a consequence of forces from outside themselves acting within a pre-existing space-time framework. Causality becomes immanent rather than transient, and what we call objects and their environment are self-generating complementary forms. . . . Process has its own logic. It is not classical two-valued logic, which runs into contradictions as soon as it is faced with processes that have properties of both continuity and transformation. What is required is a logic in which every value is an aspect of all values . . . and in which there are no absolute and atomic, logical values as in the classical scheme.
>
> B. C. Goodwin, "Organisms and Minds as Dynamic Forms," *Leonardo,* vol. 22, 1, 1, 1989

Goodwin discusses the process he calls generative transformations whereby domains of distributed potential, which are the morphogenetic field of developing organisms, give rise to actualized patterns of localized structure. This for him is the biological process of creation, and he emphasizes that genes are not sufficient causes of biological form. "Particular conditions, either of composition (gene products) or of position and velocity, select particular forms of space-time order from the set of possibilities defined by the laws governing fields, whether morphogenic, or gravitational" (p. 118). For Goodwin, the actual history of organisms (their contingent evolution) is intelligible only in relation to the logic of the biological creative process.

It may be recalled that the concept of fields first arose in physical theory to account for universal conditions that permeate space, such as gravitation. Fields are invisible and undetectable except by their effects. According to quantum field theory, though intangible, fields alone are real, while matter is simply the momentary manifestations of interacting fields. Einstein considered gravitation the very curvature of space itself, and magnetic fields impose spatial patterns, as when iron filings scattered around a bar magnet reveal the spatial pattern of its field.[2]

---

2. Classical physics recognized just two fields: electromagnetic and gravitational. Modern physics has added to these two fields: the strong field, which holds the atomic nucleus together, and the weak field, which breaks the nucleus apart in certain kinds of radioactive decay. Recently, the electromagnetic and the weak fields have been shown to be the same. It is believed that these four fields are really one field.

Historian of biology Donna Jeanne Haraway (1976) points to Ross G. Harrison (1870-1959) as a pioneer in the construction of a modern organicism in distinction to the old vitalisms[3] and mechanisms. Ross's work on the limb bud helped to lay the foundation for the controversial field concept that informed a good deal of biological work in the 1930s. The field concept was later considerably modified but still supports the organismic paradigm today. Haraway also singles out, among organicists employing the field concept, the two noted biologists Paul Weiss and Joseph Needham. Haraway remarks that by means of the field concept these three scientists found a way beyond the polar opposites such as structure and function, crystal and organism, part and whole; they unified the particle and the field.

The fact remains, according to Goodwin (1989, p. 31), that, as of the present, there are no field theories of organismic life cycles and cognitive processes adequate for an understanding of organisms and minds, of evolution and cognition. "The challenge here is to find a solution to the problem of form in dynamic, transformational terms that unite history with order, creativity with intelligibility."

Several years ago, Rupert Sheldrake, a British plant biologist, presented a theory of what he calls formative causation (Sheldrake, 1981). He postulates a set of complex, invisible fields, or spatial structures, that are responsible for the characteristic form and organization of systems at all levels of complexity. "These fields order the systems with which they are associated by affecting events which, from an energetic point of view, appear to be indeterminate or probabilistic; they impose patterned restrictions on the energetically possible results of physical processes" (1981, p. 13). Sheldrake's hypothesis does not, however, treat of the origin of forms, only their development once they have appeared. He proposes a two-way process whereby the morphogenetic fields concerned are built up from what happens in space and time; they help shape and determine living systems in the world, and, conversely, the latter exert an influence upon the fields.

At this point we may ask: how far has the discipline of biology progressed overall? The consensus according to authorities is that notwithstanding the accomplishments (including the brilliant discov-

---

3. Vitalism, it may be recalled, states that living phenomena are the effect of a nonmaterial principle which is variously called vital force, entelechy, élan vital, radial energy or the like.

eries of molecular biology) of the three approaches we have identified (which may be seen as complementary), biology still has far to go in terms of understanding and explaining major aspects and questions of life such as the origin of species, differentiation and development, regulation and regeneration, behavior of organisms, embryological functioning and brain functioning.

It may be noted that morphogenetic fields are reminiscent of David Bohm's implicate and superimplicate order behind the explicate order of quantum mechanics. Bohm and F. David Peat (1987), in a chapter on "Generative Order in Science, Society, and Consciousness," include a discussion of the generative order of life and its evolution. If the generative order is basic to inanimate matter, they remark, it is even more essential for the understanding of life.

Finally, notice the suggestive kinship among three respective ideas: morphogenetic fields integral to the dynamics of terrestrial life, invisible generative orders integral to the dynamic cosmos and its incipient life, and the earlier discussed philosophical doctrine embracing the cosmic hierarchy of existence and the involutionary/ evolutionary process in which all life participates.

Intrinsic Purposiveness

Purposiveness, which is of course a mental function, is evidenced throughout nature. In their book *The New Biology,* Augros and Stanciu (1987) take purposiveness as one of their main themes, and they conclude that it is as inalienable from life as mind itself.

The book details numerous examples of purposiveness. Birds build nests to house their young. The spider's web, the beaver's dam, and every other animal artifact serves evident purposes; in these instances, animals clearly act for an end. The frog purposely registers the forms moving in front of it. In plants, the flatness of leaves permits the interception of light— the source of energy for photosynthesis—and gas and heat exchange with the air. The pear shape of guillemot eggs ensures that the eggs will not roll off the flat cliff ledges on which the guillemot lays them without a nest. The examples go on and on.

Nature displays, too, numerous extraordinary feats of *co-ordination* to achieve specific purposes. Consider the many design features of a bird—wings, tail feathers, pneumatic bones, air sacs, breast bone and pectoral muscles, ribs, neck, feet, spinal column, pelvis, automatic hooking of feather barbules, etc. which combine to permit birds to fly.

Nature is moreover capable of extraordinary *ingenuity* in achieving a specific purpose. According to a study cited in this book, the cicada of North America live most of their lives underground. Their larvae emerge in adult form to reproduce in certain cycles depending upon the locality—seventeen-year cycles in the eastern half of the United States, and thirteen-year cycles in the southern states:

> These two numbers are large enough to exceed the life cycle of any predator. Thirteen and seventeen are also prime, so that no potential predator can coordinate its life cycles with the emergence of adult cicadas (p. 209).

Nature's ability *to combine purpose with simplicity and economy* is also remarkable. A case in point cited in the same book is that of the whale's blubber: it serves three distinct ends: food storage, buoyancy, and insulation.

Again, the slime on a fish's body accomplishes three goals with extraordinary efficiency—reducing drag, affording protection from microscopic parasites, and, by virtue of its slippery property, helping fish escape predators. Yet another example: birds' feathers serve for flight, heat regulation, protection and ornament.

Purpose, in sum, is inseparable from the very structures and organization of nature's living forms. This, in turn, suggests the interdependence of mental and bodily function, beautifully coordinated to serve the whole creature.

Nature's Surpassing Artistry—Whose Art?

Nature's creations richly display such qualities as design, form, color and texture, so much so that one would have to be exceptionally dull or unresponsive to fail to be amazed at some of nature's "appearances."

According to the zoologist/philosopher Adolph Portmann, many of life's colored creations are calculated to have a visual effect. He writes (1975, p. 68): "[They] . . . are organized precisely so that they may radiate true visual 'broadcasts'—broadcasts which are directed to watching eyes as receiving organs, and which, at the same time, function in accordance with the laws of sight and of the production of color. As the eye is made to see, so are many things in the world formed that the eye may see them."

> We may draw attention to some bird-songs, to the magnificently rich coloration of rosell parrots, to the colours and patterns of deep-sea fish (where there is practically no light) and also of butterflies, and to the perfection of colour and construction of the peacock's feathers. On the basis of sexual selection this beauty must be explained as arising from the emotional sensitivity of the peahen, which was such that it was attracted to those males who proved superior in some minute artistic creation to their neighbours. To attribute such aesthetic susceptibility to the peanhen's mind seems fantastic: indeed, on the human level this sensibility only develops as a rule with the approach of maturity. The grace of form and color of many flowers can scarcely, I think, be for the delectation of the hymenoptera. Wherever we look in nature we see the evidence of artistic exuberance far beyond the utilitarian survival value.
>
> Raynor C. Johnson, *The Imprisoned Splendour* [pp. 72-73]

The mechanists' idea about colors is that they are primarily chemical results of metabolic processes, and that their accidental accumulation in visible organs gave natural selection the possibility of using these colors in the service of pollenization or preservation or mating or signalling or for some other utilitarian purpose. But according to Portmann, investigations show that in many cases very intricate organs, even combinations of several structures, have no practical purpose, even though their development requires tremendous expenditure of developmental energy on the part of the creatures concerned.

Studies of sea anemones and worms, marine snails and many other creatures have disclosed yet another mysterious phenomenon: *none of these play any role in the fields of vision of higher animals and none have eyes with which they might be able to see one another.* Nonetheless, all of them possess colors and marking, often of great beauty.

Obviously these aesthetic features, which lack all utility, have no possibility of entering into the work of natural selection, Portmann remarks, and he calls them "unaddressed broadcasts." He places them in the biologists' category of "species specificity." There also exist special organs that have no utililty other than self-representation—organs "which do nothing except manifest the particularity of a species in the language of structures." To the unprejudiced eye, these phenomena might well seem *"as nothing other than the intentional work of an artist"* [italics added].

Portmann ends his essay with the following pregnant words:

> The organisms do not exist in order that the metabolic function may be exercised; something unknown governs the metabolic process in order that this particular organism—which ultimately is ever before us as a mystery—may be maintained for a little while. And a part of this organism is its manifest appearance, which we have called its self-representation.

Are there artists behind the scenes? Could it be that the remarkable and subtle appearances found among plants and creatures are the creative work of hidden ordering principles, or of the Archetypes of Plato's vision?

This in fact is the gist of a postulate of H. P. Blavatsky, who refers in *The Secret Doctrine* to "the conscious, intelligent powers in Nature," whose task is the fashioning of nature's forms, and whose function is reflective of their evolutionary status. (Blavatsky more generally and in depth expounds the doctrine of hierarchies and its different versions in Judeo-Christian, Syrian, Hindu and other traditions.)

May these ideas be related to the earlier discussed morphogenetic fields? May they be related to Bohm's implicate and superimplicate orders? Only time may provide an answer.

8

Of the Brain and the Mind

To consciousness the brain is messenger.
Hippocrates

Introduction

Traditionally, the human being is viewed as consisting of body, mind and spirit. More particularly (and consistent with our earlier consideration of the composite human constitution), we may take the soul to mean the mind in its fullness, with all its thinking, feeling and willing, and take the spirit of woman/man to be something beyond it, completely indefinable in terms of mind or body, but necessary to his or her existence and interaction (Cf. Wood, 1967, p. vii).

Let us now take a look at science's view of human mind or consciousness. In fact, there are two main schools of thought.

We have already noted that the majority of the scientific community still holds the view that the mind is simply reducible to the brain and "nothing more"—more precisely, to the brain's biophysical and biochemical functioning. We pointed out the drastic implications of this statement which in effect reduces the human being to an automaton, leaving no room for freedom and making nonsense of education, of law, of art, of civilization itself.

The idea of reducing mind to brain is also naive from the standpoint of physics itself. The brain, being made of physical matter, must as Margenau (1987, p. 19) remarks, contain "a variety of essences that are nonmaterial, highly elusive, incomprehensible to 'common sense,' often incapable of visualization and localization." Thus brain "stuff" is itself fundamentally non-material. Or, to state this in another way, reductionists little realize that they engage in a circular argument—an argument that begins and ends with mind—when they assert that the human mind, including consciousness and reflective thought, can be explained by activities of the central nervous system. For must not the nervous system itself be understood in terms of atomic physics, that is, in terms of the action and interaction of the component atoms of carbon, nitrogen, oxygen, and so forth? And do not these atoms, in turn, take their source from the subatomic level which is now formulated with the mind as an inseparable element of the system? (Cf. Morowitz, 1987).

Others in the scientific community are persuaded that the mind and the brain are *not* identical, however intimately linked. While these scientists are in the minority, they include in their ranks some distinguished persons—for instance, the eminent neuroscientists Sir Charles Sherrington, Sir John Eccles, Wilder Penfield, Roger Sperry, Karl Pribram, and the above-quoted Professors Henry Margenau and Harold Morowitz. However they may otherwise differ, there is total agreement among these scholars that the human consciousness of self and the creativeness of the human mind cannot be reduced to any other explanatory level. The noted biologist W. H. Thorpe writes,

> It is remarkable to find two people as different in their background, their training and their approach as Karl Popper and Jacques Monod, the one a philosopher and the other a molecular biologist, in total agreement over this point. That is to say, they are both clearly convinced of the present impossibility of reduction from the living to the non-living and from the conscious mentality to the non-mental aspect and organisation of life (Harris, 1976, p. 61).

Thorpe continues:

> Karl Popper indeed goes much further and believes that the reduction of biology to chemistry or of chemistry to physics; or the reduction to physiology of conscious or subconscious experiences which we may ascribe to animals, and still more, the reduction of human consciousness itself and the creativeness of the human mind to animal experience—are all projects the complete success of which seems most unlikely if not impossible" (pp. 61-62).

According to neuroscientist (and Nobel laureate) Roger Sperry, neuroscience has now reconceptualized the mind-brain relationship in a fundamental way which represents a direct break with the long-established materialist and behaviorist doctrine that has dominated neuroscience for many decades. Far from renouncing or ignoring conciousness, the new interpretation gives full recognition to the primacy of inner conscious awareness as a causal reality.

Wilder Penfield, the Canadian neuroscientist, spent a lifetime trying to find a full explanation of the mind in the operations of the brain. In his small classic *The Mystery of the Mind* (1975), he re-marks that there is no place in the cerebral cortex where electrical stimulation will cause a patient to make a decision or conceive a belief. Penfield's investigations led him to the conclusion that it is impossible to explain the mind in terms of the physics and chemistry of the brain, but that at the same time the mind can give direction only through the mind's brain mechanism. He thought of the brain as analogous to a computer and the mind as the programming agency. He writes (p. 80):

> Because it seems to me certain that it will always be quite impossible to explain the mind on the basis of neuronal action within the brain, and because it seems to me that the mind develops and matures independently through an individual's life as though it were a continu-ing element, and because a computer (which the brain is) must be programmed and operated by an agency capable of independent under-standing, I am forced to choose the proposition that our being is to be explained on the basis of two fundamental elements. This, to my mind, offers the greatest likelihood of leading us to the final under-standing toward which so many stalwart scientists strive.

In such statements science is beginning to close a serious rift between itself and religion, the humanities, and perennial philos-ophy.

The Mind-Brain Relationship

If the brain and the mind are not identical, the question arises as to just how they are related. The above statement by Penfield contains the suggestion that the brain is to the mind as the computer is to the programmer. The computer cannot "think" if by thinking we mean human ratiocination, which is usually purposeful and is almost al-ways colored by feeling. Moreover, a computer is necessarily pro-grammed.

Implications for the Question of the Survival of Death

One of the topics we will discuss below is reincarnation, a concept which presupposes the survival of death. Here we need only point out that to identify mind with brain is, by the same token, to deny the possibility of survival of physical death. On the other hand, the emergent view of neuroscience that consciousness is primary and

[Thinking on the part of humans] is driven either from "below" by desire or emotion, or from "above" by inspiration. Pure thought is perhaps impossible for us; abstract mathematical thought comes closest. . . . [Yet] men compute because they *want* to do so. . . . In antithesis, a computer does what it is told to do . . . being totally without self-generated drive, inspiration, purpose, or emotion. To be useful a computer must indeed be programmed for a purpose.

E. Lester Smith, ed., *Intelligence Came First* [p. 53]

irreducible to any other level of explanation is one which presents no logical difficulty for the case for survival.

Implications for the Practice of Medicine

The body-mind and the more specific brain-mind questions have an important bearing upon the understanding of health, illness and the practice of medicine.

Western conventional medicine is largely reductionistic—that is to say, it views the patient primarily as a physical body or as a physico-chemical machine, whose dysfunctional parts the doctor must repair. It neglects, by and large, to look at the human being as a whole, including the capacity for self-healing—that is so out of character with the properties of a machine—and at the human being's psychological, social and environmental conditions.

Contemporary medicine has, to be sure, made tremendous advances in certain areas, but the mechanistic approach is proving too limited. As Dr. Larry Dossey has made clear in his book *Space, Time and Medicine*, conventional medicine confuses disease processes and disease origins, treating symptoms instead of causes. It simplistically adopts the view of "one disease, one cause," ignoring the fact that health and illness depend on an interplay among physical, psychological, social, and environmental factors. Very little *preventive* medicine is practiced.

However, several decades ago a new branch of medicine arose,

This self-conscious mind of ours has this mysterious relationship with the brain and as a consequence achieves experiences of human love and friendship, of the wonderful natural beauties, and of the intellectual excitement and joy given by appreciation and understanding of our cultural heritages. Is this present life all to finish in death, or can we have hope that there is further meaning to be discovered? . . . We must realize the great unknowns in the material makeup and operation of our brains, in the relationship of brain to mind, in our creative imagination, and in the uniqueness of the psyche. When we think of these unknowns as well as the unknown of how we come to be in the first place, we should be much more humble. . . . In the acceptance of this wonderful gift of life and of death, we have to be prepared not for the inevitability of some other existence, but we can hope for the possibility of it.

This is the message we would get from what Penfield . . . and Thorpe . . . have written; and I myself have also the strong belief that we have to be open to the future. This whole cosmos is not just running on and running down for no meaning. . . . We cannot think more than that we are all part of some great design. . . . Each of us can have the belief of acting in some unimaginable . . . drama. We should give all we can in order to play our part. Then we wait with serenity and joy for the future revelations of whatever is in store after bodily death.

Sir John Eccles, "The Self-Conscious Mind and the Meaning and Mystery of Personal Existence" [Sloan, ed., pp. 52-53]

called psychosomatic medicine, which is concerned specifically with the study of the relationships between the biological and the psychological aspects of health. Psychosomatic medicine is gaining increasing acceptance and is stimulating research into the influence of the mind on the immune system, into the influence of emotions on health, and into the incidence and character of remission from cancer and other illnesses.

Numerous cases of "spontaneous remission" from illnesses and of what is called faith or spiritual healing have been reported. Conventional medicine has largely ignored or shrugged off these phenomena as aberrant, and systematic research into them is only beginning. However, in the past six or seven years a new field called psycho-neuroimmunology has emerged. This is concerned with identifying the links between the mind, the brain and the immune system, and the ways these communicate with each other.

It is becoming evident that the inner mechanisms of healing stem from the way that seemingly different systems work together, for example, the coordination of the circulatory system, the nervous system and the immune system. Beyond these, moreover, there seems to be something like a healing system that only comes into play when it is challenged or confronted by stress, trauma, disease or illness of some kind. Furthermore, the healing system appears to work together with something that has been called the belief system. Norman Cousins proposes in his book *Human Options* that the heal-ing system is the way the body mobilizes all its resources to combat disease, while the belief system is often the activator of the healing system.

Clearly, health and health care in the broadest sense comprehend physical, psychological and also social health—inasmuch as the indi-vidual's and society's health are interdependent. Emphasizing the connection between the two, Capra (1983, p. 134) notes: "Psycho-logical and social pathologies have now become major problems of public health . . . there has been an alarming rise in alcoholism, violent crimes, accidents, and suicides, all symptoms of social ill health. Similarly, the current serious health problems of children have to be seen as indicators of social illness, along with the rise in crime and political terrorism."

Health has been regarded as synonymous with a good health care system, consisting primarily of proper nutrition, absence of smoking and access to doctors and hospitals. But health is in reality far more.

Upon its establishment some forty years ago, the World Health Organization defined health as "a state of complete physical, mental and social well-being." The broader implications of WHO's defini-tion were however left largely dormant until recent years. But WHO is now, with the participation of public health experts from around the world, spearheading a shift from thinking about "public health policy" to thinking about "healthy public policy." WHO is bracketing health with wider concerns such as economics, an approach which is warmly welcomed by dissenting economists. The latter share WHO's conviction that health must be linked with work, food, housing, environment and technologies. WHO makes five recommendations in what is known as its "Ottawa Charter" (adopted in 1986 at a conference in Ottawa): ● Build healthy public policy. ● Create supportive environments. ● Strengthen community action. ● Develop personal skills. ● Reorient health services.[1]

The Possibility of Self-Regulation and Self-Transformation

As will be suggested, when we consider the domain of religion, the main goal common to religious traditions is self-transformation, for which each tradition has prescribed methods and techniques. Science is now approaching this domain from a different but complementary perspective: it is investigating the correspondences between the brain, on the one hand, and emotions and mind, on the other.

A human being is endowed with volition, something which permits choosing and creating "a visualization of desired physical, emotional, and mental behavior." So write Elmer and Alyce Green of the Menninger Foundation, in an essay on "Biofeedback and Transformation" (*The American Theosophist*, Spring Special Issue, 1984). The Greens have been studying the pyschophysiology of consciousness, and especially of creativity, for thirty years. Biofeedback is the process whereby some of a person's biological information is fed back to him or her, usually by means of a visual or audial indicator. Since a person's mind, emotions and body function interdependently, the rationale of biofeedback is to employ the physiological information deliberately to influence these components in desired ways. The method involves deep relaxation, followed by visualization of what one wants the body, the emotions or the mind to do. "What we call training in self-regulation of the body is in reality *training in self-regulation of the brain, by the mind, with volition*," state the Greens [italics ours].

Let us note parenthetically that in biofeedback we have yet another instance of the remarkable coalescence of different fields of specialization, for it represents a convergence of neuroanatomy, electrophysiology, learning theory, ethology, perception research and psychophysiology.

In their book *Higher Creativity, Liberating the Unconscious for*

---

1. See *New Options*, July 25, 1988, Issue No. Fifty.

> Until a few years ago, claims that consciousness can be expanded and transformed rested on subjective evidence. Suddenly, first in the handful of laboratories of a few pioneer scientists, then in thousands of experiments around the world, the undeniable evidence began coming forth.
>
> Awakening, flow, freedom, unity, and synthesis are not "all in the mind," after all. They are in the brain as well. . . . The subjective accounts have been correlated with concrete evidence of physical change: higher levels of integration in the brain itself, more efficient processing, different "harmonics" of the brain's electrical rhythms, shifts in perceptual ability.
>
> Marilyn Ferguson, *The Aquarian Conspiracy* [p. 67]

Breakthrough Insights (1984), Willis Harman and Howard Rheingold devote a chapter to the available "tool kit for personal breakthrough." The kit contains both traditional and new tools for self-transformation:

Even casual examination of the literature—from the yoga sutras of Patanjali to the mystical texts of esoteric Christianity, Judaism, Buddhism, and Islam—makes it clear that the tool kit is not exclusively an invention of the modern age (p. 81).

One final cautionary reminder: the study of the correlations between mind and brain are of great practical value, but we should never forget that the mind is irreducible to the brain, and that a change in the brain cannot in itself unlock a particular thought or emotion. As Ken Wilber has remarked, "No amount of EEG sophistication could help you prove or disprove Keynes' theory of macroeconomics, for instance."

9

Of Time and Causality

Causality in classical or Newtonian science is, as we know, linear and deterministic. It states that if one knew right now the positions, masses and velocities of everything in the universe, one could predict the whole future, everything that will occur. The view assumes that on the basis of present information (always supposing it to be complete), an observer could predict the whole future course of events according to the laws of determinism. This presupposes, of course, that one could stand outside the system, which we now know is impossible. In fact, strict causality has been abandoned because of the developments in science already discussed, as well as such phenomena as synchronicity, or meaningful coincidence, and other mysteries involving time. We now face a world characterized by relativity, ambiguity, non-locality and other non-linear causal states.

In classical physics, time is a steady flow from past to future, everywhere the same, untouched by consciousness and in no way affected by the universe itself or the bodies in it. But we now know that time is not the same in all parts of the universe, since its rate is affected by its frame of reference, and therefore it can no longer be seen as an absolute. Yet so strong is the grip of personal, "commonsense" experience, that all of us find it difficult to relinquish the idea that time unfolds through a series of successions, even if in certain cases those successions depend on the observer.

In fact, the time dimension of nature is more encompassing even than the conceptions of Newton and Einstein and of quantum mechanics. Determinism persists in the idea of "chance events," even though glimpses of a more underlying order suggest that the kind of causal relations which regulate events must be sought in terms of *relationships*, rather than single events.

What we rarely stop to realize is that time and causality are not physical events (ticking clocks, missed trains); they are mental constructs that are experienced differently in different states of consciousness.

In his book *Synchronicity* (1987), F. David Peat, a physicist and philosopher of science, points out that while the new physics shows the possibility of different orders of succession, it leaves unexplained the phenomenon of meaningful coincidence or synchronicity. "It is only when causality is pushed to the limit that it is discovered that the actual context in which events take place must extend indefinitely. In other words, everything that happens in our universe is in fact caused by everything else. Indeed the whole universe could be thought of as unfolding or expressing itself in its individual occurrences. It is within this global view that it becomes possible to accommodate synchronicities as meaningful events that emerge out of the heart of nature" (p. 58).

Peat's proposition that everything that happens is caused by everything else is in fact an old idea, though he comes at it in a new way. In Western thought it is spoken of as the mutual sympathy of things; in the East it is embodied in the doctrine of karma, the law of cosmic balance and harmony, which in human life becomes the law of morality. What karma signifies is that since the universe is both ordered and intelligible, every human act has meaning and is intended, purposeful. Thus individuals are responsible for their actions and must eventually bear the consequences, in accordance with the inner law of cause and effect, which nothing can circumvent.

We must not misunderstand this latter statement. It does *not* mean that everything is predetermined. To the contrary, it implies a creative universe. What it signifies for human beings is this: the reliability and the intelligibility of the cosmos make it possible for us to accomplish our aims. For instance, we cannot go to the moon unless we know the astrophysical and astronomical rules and abide by them. Put in another way, lawfulness is indispensable for freedom and responsibility; lacking a perceived order, choice and self-determination (controlled action) are impossible. Freedom and necessity are mutually defining poles.

Let us further note something extraordinary that is happening today: the mutual interdependence or causal relations of all things is graphically illustrated by our present global state of affairs—by the obvious interdependence and interaction of peoples, and of our phys-

What is randomness in one context may reveal itself as simple orders of necessity in another broader context. And vice versa, what is a simple order of necessity in one context may reveal itself as chance in another broader context. But in a still broader context, both are to be seen as extremes in the rich spectrum of orders of varying degrees that lies between them. Thus, there is no need to fall into the assumption of complete determinism (although this may in certain fairly broad contexts be a correct abstraction and approximation). Nor is there any need to assume that chance and indeterminism rule absolutely (though these too will provide correct abstractions and approximations in their appropriate contexts). No matter which system of law may be appropriate in the context that is currently under investigation, there is always room for something more and something different—something that will be more subtle and that has the ultimate potential for being a manifestation of creativity.

Bohm and Peat, *Science, Order and Creativity* [pp. 133-134]

Space is the possibility of movement, time the actuality or the realization of movement; or, space is externalized, objectivated time, time projected outward. Time, on the other hand, is the internalized, subjectivated space—the remembrance and inner transformation of spatial movement into the feeling of duration or continuity. Time and space are related to each other like the inside and the outside of the same thing. Reality comprises both and simultaneously goes beyond both of them. Those who experience this reality live in a dimension beyond the space-time continuum and experience the universe as a timeless body.

Lama Anagarika Govinda, *Creative Meditation and Multi-Dimensional Consciousness* [p. 280]

ical, ecological, social, moral (human rights, for example), economic, security and other conditions. This state of affairs corroborates in a new way the nondualistic tenet that the collective creates its own reality, by its thoughts, intentions, motives, actions and values.

Earlier we reviewed new developments in the life sciences, including the emergence of organismic or process-oriented thinking and the new sciences of complexity which build on systems theory. Whereas the traditional approach is to study nature in terms of analysis and the causal interaction of parts, the systems approach arose from the need to be concerned with the problems of wholes and wholeness—wherein causality is not just linear but multi-dimensional. This includes cases of chaos, turbulence, changes of state, transition and evolution, wherein "nature displays far more subtle mechanisms in which new and emergent properties manifest themselves and descriptions must take into account the *whole system* and not just its parts" (Peat, 1987, p. 73).

In his afore-mentioned book, Peat points out that it is becoming more and more apparent that nonlinear behavior in nature is more the rule than the exception. At the same time, the availability of high-speed computers and the recent development of new mathematical techniques make it possible to study nonlinear systems.

Nonlinear systems are much closer to the operations of an organism than of a machine. "Its understanding therefore requires new attitudes that lie closer to synchronicity than they do to linear causality, in which patterns and orders unfold out of the general background of change. Within such an approach, mind may no longer appear as an alien stuff in a mechanical universe; rather, the operation of mind will have resonances to the transformations of matter, and indeed, the two will be found to emerge from a deeper ground" (p. 73).

Chaos theory mentioned earlier comes to mind here, and it is worth noting that chaos theory implies that randomness is not something incommensurable with order but is rather a special case of a more general notion of order. Whatever happens must in fact take place in some kind of order, so that the notion of a "total lack of order" has no real meaning. As we earlier remarked, chaos theory is in this respect compatible with the karma doctrine.

In the aesthetic realm, time presents itself to consciousness in yet another way. Think of time and its various rhythms and pace in music (where intervals and pauses are all important), in dance, in poetry, in the novel, in drama. Think also of our perception of time passing; ponderous when we are caught in a disagreeable or unpleasing situation, imperceptible when we are enjoying ourselves. Does this not also reveal time's relativity?

Finally, there is the mystical state of consciousness wherein time becomes timelessness. We spoke of this transcendent state earlier (in

The mystery of time has aroused man's wonder since the dawn of history, and strongly influenced his views of self and world. A *cyclical* concept of time, which arises from observation of such natural sequences as the alternation of day and night and the renewal of the seasons, has always prevailed in the East: the Hindu theory of endlessly recurrent cosmic cycles of activity and rest (the "days and nights of Brahma"), the yogic path of the self's return to union with the All, the cyclic reintegration of man with the macrocosmic reality symbolized by the mandala in Tibetan Buddhism, and the Chinese concept of cyclic patterns of history as the natural development of an organismic world-view—all these are examples of a conception of time as a never-ending dynamic process which continually returns upon itself, not necessarily to its starting point, but rather in an ever-mounting spiral.

The doctrine of reincarnation, intrinsic to Indian religions, is an application of the cyclic view of time to the life of individual man. . . .

In contrast . . . [to this cyclical view found in the East], prior to the 20th century . . . [Western thought] was committed to a *linear* concept of time, often likened to the flow of a river. . . . The present is both the direct result of the past and the cause of the future. But . . . [this linear view] established two different values for time: the past is held to be static, closed and unalterable, while the future is dynamic, open, fluid and problematic. . . .

[The new physics] shattered the rigid causality of the physical world . . . [suggesting instead] that there is a whole range of causal possibilities which includes such things as indeterminacy, coincidence, simultaneity, and even the reversibility of time. The perception of space-time as a continuum . . . also makes it possible for us to understand that time may be one indivisible whole which only *appears* in its threefold guise of past, present and future.

Emily B. Sellon, "Causality and Synchronicity" (private paper)

Chapter 2) and will look at it again in relation to the experience of unity (in Chapter 16). It is a state of consciousness that lies beyond space-time and yet embraces space-time.

Certainly it seems evident that problems of time and causality involve all modes of thought and all apparent dichotomies, including mind and matter, the observer and the observed, space and time, physics and metaphysics, science and the arts, science and perennial wisdom, inner values and outer conditions. They will doubtless remain unresolved until they are seen in terms of a higher relationality, a deeper unity.

10

The Psi Faculties, or the Relation Between Inner and Outer

It is a fascinating example of synchronicity that both physicists and parapsychologists should use the term "psi" to indicate what is still unknown, "a curious verbal flash that may serve to indicate common ground between two disciplines" (Renée Haynes, in Koestler, 1973, p. 142).

Psi, the name of a Greek letter, is used to designate so-called paranormal faculties—telepathy, precognition, clairvoyance, clair-audience, and psychokinesis (the mind's ability to influence the movement of external physical objects, as in the fall of dice). The investigation of these faculties is traditionally the domain of parapsychology.

Telepathic, precognitive and other paranormal experiences are spontaneous more often than not. Renée Haynes has written: "Baffling, unrepeatable, uniquely personal, as such events may be, the fact that they do occur, that certain hallucinations, waking impressions, and vivid dreams can be correlated with objective happenings unknown to the person concerned, far away, long ago or not yet enacted, has repeatedly been made plain, both before and after systematic investigation began in the 1880s. . . . Many spontaneous instances of the paranormal . . . have been checked and verified by standards of evidence acceptable in a court of law" (in Koestler, 1973, p. 142).

The mind-brain problem is directly related to the subject of psi faculties. If one contends that the mind is the product of the brain, paranormal faculties must be either denied or explained in physical terms. Attempts to find a physical explanation have met with no success, and therefore their existence is usually dismissed by mechanists.

However, many scientists have changed their attitude toward parapsychology from hostility and negativity to a recognition of the field as a potentially important area for investigation.

The relationship between brain states and paranormal perceptions is a very interesting one, as Arthur Osborn (1959), a veteran investigator of this field, has noted (p. 15):

> Obviously, the condition of the brain is important for the reception of psychic impressions. One curious fact that emerges is that while the brain needs a good blood supply for alert, normal functioning, the reverse is often the case when information is being received by paranormal means as during sleep or trance. . . . Brain passivity is often the prelude to subconscious activity. It would almost seem that when the brain is not being subjected to intense sensory impacts its receptivity to other levels of consciousness is increased. This may be the rationale behind the practice of fasting and the severe austerities associated with some religious disciplines. Also, hypnotized subjects in deep sleep and unconscious at the normal level may tap sources of knowledge outside the body's physical range. These and other considerations tend to dethrone the brain as the primary instrument for gaining knowledge and to strengthen the conclusion of its being a special terminal for the reception of information from deeper levels of our awareness.

Scientific investigation of parapsychology goes back at least to the founding (in 1882) in London of the Society for Psychical Research. A more recent center of research was at Duke University, North Carolina, where the late Dr. J. B. Rhine worked for many years, beginning in the early 1930s. It may not be generally known that the ranks of those who have investigated parapsychology include some Nobel laureates in physics and medicine, professors of philosophy, and fellows of the Royal Society and the Soviet Academy of Science (Koestler, 1973, pp. 19-20).

Unquestionably, it is the new physics which has put parapsychology in a more respectable light. The notion of the space-time continuum helps us see time as an indivisible wholeness present to us now, including what we think of as the past and the future. If this is so, precognition may be a momentary glimpse into that wholeness. Again, if subatomic particles intercommunicate instantaneously across vast distances, may not human individuals have the ability on occasion to become aware of something transpiring at a distance in space? Indeed, one may argue that the psi phenomena are not a bit

Serious researchers are rediscovering and re-evaluating a broad spectrum of data that in the past have been suppressed or even ridiculed because of their incompatibility with the old paradigm. At the same time, vast amounts of new revolutionary observations are being generated by laboratory consciousness research, psychedelic therapy, experiential psychotherapies, field anthropology, parapsychology, and thanatology.

Parapsychological researchers Joseph Banks Rhine, Gardner Murphy, Stanley Krippner, Jules Eisenbud, Charles Tart, Elmer and Alyce Green, Arthur Hastings, Russell Targ, and Harold Puthoff have done meticulous scientific work that suggests the existence of telepathy, remote viewing, psychic diagnosis and healing, Poltergeist, or psychokinesis. This avenue of research has attracted the attention of modern physicists and it has become a serious theoretical challenge to incorporate its findings in the new paradigm.

> Stanslav Grof [in Grof, ed., 1984,
> [p. 16]

Besides challenging the conventional notions of physical space and time, psi research (like modern physics) poses a challenge to the customary idea of what might be called "epistemological space," i.e., the "space" that would separate the knower from the known. Parapsychology has its own "problem of measurement" which we have named the "experimenter effect" . . . [the problem of differentiating between the experimenter and his or her experiment]. Then may we not draw the same inference for parapsychology as was drawn for quantum physics? Not only is wholeness an inherent property of the phenomena observed, but the observer him- or herself is included as an aspect of this wholeness.

> Steven M. Rosen, Ph.D., "Wholeness
> and Psi," *theta*, Vol. 10, 4,
> Winter 1982

more fantastic than the phenomena of quantum physics or the relativity of space-time.

The psi faculties suggest in yet another way the inseparability of mind and matter, and more particularly the inner link between the knower and the known.

Here is a telling anecdote which F. David Peat relates in his aforementioned book on *Synchronicity* (pp. 5-6).

A young woman is visiting friends when suddenly everyone in the house smells a burnt-out candle. Despite a thorough search of the rooms no source for this smell can be found and it is certain that no candle had been lit in the house that day. . . . Later the same evening the woman receives a transatlantic telephone call saying that her father is, unexpectedly, about to undergo an operation. A few weeks later her father dies and the woman flies home to her parents' house. On the morning of the funeral the woman sees a large painting that had originally been given to her parents as a wedding present fall from its place on the wall. . . .

It is as if the young woman became a nexus into which events from the external world, past and future, flowed and out of which the synchronous phenomena emerged. The illness of her father and his eventual death, the pained reaction of her family, and her own feelings

---

The idea that all events in nature are interconnected by meaning is rooted in the occult metaphysics, which holds that consciousness is the primary field of experience, and that all events are in some way meaningful, or have a conceptual component that makes them intelligible and significant. A complementary concept in the West is the notion of the innate harmony or "sympathy" of all things postulated by Hippocrates, Philo and Theophrates. This sympathy was given as the cause of all simultaneity; it is an important element in alchemy and astrology. The great Arab (Sufi) philosopher Ibn Arabi attributed the acausality of spontaneous events as evidence that the whole universe is a theophany, manifested by the continuous creativity of the Divine Imagination—which also works in man, and makes it possible for him to perceive and participate in the cosmic process.

Emily B. Sellon, "Causality and Synchronicity" (private paper)

No form of clairvoyance gives clear spiritual vision. But spiritual vision and understanding may, if trained in that direction, lead to true and accurate clairvoyance. The trained clairvoyant . . . learns to use a steady controlled mind. . . . [Yet] spiritual vision is of another order altogether. It cannot be conveyed in picture symbols, neither can it be conveyed in any form of words. . . . Spiritual vision, moreover, changes a person, and he can never be the same afterwards as he was before. But even the higher forms of clairvoyance do not necessarily change the clairvoyant. He can still be as personal, as stupid, as silly, and as self-important as before. For clairvoyance, unsupported by deep spiritual insight, into oneself as much as into others, belongs to the personality, and indeed tends to make that personality feel more important than ever, because it feels superior to the ordinary 'blind' people around it. Sensory forms of perception draw a line between subjective and objective, the within and without. . . . A similar differentiation has, in the course of time, to be developed in the psychic organism, so that the individual knows the difference between the product of his own reflection, and that which exists in its own right outside the field of his personal mind. It is also necessary to learn to assess the difference between perception of psychic objects, such as a ghost, and visions which are in effect archetypal expressions of man's spiritual experience.

Phoebe D. Bendit, *Spiritual and Psychic Vision* (a pamphlet)[1]

appear to have enfolded within her and emerged as the phenomenon of the burnt-out candle—*before the telephone call was received.* The events which took place in that room, focusing on the phenomenon of a burnt-out candle, represent in microcosm the unfolding drama of the father's death and the young woman's return to her parents' home.

A significant question that arises in reflecting upon psi faculties is this: How are they related to spiritual vision? Is clairvoyance, for instance, a form of spiritual vision? The late Phoebe D. Bendit, a gifted clairvoyant herself and moreover a theosophist, gave the following answer: While a trained clairvoyant can put clairvoyance to

---

1. Published by the Theosophical Society in America.

many practical uses, ranging from the field of education to the fields of medicine and surgery, and from art to psychology, clairvoyance must never be confused with spiritual vision. She stressed that all forms of sensory and extrasensory perception *divide,* whereas spiritual vision *unifies*—without obscuring the differentiations realized through the senses.

I daresay that the psi faculties are at least latent in all of us, and that many of us have occasionally noticed their spontaneous operation in ourselves, whether in significant, less significant or even trite ways. They are not at all of the same order as spiritual vision, as Bendit explains. Yet they are intriguing and significant in terms of the way they confirm the interrelationship of our physical and our mental, or our inner and our outer, worlds. By the same token, parapsychology is interesting in terms of the way it enhances one's conviction about the ultimate convergence and complementarity of the different modes of knowledge and experience.

III

The Spiritual Domain

Reality is One though sages call it by different names.
The Upanishads

By whatsoever path you come to Me I shall welcome you, for the paths men take from every side are Mine.
Lord Krishna (in the *Bhagavad-Gita*)

Whereas science discloses the relational structure of the infinitely differentiated universe, spirituality provides a glimpse of the mystery of Being, the ultimate ground of the same universe, the non-temporal depth dimension of the cosmic whole.
Haridas Chaudhuri, *Being, Evolution & Immortality*

11

The World Religions: Constants and Variations

Introduction

We now turn to a different, but—as we have already hinted more than once—not an unrelated mode of inquiry, and, by the same token, to a different aspect of ourselves. This may be called faith—the religious or spiritual aspect of human nature.

Although the religious mode is different than the mode of science, the two are in principle united in their search for truth. While religion's specific concerns and methodology are not those of science, they both dwell within one and the same universe; they are, in principle, not only in harmony with one another but mutually complementary, supportive, and reinforcing. (Their relationship will be elaborated in Chapter 14.)

Religion is notoriously difficult to define because it means different things to different people, but it is entirely possible to say what the religions are about, what their purpose is. In *Many Peoples, Many Faiths,* Robert Ellwood suggests, by way of a working definition, that religion is a search for the invisible reality underlying the world—another kind of reality than what is tangible and visible and with which one's life is somehow involved. Each religion provides a map of that reality—essentially by what it says about ultimate questions, such as the origin, cause and destiny of the world, absolute or ultimate reality, and the origin and destiny of humans. Each concerns itself with the way we may come into rapport with the invisible reality.

Ellwood writes (1982, pp. 9-10):

All religions have attitudes in common that are unshared by nonreligious outlooks. They are all based on feelings, belief, and attitudes

171

which imply that humans have needs other than the physical, and live
in an environment that includes more than physical reality. . . . Religion centers around those symbols, statements, and social forms
which give visible expression to an invisible environment humans
believe to be around them, and an invisible true nature they sense to
dwell within them. . . .
Humankind seems instinctively to feel non-physical reality is more
mysterious, more ultimate, and more powerful than the physical. It
has to do with humanity's ultimate origins and most absolute relations.
It has to do with that which cannot be surpassed—the point of origin
beyond which one cannot go to a preceding stage, the relationship than
which there is none more important, demanding, or final.

Religions variously name ultimate reality: God, Allah, Tao, Brahman, Plenum/Void, and so forth. They teach that the ultimate goal for
the individual is union or mergence with the Absolute—the goal
variously known as salvation, liberation, enlightenment, nirvana,
moksha. The religions each prescribe a way, an *upaya*, for reaching
it, and these prescriptions—which are in fact intended for self-transformation— bear striking parallels one to another, notwithstanding
each religion's distinctive idiom.

While sharing these most fundamental features, each of the religious traditions is clearly a unique amalgam of distinctive practices,
attitudes, theologies and mythic or symbolic language. As C. G.
Jung reputedly remarked, each religion speaks its own language
which is impossible to imitate.

Not only are they unique, but within the fold of each of the great
faiths there is again much differentiation and variation. Some of the
teachings are even mutually contradictory, not only among the religions themselves but also within particular traditions and interpretations.

Do the diversity and contradictions impugn the truthfulness of the
religions? Hopefully, our exploration should shed light on this basic
question, among others.

First let us briefly recall both the extreme diversity of the religious
traditions and the nature of their consensus.

The Diversity

The respective major religions are richly, fascinatingly, astonishingly—or should we say bewilderingly?—diverse. A veritable kalei-
doscope of images floods one's mind in the array of Hinduism,

Buddhism, Zoroastrianism, Jainism, Taoism, Confucianism, Shinto, Judaism, Christianity, Islam, Sikhism. Each is distinctive; each claims to represent truth, and some adherents of a particular tradition claim on its behalf that it represents truth exclusively.

Upon a moment's thought, the diversity of expression of religions is not surprising. For each of the world religions is the product of a long and particular history—the product of an interplay over time among numerous specific factors and facts of history, culture and geography, including the cross-fertilization with other faiths and philosophies with which the religion came into contact over the course of its history.

Diversity is anyway a fundamental feature of existence—think of the endless diversity of flora, fauna, the physiognomies of humans, individuals' gifts and abilities, different cultures, civilizations and languages. Religious expression is not exempt from the differentiation and variation that are characteristic of all existence.

We have seen that differentiations in nature and in science are followed in turn by integrations, the formation of new unities-in-diversity. Is this principle applicable to differentiation in religious expression? Recall the example of the living embryo, in which cells specialize and then become integrated into a tissue or organ. Or take the evolution of a science, wherein there is first the acquisition of a mass of unrelated or poorly related data, which are subsequently unified by an overarching generalization or theory. Recall, too, that the evolutionary process itself is characterized by alternate novel differentiations and integrations, and that it exhibits an overall pattern and direction that are transcendent.

Can the same process hold true for religions? Can we say that the religions form an organic wholeness, or, to use a different metaphor, do they present a spectrum of distinctive but blending colors? Can we say that teachings of religions which seem to contradict each other are reconcilable as complementary aspects of one and the same many-aspected Reality? Can we say more generally that the world religions all point to one supervening Reality, to one and the same mountain top, so to speak? What follows will bear *inter alia* on these questions.

Take Hinduism, for example. It embraces a veritable maze of theologies, modes of worship, different disciplines, innumerable sects, cults and philosophic systems. Indeed, it has been said of Hinduism that nothing can be asserted about it that cannot also be denied. It contains a rich pantheon of hundreds of thousands of divine images and widely divergent approaches to Divinity, for Hinduism accepts that there are innumerable valid ways to serve and worship the One—*Brahman*—the immutable, ultimate, indescribable Reality that pervades and transcends all things. In the Upanishads (part of the Hindu scriptures; "Upanishad" literally means a "session" in the sense of sitting at the feet of a master who imparts wisdom), there is found the statement: Reality is One though sages call it by different names. The sacred classic *Bhagavad Gita,* in referring to Brahman, speaks of "the countless gods that are only my millions of faces."

Christianity is similarly characterized by abundant variation. Compare, for example, the glittering scene of a pontifical High Mass in St. Peter's to a quiet Quaker meeting in an unadorned meeting room. Christianity differentiates itself into three main divisions—Roman Catholicism, Eastern Orthodoxy, and Protestantism. Protestantism, in turn, comprises many branches, and these are again divided and subdivided. (Presbyterianism includes no less than 125 branches.) Yet Christianity is a unified faith, and all its divisions are a unity-in-diversity by virtue of their common focus on Jesus of Nazareth, called the Messiah or Christ.

Similarly, over the forty centuries since the rise of the faith of the Israelites, later to become Judaism, the Jewish religion has given rise to many different manifestations and expressions and to different types of spiritual leaders in different periods—patriarchs, prophets, legislators, priests, psalmists, sages, rabbis, philosophers and mystics or Kabbalists. Judaism in fact has never had a creed, and it is not homogeneous. This is evident, for example, in the parts of the Old Testament designated as the Wisdom Books—the books of Job, Psalms, Proverbs, Ecclesiastes, and the Song of Solomon. Of these Ellwood writes, "They are called Wisdom Books because they are primarily concerned with presenting timeless words of devotion, reflection, moral advice, and philosophy. They are remarkably diverse; to one whose view of the Bible is chiefly shaped by those parts concerned with God's Law, judgment on sin or calls to faith, substantial passages of the Wisdom Books may seem amazingly skeptical or speculative" (Ellwood, 1982, p. 264). Present-day Judaism has several branches, such as the Orthodox, Conservative and Reformed congregations. What unifies Judaism is the Torah, the Law of Moses (the first five books of the Christian Bible), and above all its understanding that God is one.

Islam, the youngest of the major religions, also has important variations and divisions, especially as it comprises an international community that cuts across many cultures. Yet it is, of the great faiths, the most homogenous. The heart of Islam is submission to the total will of Allah, the one and only God, and the belief that Allah's will for humanity is most fully given in the Koran, the book revealed through the prophet Muhammad. The Koran is for Islam the fountain source of true law and true culture, implicating every area of life, including political, economic, and family life, and of course the life of prayer. For Islam, no less than for Judaism, God—Allah—is one without a second, and both Judaism and Islam abhor idolatry. From this stems their proscription of images in their places of worship. Their aesthetic or artistic expression takes other forms. The Islamic faith in particular has given rise to dazzling art and architecture, profoundly informed by unifying principles—art which originates in Islamic spirituality and "is the manifestation in the world of forms of the spiritual realities (al-haqa'iq) of the Islamic revelation itself as coloured by its earthly embodiment" (Nasr, 1987, p. ix).

Buddhism, too, presents rich diversity and is yet a unified human experience. Even the Buddha himself is imaged in richly diverse ways:

> The changing types of the Buddha icon as it was created in the various parts of India, Ceylon, Burma, Cambodia, Thailand, Java, Laos, Vietnam, Tibet, Nepal, Gandhara . . . Mongolia, China, Korea, and Japan provide many clues to the nature, development and interchange of philosophic and aesthetic ideals in these widely scattered cultures. . . . The Buddha image is the equivalent of the Christ image in the West, but it has a more varied range of representation. . . . Most often the aim was to indicate the supernatural qualities of a supreme divinity, but sometimes it was to emphasize the earthly and human aspects of this Sage . . . who, like Jesus of Nazareth five hundred years later, was born as a man. For many years following the Buddha's demise no Buddha images were made. It was considered illogical that a truly Enlightened Being . . . could ever be represented in human form, and so the Buddha's presence in early narrative sculptures was merely indicated by an empty throne, a footprint, a royal umbrella or other symbols (Ross, 1966, p. 95).

Buddhism is divided into several major branches, notably Theravada Buddhism which prevails in southeast Asia, and Mahayana Buddhism which is one of the main religions found in much of the northern tier of Asian countries. In these latter lands, Mahayana Buddhism is again tremendously varied, in large part as a consequence of its cross-fertilization with the preceding religions and cultures of the places to which it spread.

We need not further belabor the main point: there is tremendous diversity between and within different religions, and each tradition is, notwithstanding its diversity, an unbroken continuity—a unified human experience.

Some Points of Consensus

There is the diversity, but as already said, there are commonalities. Comparative study of the major traditions reveals some striking parallels and significant points of consensus.

As previously mentioned, religions revolve about the search for God as the transcendent reality, and the individual's need to come into rapport or into right relationship with that spiritual reality. Each proposes to teach the Way to find this reality.

> Tao can be rendered simply as 'Way', just as in Buddhism, the Mâhâ-yâna is the 'Great Way', and in Hinduism, the Deva-yâna is the 'Way of the Gods', while in Christianity Christ says, 'I am the Way.' In Judaism Moses leads the Israelites out of Egypt and shows the Way to the Holy Land, so in Islam the Prophet leads the Way into Mecca. Interiorly this is the 'Straight Way' (sirat al-mustaqim; the Sufiq tari-qah = Way), the 'Straight Way' of the Gospels, and 'Red Road' of the Sioux, or 'Holy Path' (Shôdô) of the Japanese. . . . The Way can equally be envisaged as Pilgrimage (to Jerusalem, Mecca, Lhasa, Benares, Ise), or as a Quest (for the Holy Grail, the Terrestrial Paradise, the Fountain of Immortality), or a Voyage (Perry, 1986, p. 95).

The different religions' teachings for following the Way resemble each other in many respects, however differently these teachings may be couched. Held in common, for example, is the need for purity and personal disinterestedness; the belief in the immeasurable worth of every human being, in the unity of all life, and in the brotherhood of humanity; the teaching of compassion, non-violence or *ahimsa;* the principle that an individual reaps as he or she sows, known in Hinduism and Buddhism as the law of karma; the capacity of each person to attain to a state of life (mental, moral and spiritual) far above that she or he is now experiencing; the necessity of dying to or leaving a lesser life to gain a greater life; and the immortality of the soul—or, in some religions, reincarnation.

Symbolic Means of Expression

Each of the religions indeed has a universal aspect, something which becomes abundantly evident when the religious myths of all times and places are placed side by side. But it will be well to preface our remarks about this feature of the traditions by a few words about the nature of religious myth and its use as a mode of expression.

In Chapter two, we considered the limits of the powers of reason or discursive thought, noting that spiritual experience is immediate, existential, non-logical and non-verbal, and also that it is marked by paradox.

The fact is that mystics, not unlike poets and painters, have typically expressed themselves in symbolic language. That is to say, sacred literature of all times and places is characterized by frequent use of myth, paradox, allegory and symbol. Why? Heinrich Zimmer (1971, p. 25) explains the reason:

> To express and communicate knowledge gained in moments of grammar-transcending insight, metaphors must be used, similes and allegories. These are . . . not mere embellishments . . . but the very vehicles of the meaning. . . . Significant images . . . make manifest with clarity and pictorial consistency the paradoxical character of the reality known to the sage: a translogical reality, which, expressed in the abstract language of normal thought, would seem inconsistent, self-contradictory, or even absolutely meaningless.

We should not confuse metaphor or myth with fact. A religious myth is a living reality which formulates itself naturally out of the depths of experience. The events it concerns may or may not be historically true, and that is of no importance, because truth and factuality are entirely different. As Jay G. Williams (1978, p. 35) has put it, fact has to do with what has already happened, and is "finished, past, objectified and dead," whereas "Truth is open, present, no-thing, and alive. . . . Truth involves purpose, value and meaning."

The symbolic character of sacred scripture means that it is not to be read just literally. For example, the biblical story of the Exodus, the story of the journey to the Promised Land, gains much deeper meaning and wider applicability if it is read allegorically as a journey in consciousness, or an evolutionary journey—from inner bondage to inner freedom. As such, it is indeed applicable to everyone and to every society.

It is in this deeper reading of scriptures that one becomes aware of the universality or inner unity of the different religions. Each religion seems to have both an exoteric or popular aspect and an esoteric or hidden aspect, as Frithjof Schuon has clearly shown in his *The Transcendent Unity of Religions*. The two levels of interpretation are discussed in the next chapter.

A word now about what is called *category error*, that is, the error of reading scriptural statements as *factual*. This kind of error is not confined to the realm of religion: scientists, too, have been guilty of category errors, or of what Whitehead called "the fallacy of misplaced concreteness"; mechanists, notably, have mistaken their model, which is only a mental construct, for reality. It is the category errors, on the side of reductionist science and on the side of dogmatic religion, respectively, which have raised barriers between religion and science, between religion and the humanities, and between religion and philosophy. But as science now further unfolds beyond mechanism, and as spiritual insights become increasingly universalized, these two modes become progressively harmonious. It becomes evident that the two are complementary, and indeed reinforce one another.

We earlier mentioned the conflict between Creationists who read the biblical six days of Creation literally, and neo-Darwinists who explain evolution in mechanical terms, and pointed out that there is a mixture of truth and error on both sides of this controversy. Such evolutionists err in denying anything but physical variation as the cause of evolutionary development. Creationists go to the other extreme and deny evolution itself. They read the "six days" of world formation literally, not seeing them as as six great evolutionary epochs or phases.

Unlike facts, symbols are imprecise—they do not have a strictly one-to-one correspondence with that to which they refer; they are multi-valent. A distinction must be made between a sign which precisely indicates a certain condition or thing (dollar signs, for instance) and a symbol which points beyond itself and "opens the door into a larger world full of hitherto unknown features and even ultimately to the world of mystery, transcending all human powers of description" (Dillistone, 1986, pp. 12-18). The sign can be invented, but the symbol creates itself.

Frithjof Schuon defined the symbol in religion thus: "Every thing is a symbol which serves as a direct support for spiritual realization, a

> In a sense, once a myth is formed, the original intent of the author becomes superfluous. One should not think of meaning as somthing ever to be found in the text itself. On the contrary, a myth's meaning emerges anew in each age and for each individual. Meaning is born out of the interaction among the story, the ego [individual], and the unknown present. Hence there is no one meaning to any myth. That is the reason why myths have the capacity to endure through the ages. A myth with one fixed interpretation is bound to decay and soon be forgotten.
>
> Jay G. Williams, *Yeshua Buddha*
> [p.26]

mantra [sacred formula] for example, or a divine name, or in a secondary manner, a graphic, pictorial or sculptural symbol, such as sacred images (pratikas)" (Perry, 1986, p. 303).

Mircea Eliade believes that a symbol is never a mere pointer, unrelated to active human experience. It "always aims at a reality or a situation in which human existence is engaged" and in this way brings meaning into human existence. An authentic symbol serves to deliver man from his isolation and subjectivity and self-interest into an "opening toward the Spirit and, finally, access to the universal" (Dillistone, 1986, pp. 145-146).

The Universality of the World's Myths

The late Joseph Campbell asked himself, "Why is mythology everywhere the same, beneath its varieties of costume? And what does it teach?" That is the central question he asks in *The Hero with a Thousand Faces*. He points out that today many sciences are contributing toward the answer—archaeology, ethnology, orientology, folk psychology, and, most of all, psychology. "The bold and true epoch-making writings of the psychoanalysts . . . Freud, Jung, and their followers have demonstrated irrefutably that the logic, the heroes, the deeds of myth survive into modern times. . . . The latest incarnation of Oedipus, the continued romance of Beauty and the Beast, stand this afternoon on the corner of Forty-Second Street and Fifth Avenue, waiting for the traffic light to change" (1972, p. 4).

Campbell comes to the conclusion that although there are differences between the numerous mythologies and religions of humanity, these are superficial and peripheral compared to the similarities. Once these have been understood, "the differences will be found to be much less great than is popularly (and politically) supposed" (1972, Preface).

In myth the psyche deals with basic problems and provides solutions which are directly valid for all humanity. Campbell takes the hero as one who has been able to win past his personal and local historical limitations to the attainment of discrimination or *viveka*, as it is called in Hindu and Buddhist philosophy. Having died to his limitations, he is reborn as eternal man, "perfected, unspecific, universal." All the religions teach that the transfigured hero returns to teach the lesson learned.

> The standard path of the mythological adventure of the hero is a magnification of the formula represented in the rites of passage: separation—initiation—return. . . . A hero ventures forth from the world of common day into a region of supernatural wonder: fabulous forces are there encountered and a decisive victory is won: the hero comes back from this mysterious adventure with the power to bestow boons on his fellow man (p. 20).

Whether we speak of Prometheus, Aeneas, Moses, Buddha or Christ, the heroic journey holds true.

F. C. Happold describes the universal features of this myth in *Religious Faith and Twentieth-Century Man* (1966, p. 109):

> Though there are a good many variations in detail, all follow the same general pattern. The hero's mother is commonly a virgin, his father a divine king or a god. The circumstances of his birth are unusual. In some versions of the myth, attempts are made to kill him and for safety he has to be taken into a distant country, where he spends his youth and early manhood. Eventually there is a return and, sometimes after a victory over the king, or it may be over a giant, a dragon or a wild beast, he himself becomes king. Or there is the story of a dark journey which the hero-god is called upon to make, or a descent into the waters where the fight with the dragon takes place. The story of a mysterious and significant death, followed by rebirth or resurrection, is a universal or almost universal element in the myth. This death not seldom takes place on a hill, and the dying hero-god hangs on a tree, and is an offering of a god to a god.

He also cites Jung and Toynbee among others who have pointed out that the myth of the divine-human hero is ubiquitous, recurring throughout history under diverse names—as Zagreus among the Minoans, Tammuz in the Sumerian World, Attis among the Hittites, and so forth.

What does this universal myth signify? It does no less than address the most fundamental dilemma of every human being: the need to accommodate two seemingly opposed dimensions of existence: our everyday, changing world, on the one hand, and the eternal, unchanging reality beyond space-time, on the other—or, in Happold's phraseology, the two opposing urges—one towards selfhood, individualization, and separation; the other towards the remedy of loneliness by union with something bigger than self. These two urges are in constant conflict.

The myth of the divine-human hero, then, permits us to bridge the two poles of our existence; by the same token, it permits the creative process of self-transformation and self-integration.

Jung emphasized that the myth of the divine-human hero needs to be reclothed from time to time in contemporary garments. If so, what garments will we fashion for it? My own feeling is that the collective unconscious is groping today toward the deeper truth of the unity of the human family—its oneness beyond distinctions of race, color, religion, nationality and ideology, and that a myth will sooner or later emerge which embodies and expresses this new level of integration.

Faith in Ultimate Reality

Most fundamental to all the religions is the belief in an absolute or ultimate Reality. However they name it, and irrespective of the different ways of understanding God or the Absolute, religions look upon ultimate Reality as infinite, omnipresent, and intellectually unknowable. What this striking consensus means, as we said at the outset, is that peoples and nations possess one and the same basis— the deepest of bases—for a set of values and principles by which to live. They are essentially at one, for, in spite of all differences, "the Holy-Itself, the Absolute, transcends and judges all the religions," to borrow a phrase from Paul Tillich.

For this reason, fanaticism and bigotry are never justified; no religion can claim to have the last word of truth. At the same time, the fact contradicts the relativistic belief that there is *no* truth.

We will enlarge on these two opposing and far-reaching statements, but first we will discuss the spiritual meaning which lies beyond all creeds and dogma.

Exoteric and Esoteric Religion

During the past half century, an extensive literature on mysticism has been published, all testifying to the fact that all the major religions have a mystical aspect or level of meaning, in addition to their popular or exoteric interpretation and texts.

The more esoteric stream, as compared to the exoteric or popular doctrines, interprets the concepts fundamental to all religions in subtler or more symbolic ways—concepts such as deity, creation, liberation or redemption, the self, evil, death, and immortality.

In *The Transcendent Unity of Religions,* Schuon (1953) defined the perspective of popular religion as that of "an irreducible dualism and the exclusive pursuit of individual salvation—this dualism implying that God is considered solely under the aspect of His relationship with the created and not in his total and infinite Reality, in his Impersonality which annihilates all apparent reality other than Him" (p. 62).

Again, Agnes Arber (1967), in *The Manifold and the One,* remarks that repeatedly, in the philosophies and religions of widely different races and epochs, the view has appeared that within truth itself higher and lower levels may be distinguished, and that only the ranges forming the lower levels are within the reach of the majority of humans. "These lower levels can be reached by means of imagery, pictorial thinking, and ritual, which depend primarily upon the bodily senses and emotions, and do not demand abstract intellection. On such planes the desire is for a Deity with the attributes of personality—the Saguna Brahman of the Upanishads; at the higher levels, on the other hand, the conception of Deity is equated with the idea of the Absolute or Suprapersonal Whole, concerning which nothing can be predicated—the Nirguna Brahman (p. 45).

Schuon points out that the traditional *forms* of religion are (by definition) unavoidably limiting. At the same time, however, a religion's forms are indispensable to it; if they were discarded, the religion itself would cease to exist. He believes that the unitive consciousness finds the forms *transparent; it sees through them the formless, trancendent wholeness.* A given religion, then, may be

> The Hindu masses' meticulous observance of immemorial ritual, often childish and superstitious in the modern view, is balanced by the presence in Hinduism of many great teachers and disciples of a purified faith rooted in humanism and universalism. . . . Down the centuries India's greatest religious leaders have all been "iconoclasts" in one way or another.
>
> Nancy Wilson Ross, *Three Ways of Asian Wisdom* [p. 16]

> The religious consciousness is not exhausted with the emergence of the classic systems of institutional religion . . . new religious impulses may and do arise . . . the longing for new religious values corresponding to the new religious experience finds its expression in a new interpretation of the old values which frequently acquire a much more profound and personal significance, although one which often differs entirely from the old and transforms their meaning. In this way, Creation, Revelation and Redemption, to mention some of our most important religious conceptions, are given new and different meanings reflecting the characteristic feature of mystical experience, the direct contact between the individual and God.
>
> Gershom Scholem, *Major Trends in Jewish Mysticism* [pp. 8-9]

read at different levels, and the deeper the level, the more the universal meanings of the religion come into view.

Now, what, in turn, is the connection between religion and perennial philosophy? It is this: the perennial philosophy is founded on mystical perception. It is mystical perception translated into philosophical statement. Thus the perennial philosophy and mysticism are intimately related but are not synonymous.

Something of the difference among the three categories may be illustrated by an example: the way Christ's relationship to God is interpreted. In popular, exoteric religion, Christ is God. Mystical Christianity perceives the relationship differently; it is not so much that Christ *is* God but God is *in* Christ. Perennial philosophy, in turn, speaks of an impersonal or universal spark—the Divine Self or the

"Revealed" religions generally represent attempts to make . . . [the] Supreme Absolute accessible and comprehensible to mankind in general. This can be done only by reducing the ultimate conception from the level of Godhead down to that of God, and confining the latter term to a . . . personal and anthropomorphic [significance]. . . . A two-story conception of truth is found in the Upanishads; in the Islamic and Sufic traditions; and also in the writings of Nicholas of Cusa and Bruno—to cite merely a few typical instances. It must be recognized, however, that to speak of the levels of truth as though they were sharply separated and discrete does not give a fair impression. The levels grade insensibly into one another, and the lower phases— in which symbols are taken literally at their face value—when fully developed point beyond themselves to the higher.

Agnes Arber, *The Manifold and the One* [pp. 45-46].

Reality affirms itself by degrees, but without ceasing to be "one," the inferior degrees of this "affirmation" being absorbed, by metaphysical integration or synthesis, into the superior degrees. . . . [The] exoteric point of view cannot comprehend the transcendence of the supreme Divine Impersonality of which God is the personal Affirmation; such truths are of too high an order, and therefore too subtle and too complex from the point of view of simple rational understanding, to be accessible to the majority or formulated in a dogmatic manner.

Frithjof Schuon, *The Transcendent Unity of Religions* [p. 53]

Christ-Nature or the Buddha-Nature—identifying itself with or shining through each person. This divine nature was perfectly exemplified in the Christ, but it can shine through anyone who purifies his or her consciousness, so as to be transparent to the inner light.

To close this chapter, and by way of invoking the next subject, let me quote something that Marco Pallis, the noted scholar of religion, has written:

What one always needs to remember is that traditional forms, including those bearing the now unpopular name of dogmas, are keys to unlock the gate of Unitive Truth; but they are also (since a key can close, as well as open, a gate) possible obstacles to its profoundest knowledge: all depends on how the forms are envisaged and used at different stages of the Way. It is by his active exercise of the faculty of metaphysical insight conferred on him that man is enabled to situate, and eventually to transcend, distinctions of religious form, but without blurring or betrayal of that which provides its efficient cause for each form as such. Living his own form faithfully and intensely a man will live all "other" forms by implication (in Perry, 1986, p. 10).

This statement admirably suggests not only the idea of the different levels of interpretation but also that of the inner unity of the world religions. We turn next to the subject of that inner unity.

12

The Essential Unity of the Religions

Truth Is One

We have distinguished between Truth with a capital *T*, and religious, scientific and ideological truths, all of which are subject to refinement and reformulation *ad infinitum* and can never be equated with Truth itself. This being so, no particular religious dogma or revelation can claim to be the final word of truth. And we have tried to show that the nondualistic perspective undercuts dogmatism and the fundamentalist, orthodox claim for the eternal validity of scripture, whether it be Jewish, Christian or Muslim. Chaudhuri (1977) put the issue thus: "God is not to be exclusively identified with any particular historical figure such as Buddha, Krishna, Christ, Moses, Mohammed, etc. They are all manifestations in history of the one suprahistorical creative intelligence that guides the course of history" (p. 19).

As the ancient Vedas say, "Truth is one; sages call it by different names."

What About the Contradictions?

But if truth is one, how can we explain the contradictions among and even within the different religions?

The explanation lies in the paradoxical nature of truth—the fact that existence is pervaded by pairs of opposites which are in reality inseparable polarities.

The Judeo-Christian tradition emphasizes the meaningfulness of history; in the Bible, God intervenes and reveals himself in world events; the Koran gives positive prescription regarding the social order. Hinduism, by contrast, regards the phenomenal world as *maya*, or illusion. It teaches that the individual must seek release from the cycle of incarnations in order that his individuality might merge with the World Soul, Brahman.

These are two opposite positions, one appearing to associate God closely with physical life, the other denying that life's reality. Which is true, which false? The fact is that the question is wrong, based on a false premise. The two positions are not contradictory, for they reflect two different truths. They represent the two poles of existence that are mutually defining and that we must accommodate and keep in balance: the timeless and the temporal. Overemphasis of the temporal dimension produces shallowness, intolerance and materialism. Overemphasis of the timeless dimension produces other-worldliness, and a disdain for earthly things.

The integration of these two attitudes towards physical existence equally means the unification of Eastern and Western thought, leading to deeper world understanding. Lama Govinda (1976) wrote:

> The danger in the West lies in the overemphasis on the this-worldly pole of individuality, of egocentric activity, of self-assertion and will-power. The danger in the East lies in the overemphasis of the universal pole, the metaphysical, the negation of the value of individuality, which leads to a passive dissolution in a formless unity. Both attitudes contradict the innermost law of existence, the one by denying universality, the other by depriving individuality of its value. The latter would actually contradict the idea of a divine (or divinely evolved) universe . . . because it would amount to the accusation that the godhead had meaninglessly created individual forms and beings. . . .
> To a god the finite would be as great a necessity as the infinite is to man, because only the finite gives meaning to the infinite. Only a man of spiritual maturity and deep insight is capable of appreciating the true value of the finite in the uniqueness of its momentary appearance. This is why only the greatest among us are capable of understanding the simple things of life in their true depth and significance (p. 205).

We all wrestle with a pull in two directions—toward the practical and mundane, on the one hand, and the transcendent, on the other. As if this were not enough, religions offer us two opposite routes to the transcendent pole. For they speak of the Affirmative Way to God and of the Negative Way to God.

In Hinduism these two opposite ways are expressed perhaps more extremely than in other religions. The Affirmative Way in Hinduism

> Integral nondualism reconciles the mystical truth of formless
> Being with the rationalistic theory of forms and ideas. . . .
> Forms and ideas are no less real. . . . Realization of the form-
> less transcendence is essential for attaining spiritual depth and
> universality of outlook, whereas realization of the reality and
> value of forms, ideas, determinate principles . . . is essential
> for human progress in scientific, technological, social, eco-
> nomical and political spheres. . . . Integral nondualism recon-
> ciles mysticism with evolutionism. . . . But ancient mysticism
> was not fully aware of the reality and importance of evolution
> and history. Dazzled by the glory of the eternal, it minimized
> the importance and value of time. . . . It is through participa-
> tion in history that [man] can evolve and manifest the unsus-
> pected glories of his inner being.
>
> Haridas Chaudhuri, *Being, Evolution*
> *and Immortality* [pp. 32-33]

means using things found in the realm of the many—art, images,
rites, temples—to raise one's love to the infinite; the Negative Way,
in contrast, is the way of asceticism, the way of austerity—of finding
the One by not being distracted or diverted by the blandishments of
the multiplicity of things which are the Other. Here again, two seemingly opposite Ways are in reality an inseparable polarity.

What is needed, again, is to strive for balance and wholeness. As
Lama Govinda (1976) has put it: "The overemphasis on unity is as
great a fault as the overemphasis on duality or plurality. If we conceive duality as the irreconcilable opposition of two independent and
mutually exclusive principles, and not as the necessary polarity of
two mutually complementary aspects of reality or of a higher unity—
or if we cling only to one side, under complete exclusion or negation
of the other—then indeed, we suffer under a serious illusion. If we
try to deny the fact of polarity (imagining that reality consists only in
unity) then we simply close our eyes to the most evident reality"
(p. 205).

The solution is what Buddhism has termed the Middle Way or the
razor-edged path, which avoids both pitfalls by perceiving their complementarity.

Empathizing with Different Religions

In our increasingly pluralistic society, many people—including religious and not particularly religious people—have discovered that the different religions and their practices and customs are thoroughly fascinating in many ways. More than that, some people have discovered in themselves an empathy for or a receptivity to religious altars of a very different kind from those into which they were born. If we reflect on it, this is very understandable, for when the age-old truth is put forward in a new guise, it appears fresh and immediate.

I found illuminating Robert Ellwood's observations on this point (1982, p. 3): "More than once, as one explores the most alien-seeming of humankind's religious symbols and scriptures, one may find oneself saying, 'This was made or said by human beings like myself. I know why they produced it; something in me has felt the same way'." In a talk of Ellwood's I once heard, he, an occidental, described his experiences while travelling to different places of worship in the East:

> As I visited various Shinto shrines and Buddhist temples, I could not help feeling that there was present in Shinto shrines a sort of real spiritual presence, not infinite God exactly, in the Western sense, but something more along the line of what we would call Angelic or Devic, a powerful presence associated with deep woods and trees that usually surround the ancient Shinto shrines—a spiritual presence strongly associated with a local particular place, nature and its environment, and its cultural heritage. In Buddhist temples, one gets the feeling of the presence of an infinite intelligence, infinite mind, which is supremely represented by the Buddha and Bodhisattva and their enlightenment. Thus I get a feeling of spiritual reality and yet not necessarily absolute spiritual reality in the religions of the world.

That we should be capable of resonating with different religions is but natural. Are we not all sprung from the same source? Do we not all belong to one and the same infinitely interconnected universe?

Moreover, as Ellwood implies above, and as earlier suggested, different religions address different aspects of our multi-faceted existence. Accordingly, each exerts its own appeal and none can be absolutized.

Different Paths Up the Same Mountain

Scholars have used different metaphors for the essential unity of religions underlying their diversity. A well known analogy is this:

Whether we listen with aloof amusement to the dreamlike mumbo jumbo of some red-eyed witch doctor of the Congo, or read with cultivated rapture thin translations from the sonnets of the mystic Lao-tse, or now and again crack the hard nutshell of an argument of Aquinas, or catch suddenly the shining meaning of a bizarre Eskimo fairy tale, it will be always the one, shape-shifting yet marvelously constant story that we find, together with a challengingly persistent suggestion of more remaining to be experienced than will ever be known or told.

Joseph Campbell, *The Hero with a Thousand Faces* [p. 3]

The unconditioned purity of infinite Truth is white light. The religions are its refraction into a rainbow of different hues. The colors are both beautiful and distinctive; they blend into one another; they constitute a harmonious spectrum; each reveals a different aspect or quality of the Light of which it is an emanation.

Huston Smith, in *The Religions of Man,* invoked another image, that of a mountain (1965, pp. 85-86):

It is possible to climb life's mountain from any side, but when the top is reached the pathways merge. As long as religions remain in the foothills of theology, ritual or church organization they may be far apart. Differences in culture, history, geography, and group temperament all make for different starting points. Far from being deplorable, this is good; it adds richness to the totality of man's religious venture. . . . But the goal beyond these differences is the same goal.

That is to say, the great religions are "the well-trodden paths," to use a familiar phrase, up one and the same mountain. These paths or ways originate in different climes and epochs of history. Their teachings are in the nature of "guidebooks" for the pilgrim who essays the long struggle to the peak. The instructions are rather different at the outset of the climb, since the approaches may be distant from one another in time and place. But as the pilgrim mounts, the paths converge, terrain becomes more and more uniform, the sharp differences and contradictions gradually disappear. At the summit, often hidden from sight in the lower reaches of the path by "the cloud of unknowing," lies the supreme goal: wisdom, salvation, the Kingdom of Heaven, enlightenment, union with God.

But what is the real purpose of the comparative study of the religions? Is it enough to discover the ideas and doctrines they hold in common, and to see their complementarity and mutual harmony? No, that is not enough, because, to reiterate, intellectual knowledge even of a unitive sort cannot deliver the experience of unity. At risk of putting my whole argument in question, I must admit that it is not enough merely to accept the idea of unity. It must be *lived*. Safe to say, we all have far to go in integrating our head and our heart. As depth and transpersonal psychologists tell us, we have yet to awaken from our dreaming. The heart of religion—and equally the heart of unitive philosophy, which is a way of life—is the actual living of or by the spiritual intuitions. That is why Blavatsky, for one, emphasized that it is in living one's religion that one finds its unity with other religions. Or as Chaudhuri put it, comparative studies "must accompany the gradual transformation of one's own being in the light of truth" (1984, p. 34).

These reflections remind us *inter alia* that the paths up the mountain, that is, the great religious traditions, are given to guide us, but the journey is essentially a matter of personal dedication, a one-of-a-kind, unique pilgrimage for each of us. Just as a spring waters many plants, so one mountain offers many paths to its summit.

13

Religion: Past, Present and Future

In the *Rig Veda*, which is perhaps the oldest scriptural text of a living tradition (Hinduism), we find an extraordinary statement: "The fairwinged One who is but one, inspired poets, by their incantations, shape in many ways" (meaning that inspired poets, by their incantations, shape the One in many ways, notwithstanding that the One is but one). Elsewhere in the Hindu scriptures (in the *Srimad Bhagavatam*) is found the declaration: "Truth has many aspects. Infinite Truth has infinite expressions. Though the sages speak in divers ways, they express one and the same Truth."

The *Rig Veda* had its origin in the even older hymns of the ancient Aryans, who came into India through the Himalayan passes at about the time Moses was leading the Israelites out of Egypt, that is, around 1500 B.C.E. The Aryans were the ancestors of Northern Europeans (and their language, Sanskrit, is ancestral to European languages). The Aryans brought with them their own bardic priests who were already in possession of the ancient tradition, passed on through oral teachings. Of these ancient teachings it was said that they were "born of the very breath of God." The root of the Sanskrit word *veda* is *vid*, "to know"—"to have divine knowledge." (In English we have the related word "wit"; in Russian the same root is found in words connoting seeing, appearance or vision, an example of the common lingual ancestry.) The vedic scriptures are designated in Hinduism as the "eternal revealed."

All this would seem to be consistent with the postulate that a core wisdom goes back immemorially, and that it was revealed to humanity in glimpses even in the early dawn of culture. History would appear to support the idea that each civilization or peoples drew forth a measure of that Wisdom Religion, consistent with its own needs, its state of consciousness, its temperament, its circumstances, its problems. In one way or another, that essential wisdom has leavened every civilization down the ages; no people have been totally abandoned or denied the light. Arnold Toynbee, the historian, rhetorically asks: What would humanity and its cultures have been without its greatest benefactors: such towering teachers as Confucius and Laotze, Zoroaster, Socrates, the Buddha, the Prophets of Israel and Judah, Jesus, Muhammad?

Notwithstanding that religion has been an indispensable leavener of civilizations, religion, as history shows, has also been (and alas still is) the ostensible cause—perhaps the foremost cause—of division, conflict, hatred and war, as Pitirim Sorokin, the sociologist, thoroughly documented. Religious wars are in fact the most destructive of any, and enormous human suffering has been perpetrated in the name of religion, as we unfortunately still witness. The fault, of course, lies not with the religions but with zealots who pervert religion for purposes of political or personal power.

Like everything else, religions are not static. Living traditions undergo change in the course of time. History shows that at times a religion may degenerate into sectarianism, dogmatism, fanaticism, aggressive proselytization, and the like. At other times, the tradition may experience renewal, revitalization. History also shows that at a time of cultural and religious decline, a great teacher may arise to remedy the existing need. In the cases of Buddha, Jesus and Muhammad, the teacher's work gave rise to yet another religion, one shaped by his spiritual vision, but also addressed in smaller or larger degree to the specific concerns and conditions experienced by his followers. The mother religion meanwhile may survive—as does Judaism in the case of Christianity and Islam.

This phenomenon illustrates the familial relationship among the religions, as Geoffrey Parrinder (1987), an English historian of religion, notes:

> To Christians, Judaism is our mother, or perhaps it may be said that to Protestants our own church of England or another is our mother, the Roman Catholic church is our grandmother and Judaism our great-grandmother. There are close family ties and a common spiritual heritage. Judaism, Christianity and Islam are called the Semitic religions, by descent from the mythical Shem, but more significant religiously is descent from Abraham or Moses. . . . Abraham was the progenitor of all true believers in one God. . . . And the vulgar objec-

Religion . . . has been used—and is still used—as a subtle ideological weapon in the game of power politics, of social exploitation and world domination. It has helped make the rich richer and the poor poorer. It has acted a stumbling block to the betterment of the social, economical and political conditions. . . .

But in ultimate analysis, the blame for the aforesaid situation lies not with religion, but with the perversity of human nature. . . . Religion is . . . man's way of living in the name of truth. There is no complete escape from religion, since the very opposite of religion becomes a new kind of religion. . . . The fundamental requirement of the present age is to divest religion of its supernaturalism, other-worldliness, pessimism, and dogmatism. Religion has to be reconstructed as a steadfast devotion to such higher values of life as truth, beauty, love, social justice, economic equality, political liberty, international peace. . . . It has to be reconstructed as a clarion call to man's self-development as a free and creative unit of the cosmic whole, as a unique focalization of the Supreme Being . . . as an optimistic affirmation of life in this world, with a vibrant sense of rootedness in the eternal and creative vision of the future.

Haridas Chaudhuri, *Modern Man's Religion* [pp. 20-22]

tion that we worship God whereas the Muslims worship Allah and the Jews worship Jehovah (whose name is too sacred for them to mention), has little more sense than to claim that the English worship God while the French adore Dieu, the Germans Gott and the Spaniards Dios. There are many names, and many and imperfect understandings of him, but there is one God, who is over all, blessed for ever. (p. 124)

What kind of change is religion undergoing today? The picture is confused. One conspicuous trend is toward a reversion to fundamentalism which demands a literal reading of scripture and leads to the kind of absolutism that breeds fanatics. At the same time, we witness a marked trend toward inclusiveness and universality. Both trends are undoubtedly related to all the other planetary developments taking place, including the politico-socio-economic. In particular, the extraordinary appeal of fundamentalisms of one kind or another may be

The Neolothic world became the world of the Bronze Age, the Iron Age, and the age of the ancient agricultural empires in the Near East, India, and China. In this age came a remarkable turning-point in human spiritual life. . . . The pivot of this great change was the fifth century B.C.E., approximately the time of the Buddha, Confucius, Lao-tzu, and Zoroaster. In Hinduism it was the time the old Vedic religion was beginning to give way to the mystical wisdom of the Upanishads and the outlook symbolized, at least, by the Krishna of the *Bhagavad-Gita*. Further west, it was roughly the time of the great Hebrew prophets and the earlier Greek philosophers. All across the globe momentous stirrings were underway as one spiritual age was yielding to another. The philosopher Karl Jaspers called it the Axial Age; its later fruit includes Jesus and Muhammad and their religions, but in a real sense the latter was probably the "seal of the prophets" as claimed by Islam, for one does not envision new world-scale religions starting today in quite the same way as in the days of Jesus or Muhammad. Theirs was a unique work belonging to a unique era in human life.

Robert Ellwood, *Theosophy, A Modern Expression of the Wisdom of the Ages* [pp. 178-179]

Change brings uncertainty, and uncertainty invites a leap into the known or, at least, what is assumed to be known—a religious text, a romanticized dream of an earlier and simpler age, a source of authority that can justify the assertion of order, not to mention the iron fist. The specific character and causes of fundamentalism undoubtedly vary from society to society, but its presence across different societies is striking. It is paralleled by widespread skepticism about the great ideologies that arose in nineteenth-century Europe and have subsequently informed political life almost everywhere. There is even widespread skepticism about the value of any imaginative or utopian aspirations for the future.

R. B. J. Walker, *One World, Many Worlds* [p. 14]

understood in the context of today's widespread political and economic disarray.

Certainly, there is no lack of interest in religion. "One of the paradoxical aspects of the crisis of doubt, defeatism and disillusion through which the Western world is passing at the present time," writes Marco Pallis, "is the existence, among the educated public in all countries, of a never-ending demand for information concerning religious teachings and practices in all times and climes. Hardly a day passes without some freshly translated text . . . being added to the list of works in print. Metaphysical treatises of the profoundest kind, records of mystical experience in every conceivable form, instruction on yogic methods formerly only divulged to initiates, illustrations of the treasures of sacred art . . . all this . . . continually . . . [expands religious documentation]" (in Perry, ed., 1986, p. 7).

Pallis makes mention of the anthropological explorations into tribal civilizations in Africa, Polynesia and the Americas that reveal something of the spiritual lore and concomitant rites and customs of these civilizations. "What for the Nineteenth Century amounted to sheer superstition, childish when not abominable and in any case beneath the notice of sophisticated men, is now, on closer examination, found to provide food for envy more readily than for contempt" (p. 7).

As Chaudhuri (1984, pp. 64-65) remarks, we have the inestimable privilege today of access to the vast cultural heritage of the human race; we are "able to live in the free company of the world's master minds." Modern religion is "open-minded receptivity to the light of truth streaming in from all corners of the globe."

I share the view of those who see the emergence of a new form of spirituality in the world today. Two factors above all seem to be bringing it into existence: the revelations of science which impact upon philosophical and even spiritual consciousness; and the intensity of global communications and interdependence (which have both positive and negative fall-outs).

These two major factors, combined, are beginning to foster a new form of spirituality in the world. Admittedly the impulse is only in a small, but growing, minority of individuals who are recognizing one another as "co-conspirators" (breathers together) to use Marilyn Ferguson's phraseology based on Teilhard de Chardin's use of "conspiracy."

What is this new spirituality like? In brief, it is associated with individuals who look less to an outer than to an inner authority. Such people are more inner-directed, drawing on their own resources for peace and strength. Most importantly, they are imbued with the conviction that humanity is one family, and that race, religion, culture, sex and color are superficialities, irrelevant to the human condition. This attitude fosters a new type of activism, one which is not just parochial. Its philosophy is often captured in the phrase, "Think globally, act locally."

While such individuals are freshly receptive to the wisdom reposing in the world's sacred scriptures, their chief altar is within themselves. For they have discovered the ability to enter a realm of stillness within, a state wherein time and reality are somehow stretched and slowed, and wherein all affairs, personal and not personal, assume a different complexion. Paradoxically, the achievement of such a unitive state does not negate personal life or remove its problems; these remain just as clear if not clearer, but they are less disconcerting, less immobilizing. Moreover, the problems—both those that are personal and those that relate to others —seem paradoxically both one's own and yet detached from one. One is both calmer and more energized, and there is at once a sense of acceptance and of intentionality that is the opposite of indifference.

This sketch is an attempt to suggest the changing religious attitudes engendered by a commitment to the whole—the unitive dimension of religion.

Paul Tillich (1969) described a conception of religion which extends beyond its traditional usage, but does not negate it. So conceived, religion entails encounters or experiences of "the Absolute as absolute above all derived absolutes in the different realms. . . . It experiences direct knowledge, or the moral imperative, or social justice, or aesthetic expressiveness. . . . [It] is the experience of the holy in a particular place, or time, in a particular person, book, or image, in a particular ritual act, spoken word, or sacramental object" (p. 131). For Tillich this is a direct experience, and it extends beyond conventional religious institutions to include the secular domain, which thereby is made sacred.

Robert Ellwood (1982) has remarked that eminent voices have been predicting the withering away of religion at least since the eighteenth century. And he asks: Is this likely? Without attempting to

When a person rediscovers that his deepest Nature is one with the All, he is relieved of the burdens of time, of anxiety, of worry; he is released from the chains of alienation and separate-self existence. Seeing that self and other are one, he is released from the fear of life; seeing that being and non-being are one, he is delivered from the fear of death. Thus when one rediscovers the ultimate Wholeness, one transcends—but does not obliterate—every imaginable sort of boundary, and therefore transcends all types of battles. It is a conflict-free awareness, whole, blissful. But this does not mean that one loses all egoic consciousness, all temporal awareness. . . . [For] wholeness is not the opposite of egoic individuality, it is simply its Ground, and the discovery of the ground does not annihilate the figure.

Ken Wilber, *Up from Eden* [pp. 11-13]

With the realization of our global identity, we should increasingly find ourselves experiencing the sacred as something universal in humankind. Balancing this new universality, we should see at once a new fascination with roots and traditions. We should find ourselves feeling the fact of our different religious belief not so much as a threat, but now as a rich source for learning. We should more and more be able to appreciate how the one comes alive through the many.

Charles M. Johnson, M.D., "Beyond Knowledge—Toward Wisdom," *Noetic Sciences Review,* Winter 1988, No. 9

foretell the future, he vouchsafes the comment that "the relation of religion to its times is usually more complex and mysterious than appears on the surface" (p. 384).

We will let Tillich (1969) have the final word here, because his particular assertions accord so well with the tenor of our approach to reality. Tillich said that every religion has a depth that is concealed by that religion's particularity, and that the struggle to liberate religions from this distortion must never cease. He then remarks: "Therefore in our dialogues with other religions we must not try to make converts; rather, we must try to drive the other religions to their own depths, to that point at which they realize that they are witness to the Absolute but are not the Absolute themselves" (p. 149). A religion is all the truer the more it points beyond itself to that for which it is a witness and of which it is a partial manifestation. In its encounters with other religions, the desirable aim is to break through mutually to that point at which the vision of the holy-itself liberates us from bondage to any of the particular manifestations of the holy. For it is the Absolute that we need and that we cannot live without—something we take with unconditional seriousness in whatever language we express it. We need, far more than we have now, an ultimate meaning in our daily lives.

14

Religion and Science

*Both religion and science strive after truth and can therefore
exist side by side without contradicting each other and without
impeding each other. But this does not mean that they can be
amalgamated, because their essential difference is not so much
in their aims and objects as in their methods. The method of
scientific research is outwardly directed; that of religion in-
wardly; and each of these methods can achieve its best results if
it follows its own inherent laws.*

Lama Anagarika Govinda, *Creative Meditation and Multi-
Dimensional Consciousness*

An Intimate and Beneficial Relationship

Empirical science cannot provide knowledge which is not accessible to its methodology, for this requires totally different instruments
(cf. Huston Smith's classical work, *The Forgotten Truth*). Yet the two
domains, science and religion, have, in principle, an intimate and
beneficial relationship. Albert Einstein stated accurately and in a
most expressive way, to my mind, the relation between science and
religion: "Religion without science is lame; science without religion
is blind!"

But the words "in principle" are used intentionally. Earlier we
referred to the still smoldering conflict between science and religion
over the question of evolution—a conflict born of category error on
both the Creationist side and the side of the neo-Darwinians. Broadly
speaking, all absolutists, including fundamentalists and fanatics of
every shade, are likely to be in sharp disagreement with those outside
their immediate faction, for they cannot tolerate even slight cracks in
the facade of their monolithic belief. Thus they feel themselves
surrounded by threats, and wall themselves in against their enemies.
In similar fashion, scientism, as distinguished from science, erects

false barriers when it insists that only empirical science can discover what is true, and that what science does not discover must be untrue. Yet, as we have said, the essential harmony and complementarity between religion and science come into view when the scientific enterprise has a holistic orientation, and the religion is universal.

Einstein's scientific pursuits reinforced his spiritual perceptions because those pursuits made him aware of the pervasive intelligence in the cosmos. "My religion," he said "consists of a humble admiration of the illimitable superior spirit who reveals himself in the slight details we are able to perceive with our frail and feeble minds. That deeply emotional conviction of the presence of a superior reasoning power which is revealed in the incomprehensible universe, forms my idea of God" (Barnet, 1968, p. 109).

Science is, moreover, indirectly impacting upon and universalizing human consciousness through the technologies of mass production, mass commerce, mass communications, mass media and mass travel, which it has made possible. These developments have brought about a mutual encounter and virtual convergence of everything human beings are engaged in, including cultures and faiths; for instance, we encounter each other's religions and myths on the printed page, on the television screen, and by actually visiting exotic shrines and temples in the course of our touristic and other travels. The commingling of cultures and faiths that is thus occurring is surely a richly broadening experience. (This set of developments is however a double-edged sword. For instance, the increased interdependency of nations that has been brought about by mass industrialization is a factor in greater religious friction and conflict, on the one hand, and is impelling nations toward cooperation, sharing and mutual tolerance, on the other.)

To return to Einstein's words, the fuller passage (in his book, *Out of My Later Years*) is very much worth quoting (1977, p. 26):

> Even though the realms of religion and science in themselves are clearly marked off from each other, nevertheless there exist between the two strong, reciprocal relationships and dependencies. Though religion may be that which determines the goal, it has, nevertheless, learned from science, in the broadest sense, what means will contribute to the attainment of the goals it has set up. But science can only be created by those who are thoroughly imbued with the aspiration toward truth and understanding. This source of feeling, however, springs from the sphere of religion. To this there also belongs the faith in the possibility that the regulations valid for the world of existence

In both science and religion frontier knowledge is disclosed only through the use of instruments. . . .

What are the mystical counterparts of such instruments? Basically they are two, one of which is corporate, the other private. For collectivities—tribes, societies, civilizations, traditions—the revealing instruments are the Revealed Texts, or, in nonliterate societies, the ordering myths that are impounded in stories. . . .

These revealed canons are the Palomar telescopes that disclose the heavens that declare God's glory. . . . There comes a point when the mystic's instruments cannot stop with being external and must become—himself. All knowing involves an adequation of something in the knower to its object, but in the kind of knowing that is at issue here, this epistemological something cannot be limited to the knower's mind and senses. When Blake tells us that "if the doors of perception were cleansed everything would appear to man as it is, infinite," the doors in question involve the total self. "It is a fact, confirmed and reconfirmed by two or three thousand years of religious history," Aldous Huxley wrote, "that Ultimate Reality is not clearly and immediately apprehended except by those who have made themselves loving, pure in heart, and poor in spirit." These are the tools for facilitating the mystic's key perceptions that solve all riddles at a stroke and define reality from that point on.

Huston Smith, *The Forgotten Truth*
[pp. 114-115]

are rational, that is, comprehensible to reason. I cannot conceive of a genuine scientist without that profound faith. The situation may be expressed by an image: science without religion is lame, religion without science is blind.

Teilhard de Chardin (1965), himself both a scientist (a distinguished one) and a mystical Christian, declared that religion and science "are the two conjugated faces or phases of one and the same complete act of knowledge" (p. 285).

And Thomas Berry, the cultural historian, after fifty years of study of human cultures, has concluded that the scientific enterprise is the most sustained meditation ever carried out on the universe, and furthermore, that what has been discovered in the scientific era has to be regarded as equally important with the revelations of the great religions (Cf. Swimme, 1986).

Let us, however, never forget that neither religion nor science can articulate final truth. For truth, like reality itself, is ineffable. It transcends both modes of knowing and embraces both.

Science and Mysticism

There is a vogue today to compare science and mysticism. The comparisons are sometimes not surprisingly confused, given the abstractness of the subject. Yet the trend is surely a significant and positive sign of our times. It is part of the impulse toward a synthesis of knowledge, itself part of the human drive toward unity.

Ken Wilber, for one, has compiled (1984) excerpts from the actual writings on mysticism by the founders and grand theorists of modern physics, including Einstein, Schroedinger, Heisenberg, Bohr, Eddington, Pauli, de Broglie, Jeans and Planck. This is a fascinating book, but in his analysis of these writings Wilber is at pains to caution against prevailing confusions, and this, I think, causes him to over-emphasize that "these theorists are virtually unanimous in declaring that modern physics offers no positive support whatsoever for mysticism or transcendentalism of any variety, and this notwithstanding that all these individuals were mystics of one sort or another. Their general consensus was that modern physics neither proves nor disproves, neither supports nor refutes, a mystical-spiritual worldview" (p. 5).

Wilber points out that these physicists regarded the current vogue of using physics to prove or disprove the existence of God, or some religious ideology, to be inappropriate and even reprehensible, and that they emphasized that physics is a different domain whose function has nothing to do with any such purpose. According to Schroedinger, for example, religion's "true domain is far beyond anything in reach of scientific explanation."

Unquestionably, science and mysticism are two very different approaches to reality. Science looks outward at the external world, whereas mysticism proceeds by introspection or direct perception. Yet Einstein was right when he said that science and mystical religion reinforce each other, for since there can be only one reality, both share the same goal. The advances of each should make reality itself more accessible.

As we earlier saw, physics carries out its inquiry into nature with tremendous fidelity; that extraordinary group of scientists of the early twentieth century winced, but accepted the results of their mathematical equations and their experiments, even though these brought down about their ears the whole framework of classical physics. In the measure that physics succeeds in grasping aspects of the cosmos—and there is no doubt that it is opening up some hitherto unknown areas—science is allowing humans to transcend their bondage to physicality. In so doing, we are forced to acknowledge the power and pervasiveness of intangibles, as well as the extraordinary consistency of nature. In all this, contemporary science tends towards the view of perennial philosophy. But if Einstein's statement is correct, science's support of mystical religion must be by virtue of the discovery of the beauty, simplicity and elegance of the cosmic order. As for mysticism's reinforcement of science, it must be actual, or so many great physicists should not have been attracted by mystical thought.

Why were they attracted? Wilber believes the reason is modern physics had discovered that it was not, after all, contacting ultimate reality. This was indeed, as we noted, one of physics' significant new insights. However, I wonder if that is the whole explanation.

For one thing, some of the fathers of the scientific revolution, including Descartes and Newton, were *also* mystically inclined. It seems to me that the ability to see into the order of nature and perceive that the human mind can state that order mathematically often goes hand in hand with mystical perception. Indeed, outstanding individuals are often gifted not in just one but in many ways; we can all think of examples such as Leonardo da Vinci and Benjamin Franklin. Many of the gifted people mentioned in this book are also multi-faceted, and do not limit their search for knowledge and understanding to just one discipline.

Secondly, it seems to me that many scientists were stimulated by the paradoxical nature of quantum physics, which points so suggestively to a metaphysical reality.

Is There Such a Thing as a Mystical Science?

The range of questions that have intrigued the human mind and given rise to the growth of science and of knowledge in general is immensely broad, and is far from having been fully mapped as a whole body.[1]

Unmapped as yet are the regions of thought that lie at the interface of physical and mental apprehensions, including some ancient as well as some new disciplines. Among the latter is that of parapsychology, whose field includes both physical *and* mental phenomena. There are a number of other areas of experiment and experience which involve both physical energy discharges and changes of state in consciousness, such as Kirlian photography, plant response, biofeedback and psychic or spiritual healing. Where do these fit into the general framework of knowledge? Where do the occult arts such as astrology and alchemy and divinatory systems like the *I Ching* and the Tarot fit? Most mainstream scientists dismiss all these as nonsense. Yet the ancient arts of divination seem to suggest "a fundamental relation between man and cosmos. The macrocosm/microcosm doctrine and the system of correspondences which occultism [the term is defined below] teaches . . . furnish such a principle of relation. Indeed, they point to a basic isomorphism" (Emily B. Sellon, in a private paper).

Where on the map should we place yoga and Zen, two ancient spiritual practices that are rigorous scientific disciplines based upon carefully systematized principles? One definition of yoga is "union of the individual self with the divine life that pervades the universe." Zen is likewise a discipline developed to produce a transcendent state of consciousness, a direct insight into truth.

Mapping some of the as yet miscellaneous types of knowledge will require finding the natural laws that can explain them. It will also require extending our picture of reality to accommodate them. But a "picture" of reality is a state of consciousness; the spectrum of knowledge is a spectrum of states of consciousness. Can one conceive of an ultimate state of consciousness which embraces and synthesizes the subjective insights of mysticism, philosophy and science?

If one accepts the many allusions to such a "mystical science" made in the past, the answer will be in the affirmative. These references point to a secret or "occult" science, cherished by the cognoscenti, hidden from the ignorant and profane. Such an occult science demanded much of the aspirant to knowledge. H. P. Blavatsky de-

---

1. For a fascinating and instructive essay on science and the possibility of extending it beyond what we call empirical science, see Wilber, 1983, Chap. 2, "The Problem of Proof."

The *referent* of transcendental perception [in Zen], its very data, cannot be perceived with the mental or sensory eyes. Satori takes as its referent, not sensory objects out there and not mental subjects in here, but nondual spirit as such, a direct apprehension *of* spirit, *by* spirt, *as* spirit, an apprehension that unites subject and object by disclosing that which is prior to both, and an apprehension that therefore is quite beyond the capacities of objective-empirical or subjective-phenomenal cognition. As Hegel put it, this is "Spirit's return to itself, on a higher plane, a level at which subjectivity and objectivity are united in one infinite act." This trancendental apperception arises when I am aware, not simply of myself as a finite individual standing over against other finite persons . . . and things . . . , but rather of the Absolute as the ultimate and all-embracing reality. . . . [This knowledge] is a movement in absolute consciousness . . . that is, in the self-knowledge of Being or the Absolute. This direct, immediate, intuitive apprehension of Being—*not* by the eye of flesh, and not by the eye of mind, but by the eye of contemplation—is satori.

Ken Wilber, *Eye to Eye* [pp. 60-61]

---

fined it as follows: "Occultism is not magic, though magic is one of its tools. Occultism is not the acquirement of powers, whether psychic or intellectual, though both are its servants. Neither is occultism the pursuit of happiness, as men understand the word; for the first step is sacrifice, the second, renunciation. Occultism is the science of life, the art of living" (*Lucifer,* vol I, p. 7, published some time between 1887-1891).

15

Karma: The Ultimate Law of Wholeness

Our survey of science and religion in the preceding chapters suggests that the physical, mental and spiritual levels of existence are dynamically interconnected by virtue of the pervasive holistic principle. We shall find this principle equally operative in the politico-socio-economic sphere when we survey it (in Part 4). But let us now consider the principle itself in terms of one of its most universal and comprehensive formulations: the law of karma.

The universal law called "karma," to which we have already referred in several contexts, is fundamental to Hinduism and Buddhism as well as to theosophy. As a moral law, karma is taught in Western religion under the rubric, "We reap as we sow." But in Eastern thought the concept is extended to a cosmic principle governing all relationships: an inclusive law of balance and harmony. As such it correlates the cosmic with the human order, personal with societal morality, and a given society's morality with its existential conditions. Thus conceived, it is a truly universal principle which operates throughout nature and which nothing can escape. In this sense it is the most unitive as well as the most comprehensive expression of the wholeness, the interrelatedness of all things.

"Karma" is a Sanskrit word which means literally "action" or "work" and the "force" of that action. When an action is performed, a sequence of events is bound to occur, depending upon the kind of action and the force with which the action was performed. Likewise the reaction, or effect, is governed by the motivating force—the stronger it is, the stronger the reaction—until equilibrium is restored and harmony reigns again. But as we shall see, karma implies much more than a restoration of balance and harmony: it is a future-oriented process—integral to the cosmic evolutionary process. How karma accomplishes its extraordinary feats is of course a mystery; as we saw, science has not, up to now, fathomed causality even in the realms of physics and biology. One may bear in mind, however, that karma is associated with the system of thought outlined at the outset: a nondualistic philosophy which postulates that the universe is a multi-levelled, living whole, within whose (unimaginably) vast spectrum, levels are infinitely interconnected, interwoven into a living, co-evolving web of relations.

We are interested here primarily in the application of the law of karma to our own life, individually and collectively. Perhaps the first thing to note is the significant difference between the general condition of existence at the levels of the mineral, plant and animal kingdoms, on the one hand, and that obtaining for humankind. For most living organisms, the web of existence is their natural world, but human beings, endowed with self-consciousness, distance themselves from nature's processes through the power of choice and its corollary, responsibility. What this means in terms of karma is that when a human being disturbs the natural order—that is, acts deliberately to the disadvantage of others—that disturbance eventually redounds upon its originator.

Put in another way, human beings, as doers and also as responders to others' actions, bring karma into play. In its ethical sense, the law of karma states: as you sow, so you reap; like action, like consequence; violence begets violence, hatred begets hatred, love begets love. The law can also be expressed thus: he who lives by the sword, perishes by the sword; conversely, he who lives in the love of truth fosters love.

In a world where so much inequity prevails, and where greed and personal interest so often seem to succeed, karma alone redresses inequities and teaches us by experience the effects of human action. And in the social domain, we are shown that we create "the world" we know and experience, with all its problems. This idea of the long-term effects upon the world (which of course includes man's relation to nature) is now becoming accepted by most thinking people (due to the weight of evidence) and even— reluctantly—by governments.

Individuals are slower to perceive that their own actions are so far-reaching. Wars may be started by governments, but they are fought by people, and if people refuse to fight, armed conflict cannot occur. Violent thoughts or intentions are endemic in our world, as is the craving for pleasure and power, and these thoughts/desires and the

The entire universe is . . . woven into one web of karma, mental events being correlated with physical ones and vice versa. . . . Because of the inter-plane correlation, any fact in the universe, physical or psychic, can be reduced to its physical plane correlates. He who is determined to find the cause of everything on the material plane alone will always be able to find, not indeed its "cause," but at least a set of material correlates which will appear to explain the particular phenomenon. Nevertheless, the opposite method, that of accounting for physical events in terms of their psychic correlates, is a truer and more fundamental one. The lower levels hang from the higher.

Sri Krishna Prem and Sri Madhava
Ashish, *Man the Measure of All
Things* [p. 225]

Karma is essentially a doctrine of the intricate reciprocations between forces and action. . . . When expressed on a cosmological scale, this force-action is a stupendous power that propels the universe and life; when expressed in the ethical sense, it is an unfailing, impersonal law that effectuates the moral order, "dispensing" natural rewards and retributions. Metaphysically, karma is a creative energy brought forth by the collective actions of certain groups; it sustains the order and function of a particular universe in which these groups reside. Ultimately, karma is a mystery, a marvel that evades human comprehension.

Garma Chang, *The Buddhist Teaching
of Totality* [p. xxiv]

actions they cause bear fruit. To the degree that the individual exercises personal power over others or causes pain, he or she bears the responsibility for such actions.

The immediate response to such statements is that people are seldom punished for their actions unless these are directly criminal. But such a view fails to consider the many long-term consequences, including the effects on character, health and human relationships. Immediate benefits such as money and power may be achieved, but observation and experience show that action for personal advantage,

Man has always pondered the nature of his action, seeking
either to escape the consequences of his acts or to modify the
results in such a manner as to insure no harm will come to him.
To accept full responsiblity for all our choices, and hence for all
our actions, requires often more courage than we possess and
maturity we long to achieve yet seemingly cannot attain. . . .
Choice—self-conscious choice—is a specifically human capability; to abrogate our right to choose between alternatives . . .
is to forfeit some part of our humanity. To permit others to
make our choices for us is in itself a choice. . . . Out of our
choices . . . arises the complex pattern of our existence, each
choice weaving the invisible web of circumstances in which we
find ourselves enmeshed. . . . Throughout all nature, the interconnectedness of life in its manifold forms is evidenced, a
universal law of harmony revealing itself again and again in
innumerable patterns. . . . We may be too close in time or too
near in space to observe with any accuracy or understanding the
outcome of our choices, but to say law is not operative or
pattern is not to be found is to fail to perceive the larger truth
that order could not be anywhere were it not everywhere, harmony could not be achieved were lawfulness a sometime thing.

Joy Mills, *Karma* [Hanson and
Stewart, eds., 1981, pp. vii-viii]

and "success" earned at the expense of others, carry with them a
complex of consequences. Persons who achieve success at the expense of others deliver themselves into the bondage of the terms of
that success. Indeed, the more important causes of human bondage
lie within our hearts and minds, not outside them. We are prisoners of
our habits, of our fears, our desires, our hopes and our social interests. We are prisoners of our prejudices and of our worldviews.

In a deeper sense, these limitations are due to ignorance or (in
Sanskrit) *avidya*. *Avidya* connotes, more precisely, the condition of
not seeing things as they are—of misconceiving one's true nature as
the ephemeral and mortal personality and identifying the self with its
limited view of life's purpose and meaning. The consequence of such
identification is that the self is perceived in terms of material advantage, prestige, power, respect and love. While these are undeniably

good in themselves, to *seek* them as the goal of life is to be bound by the terms of personal motives and selfish action. Karma implies that *inner freedom is something which has to be earned and won by ourselves*—it cannot be granted to us from without. And we are free only in the degree to which we observe the laws of our higher nature which give us the power of choice. Since we do not live in isolation but, on the contrary, are all intrinsic elements within the web of life and relationships, individuals, far from being negligible, are the strands which support the whole edifice; if these are seriously weakened, the culture will suddenly collapse.

In the light of today's societal and environmental problems, it becomes more and more apparent that we create our own world. It is all too clear (and we will substantiate this extensively in Part IV) that the present global problems—from hunger to terrorism, from desertification to the threat of nuclear war, from ozone depletion to the permanent war economy—are of our own making, the consequences of our collective values, intentions and actions.

It is important to note, as Sir Edwin Arnold does in *The Light of Asia*, that karma is "an immutable law of absolute Love, Justice and Mercy," not only of retribution. The idea so often proposed that karma is punitive in its action stems from a limited conception of justice and judgment. As Blavatsky emphasized, karma is *not* inexorable fate, for it is we ourselves who are the planners, designers and creators of causes whose effects this universal law adjusts. Far from precluding the freedom and creativity of human beings, it is inner law which makes them possible. Scientists can accomplish the feat of sending man to outer space by obeying the necessary physical and other natural laws. Similarly, by obeying moral law in the choices we make individually and as a society, we could create a better world. (Better choices imply of course a change in our motives and values, which in turn depend on our state of consciousness.)

Blavatsky emphasized that the aggregate of individual karma becomes that of the nation to which the individuals belong, and that the sum of national karma is that of the world. She further stated: "No man can rise superior to his individual failings, without lifting, be it ever so little, the whole body of which he is an integral part. In the same way, no one can sin, nor suffer the effects of sin, alone. In reality, there is no such thing as 'Separateness'" (1946, p. 203).

Or, in Donne's beautiful phrase, "No man is an island."

One of the troubling questions which arises in considering the world as a whole relates to the inequities we perceive on every side among individuals and elements of societies as well as nations. The idea that karma will redress all apparent injustice at some future time is philosophically comforting, but not if the individual is left out of the equation. Will the lost opportunities recur? The answer to this question (if one leaves out the problem of heaven or hell) can only be found in the concept of individual continuity through cycles of rebirth which make possible the fruition of karma.

For this reason, reincarnation is usually (but not always) tied to the doctrine of karma, as in Hinduism, Buddhism, and theosophy. When accepted, reincarnation unquestionably gives karma deeper levels of philosophical and personal meaning.[1]

Without claiming "permanence" or "eternal life" for the individual, reincarnation nevertheless implies that there is a self that transcends the immediacy of personal existence and endures to be born again. The wholeness which constitutes the human being thus embraces death as an integral part of life—part of the natural cycle of birth-death-rebirth. Reincarnation suggests that an individual's evolution proceeds over many lifetimes instead of just one—in a way that is at once continuous and discontinuous (reminiscent of quantum and other phenomena and processes that we have discussed).

The twin doctrines of karma and reincarnation suppose that all we are in mind, emotions and physical body (as distinguished from our universal Self), and our present circumstances, is the result of our own past action, either in the present or in former life experiences, and that we are shaping our future at every moment by our thoughts, intentions, actions and our way of meeting present problems and challenges.

By virtue of karma, from day to day we sow the seeds of what we shall be in our next incarnation. Periodically, we are impelled to return to physical existence in order to continue our unfinished business, so to speak. Blavatsky wrote that "Karma is the force that

---

1. The idea of rebirth or reincarnation has suggested itself to countless people and to peoples in different times and places. See, for example, Head and Cranston (1977), which compiles massive documentation demonstrating this historical fact. It is also interesting, as this volume shows, that the mythical allegory of the immortal phoenix which repeatedly rises from its ashes has appeared in different versions among Christians, Jews, Persians and in far-apart cultures, including the ancient Irish, the Japanese and the Turks.

The most important field of human activity today has no accepted name. It includes a part of religion, philosophy and ethics, of metaphysics, mysticism, psychology and social service. It concerns the development of character, the cultivation of the best and the elimination of the worst of the complex thing called self. It is the whole field of the inner life as distinct from the world of everyday affairs, and yet it has immediate effect in the littlest occupation of the day. It is the art of life, the science of right living. It is the most important field of human activity today because all others, alone or collectively, have no sufficient effect upon our individual and collective behaviour to save mankind from its present tendency to self-destruction. It is the Way, as old as man, from desire to peace . . . it concerns the right relationship of all parts to the whole, and is therefore the concern of all humanity.

Christmas Humphreys, *Walk On!*
[p. 5]

No individual exists in its own nature, independent of all other factors of life. . . . Since no first beginning of any individual or of any inner or outer phenomena can be found, it means that each of them has the totality of the universe at its base. Or, if we want to express this from the standpoint of time, we could say that each of these phenomena, and especially every individual, has an infinite past and is, therefore, based on an infinity of relations, which do not and cannot exclude anything that ever existed or is liable to come into existence. All individuals (or rather all that has individual existence) have, therefore, the whole universe as their common ground, and this universality becomes conscious in the experience of enlightenment, in which the individual awakens into his own true all-embracing nature.

Lama Anagarika Govinda, *Creative Meditation and Multi-Dimensional Consciousness* [p. 10] impels to Reincarnation, and that Karma is the destiny man weaves for himself."

It seems to me that most of us would need more than one lifetime to realize even a small portion of the infinite potential that is within us. Karma, combined with reincarnation, permits far more than than the discharging of adverse past conditioning. It provides the necessary time for completion of our grand journey in consciousness toward enlightenment and the full realization of unity. For, as Lama Govinda has pointed out, given our divine origin, the past is also a guarantee of a sublime future.

In sum, what karma immediately implies for us is that all things are bound together in a multi-levelled web of relationships which grows through time—effects following causes and becoming in turn the causative factors, in an unending process of growth and development. These time-binding relationships are in one sense determined, since they are the result of past action, but in another sense they are liberating. For each of us has the power (if we would but exercise it) of transcending our circumstances. The insight that we are an indispensable part of a whole world which is continually being recreated by our own actions gives us a tremendous sense of responsibility, but also of fellowship in a great work.

16

More on the Spiritual Implications of Wholeness

Experiencing Unity

Let us look further at the meaning and implications of radical wholeness. For the individual, this essential unity with others is expressible through sympathy, empathy, solidarity, compassion, love and identity. Now all of these feelings issue from a level that is deeper than reason, though reason upholds them. As earlier explained, a sense of unity arises from the intuitive or spiritual or mystical level of consciousness. Involved is a shift of consciousness from the ordinary rational level to a trans-rational level.

It is worth underlining that this experience is not confined to the rare mystic.

People often experience unity with another being they love. They know the experience of unity with nature, i.e., a spontaneous feeling triggered by a particular encounter, whether it be with a landscape or beautiful rose or an expanse of water. A person may likewise experience an identity with a work of art, a poem, a musical work, a novel or a play.

Before a beautiful landscape, for example, one may suddenly, spontaneously, feel *it* to be a unity, and invariably this is accompanied, consciously or unconsciously, by a feeling of *oneself* becoming *whole* and *at one* with nature. The landscape naturally comprises a myriad components, such as numerous trees and shrubs, perhaps some animals, perhaps man-made structures, certainly the varying contours and textures of the land, the configurations of color and pattern of land, sky and water. Yet all these meld into a unity that includes the experiencer. And as we well know, this is invariably refreshing, even bliss-making.

Take as another example experiencing a fine musical work, such as a symphony. The numerous different elements—notes, melodies, tempi, movements, instruments, players of those instruments—become a whole, as does the work itself, which is in some mysterious way incomplete without the listening ear.

The piece of music can of course be experienced in memory as well as in performance. I recently came upon an illuminating passage concerning the nature of this type of experience—in Roger Jones's book *Physics as Metaphor*. Jones writes that when held in mind, the musical work is not in time as it is when listened to in performance, "any more than our ideas, recollections, and dreams may be thought of as existing in objective time. [When apprehending or appreciating the work in mind] one has a sense of it as a unified thing with a character and value of its own, like a cherished friend. One could not begin to say all that it means, or to define it. It is held in the mind as a unique, known, and valued entity. The full work is felt, not as evolved and laid out in time, but as capsulized and unified. . . . The same is true of a movie or novel after seeing it or reading it" (1982, p. 92).

We tend today to be far more conscious of our separateness, our individuality, than of our unity. But everyone has a conscious or unconscious drive toward unity; that urge is fundamental to all religious faiths as well as to science. In the latter it takes the form of a search for elegance and simplicity.

The drive towards unity takes many forms and is expressed in many cultural values: the importance of kinship and family ties, membership in clubs, fraternities, professional societies, political parties, religious groups, patriotic organizations. These are all outward signs of the impulse toward kinship, which unfortunately is as often exclusive as inclusive, when we misguidedly take compatibility for sympathy.

The search for unity takes on a different cast when the individual is motivated by the will to break down barriers wherever they may be found. Such efforts range from a commitment to helping others through various kinds of service to the determination to break down the inner obstacles to unity through the practice of love and compassion. This intent is being evidenced in the widespread interest in the practice of meditation, which is recognized by many as the means *par excellence* for self-integration (overcoming the inner warring be-

Our life has value only because and in so far as it realises in fact that which transcends time and existence. Goodness, beauty and truth are all there is which in the end is real. This reality, appearing amid chance and change, is beyond these and is eternal. . . . For love and beauty and delight . . . do not die, since the Paradise in which they bloom is immortal. That Paradise is not a special region, nor any particular spot in time or place. It is here, it is everywhere where any finite being is lifted to that higher life which alone is waking reality.

> F.H. Bradley, *Essays on Truth and Reality* [p. 469]

The Absolute is the ultimate ground of all such values as truth, beauty and goodness. They are relational, not intrinsic characteristics of the Absolute. . . . Beauty is the Absolute insofar as it is felt or immediately perceived in sense-impressions. Goodness is the Absolute insofar as it is expressed in integrated actions. . . . Truth is the absolute *qua* known or revealed to the mind. . . . It is the value that emerges from the mind's contact with the Absolute. Now, the mind's contact with the Absolute is knowledge. . . . Truth is therefore the object of knowledge. But human knowledge is always by its very nature relative. It is what the knowing mind gains by contemplating Being under certain circumstances from a certain standpoint. In thus contemplating Being it is always a particular aspect, characteristic, or dimension of Being which is revealed at a given time. Truth as an object of knowledge is, therefore, always a definite perspective of Being. It can hardly be absolutely equated with the Absolute. . . . But yet the Absolute is not unknown and unknowable, as agnosticism would have us believe. Because the Absolute is increasingly unveiled in respect of its various aspects in the gradual expansion of our knowledge. In its essence, the Absolute is immediately encountered in our intuitive realization or nondualistic experience.

> Haridas Chaudhuri, *Being, Evolution & Immortality* [pp. 71-72]

tween the opposites) and for a sense of alignment with the cosmos and with one's fellow beings.

Inner harmony makes for outer harmony, as we know. Given the development at present of a global society, one's ability to feel empathy and solidarity with other people irrespective of their creed, culture, color and sex assumes new significance and urgency. The interest in meditation and the emergence of a global society seem to be remarkably synchronous developments.

The Higher Values: Categorical Imperatives

Those who have a sense of unity and wholeness in some measure cannot doubt the validity of the higher values such as truth, goodness and beauty.

On the other hand, knowledge and values have largely been separated from each other in the modern era, a separation induced by classical sciences' emphasis on "pure objectivity." Physics in the twentieth century unexpectedly discovered the falsity of this ideal, as we saw, but because of the lag between scientific discovery and its absorption into the cultural worldview, many people still espouse "value neutrality," and believe that individual choice and behavior are purely personal and without social consequences. Still more pervasive and destructive is the position taken by linguistic analysts and deconstructionists, that values and meaning are entirely relative, and that the form (of language) alone has significance and can be discussed.

Many have lamented the general loss of meaning attendant upon this state of thought. David Bohm remarks, "Thus, the universe is now pictured, according to modern science, as a vast space full of dead matter moving mechanically, while man is a tiny creature living on a mere speck of dust in this space, trying desperately to make his life seem worthwhile by projecting his own arbitrary and inevitably petty ends and goals" (in Sloan, ed., 1984).

Fortunately, this picture is being eroded by science itself, which now images the world more like a flowing wholeness, or a living system, or a flow pattern, or a self-organizing and evolving universe. All these terms may be metaphorical rather than definitive but they point to the fact that the cosmos and its component entities are one whole, linked together by meaning.

[By *the good* as an eternal and supreme value Plato and others have meant] not any particular good, nor even the general good of mankind, but rather the very essence of goodness. This not only acts to sustain what is good, to propagate it and make it flower, but it is in itself of the quality of perfect love, harmony, beauty, and wholeness (which was generally what was meant also by the divine). . . .

[However] . . . both in religion and in politics, it is just those who were convinced of the absolute goodness of what they were doing who often ultimately produced the greatest evil. So it seems that, at the very least, the notion of absolute goodness can be consistent only if it has absolutely no definable content (so that it evidently could not be held in any form of knowledge). What could be meant by such a notion?

In answer . . . one might suggest that what is required is not an intellectual understanding of the subject but rather an *act* of turning toward the ultimate good. . . . [However] is a human being actually free just to *will* to turn away from such self-centeredness toward the highest good? This does not seem to be so. Indeed . . . considering just the narrower and easier content of science, it is evidently not possible even for a highly competent scientist, by means of choice or will, to make himself as free of ego-based blocks and barriers in his thoughts in his own subject as were, for example, Newton and Einstein. . . .

Only the intense energy of insight[1] . . . can dissolve all kinds of blocks and barriers, including even those that are responsible for self-centeredness.

> David Bohm, "Insight, Knowledge,
> Science, and Human Values" [Sloane,
> ed., pp. 28-29]

The current attempt to see the self in terms of a computer is to be self-alienated and alienated from nature, and from the living cosmos itself. Such a view is hostile to the cultivation of meaning and value, and thus to the development of a sense of the whole. As already

---

1. Bohm defines insight as an act of perception, permeated with intense energy and passion, such that it can dissolve habitual rigidities of the mind that cause it to avoid challenges.

shown, it leads to the widespread aberration of relativism. But even while we recognize that all statements, whether they be religious, philosophical or scientific, are only relatively true, only *contingent* truths, these must have some ground above and beyond opinion or, in other words, some relation to truth itself, even though this escapes all its statements.

Goodness, truth and beauty were repeatedly affirmed by Plato as fundamental attributes of the universe, and as such, representative of the highest Reality. These in turn give rise to the archetypes or ideals from which all things derive their nature. Although we cannot define these three ultimates, we can know and recognize them directly in the requisite state of consciousness (Weber, 1975). Thus, when we speak of goodness, we do not mean a particular good but the essence of goodness. Particular expressions of goodness will vary, but the abstract ideal of the Good is everlasting.

Illuminating, too, is Paul Tillich's explication of absolute and relative values. Tillich affirmed "the unconditional character of the moral imperative [of Kantian thought], regardless of its content, and the principle of justice—acknowledgement of every person as a person." Of the principle of love or compassion or *eros* or *agapé*, he asserted that it "contains and transcends justice and unites the absolute and the relative by adapting itself to every concrete situation." In encountering reality, whether by cognitive, ethical, aesthetic, or other means, we come upon "structural absolutes without which life in these realms would be impossible" (1969, pp. 125-127). Plato spoke of the archetypes. Correspondingly, mythologists tell us that these structural absolutes evidence themselves as the recurring myths of the world.

How could one absolutize justice, whether economic, social, political or legal? How could one define ethics for all time? Such values are relational, and are reached by consensus; no society or individual can lay down fixed and everlasting rules for economic and social justice or human rights, for these must be determined in the context of human life. Each case has to be considered on its own merits. As one writer, Charles M. Johnston, put it: "Moral truth should become at once an increasingly important concern, and recognized as profoundly time and context relative. Integration will bring with it an ever growing recognition of the importance of grappling with ethical questions, both personally and culturally. And at the same time it will

Under the shocking impact of modern skepticism and nihilism, a healthy catharsis is taking place today in man's religious consciousness. The elements of undying value in religion are getting sifted from the elements of outgrown usefulness . . . breathes there a man who could call in question the value of religion as devotion to truth? Total concern for truth, wherever it may be found and whithersoever it may lead, is indeed the most precious ingredient of human nature. Is there an atheist who would fail to appreciate the grandeur of love and of the spirit of sacrifice for the good of others? Is there any nihilist who would withhold admiration from a life of dedication to social service or international peace? . . . At the very center of man's religious consciousness lies hidden his growing sense of higher values—his love of truth, beauty, justice, freedom, peace and progress.

Haridas Chaudhuri, *Modern Man's Religion* [pp. 15-16]

bring whole new ways of thinking about these issues, ones that ask that we step beyond dogma and condemnation, to confront each moment's relationship to life" (*Noetic Sciences Review,* Winter 1988).

IV
Society

Thank God our time is now
When wrong comes up to meet us everywhere
Never to leave us till we take
The greatest stride of soul
Men ever took.

Christopher Fry,
A Sleep of Prisoners

17

Societal Affairs: A Planetary Overview

To rethink development is necessarily to go beyond identifying the patterns of inequality that give substance to the scenario of Two Worlds. It is to call into question conceptions of what it means to be human. . . . [It is] to engage the deepest processes of social, cultural, and ethical life. . . . It challenges the presumptions of a civilization.

R. B. J. Walker, *One World, Many Worlds*

Introduction

Society consists of and is determined by relationships. These include the relationships of individuals, groups and nations with each other, with nature and, of course, with Reality, however defined. How we individually and collectively approach, face and interpret the problems engendered by relationship determines the character of our society.

The crucial global dilemmas we witness today may be understood as acute problems of relationship, such as those between industry and the natural support system, politics and violence, rich and poor, men and women. As the problems emerge in their extremity, we struggle to grasp their cause, to come to grips with them, to do something about them.

If, as holistic philosophy proposes, life is a school of experience, then the present time of crisis and danger is also a time of opportunity. One may also invoke the language of twentieth-century science, systems theory and transpersonal psychology. In those terms, the crisis may be appraised as a perturbation of the "open system" severe enough to offer the possibility of a "quantum" leap into a higher orbit of consciousness.

In the present chapter, we traverse a wide range of subjects, from economics to the United Nations, from third world conditions to disarmament. Whereas these different concerns are customarily discussed under separate rubrics, and not all in one short book, the fact is that they are all interconnected and integral to one and the same politico-socio-economic system and to one and the same planetary ecology.

No single individual, obviously, can encompass this vast, complex and dynamic domain, and certainly not the present writer. Nor can anyone predict the future, especially in an age of rapid change such as the present. Even the most skilled futurists, as they try to understand what is really happening by monitoring present developments in order to project future trends, do not always find the larger patterns clear. Indeed, given the dynamics of the world economy, the possibilities before us remain very obscure.

Our aim is limited to an attempt to draw out some of these dynamics, to see how actions and values espoused by people individually and collectively create their society. At the same time, by considering such a broad range of concerns so briefly, my hope is to facilitate my own and my readers' overall process of integration.

We shall certainly not attempt to investigate, let alone prescribe, *strategies* for societal improvement and change. Nevertheless, we shall be interested in the *spirit* of change and how it is expressed (by means of ideas, proposals and actions) by the collective and individual agencies and actors concerned—a category that in the final analysis includes everyone.

The uncertainties of the complex politico-socio-economic-technological-ecological system are legion, needless to say. But inasmuch as we are inquiring into the reality of wholeness, we will take as inclusive an approach as possible.

The Values of the Industrial Era

First it will be well to outline some of the chief features of economics and industry, the former representing the theory for the latter. We will be especially interested to see how industry and economics are interwoven with everything else, including their environmental, social, political, cultural, moral and spiritual implications.

Industrialized societies are today dominant in the world. As we well know, the economy and the state of industry are a primary focus of these societies. But material concerns have not always been the main focus of Western culture, any more than of Eastern culture. It is important to understand that this emphasis is historical rather than simply natural. Think, for example, of European Medieval society, in which the emphasis was far more on religion than on material concerns. The Church taught that earthly existence is a short prelude to eternal life, and it laid down the moral code for people to follow in preparation for that life. It also influenced commerce by condemning the charging of interest as usury, and regarding profit as greed. The merchant and craft guilds, which existed in the towns that had grown up by the eleventh century, functioned to prevent competition and to regulate the economic life of the towns (Spanier, 1985).

As merchants and manufacturers began to rise in importance, early economists championed the cause of this emerging business class against the landed gentry and other forces of tradition. They denounced the status quo, supported the "bourgeois revolution" and laid the base for the industrial and corporate revolutions that followed (Power, 1988, p. 7). In the course of time, however, economics ceased its critical mission and instead began to defend the new capitalist system (Power, 1988).

Today, governmental administrations and policy-makers rely heavily on economists' advice, but conventional economics is too narrowly focused (on monetary and commercial values and profits), is philosophically shallow (positing the Rational Economic Man), and the tool-kit it utilizes is outmoded (by today's globally interdependent economy).

Economists concentrate on quantifiable or measurable values. Conventionally, economics has not been concerned with the immeasurable values implicit in its economic models. But in reality, economics, and its sister disciplines sociology and political science, are sciences/arts that bear fundamentally on the *quality* of societal life. By their nature, they cannot be quality-neutral; in fact they are quality-laden, both positively and negatively.

To put the matter in another way, conventional economists share the mainstream outlook of which we spoke at the beginning of this book: the reductionistic idea of reality, with its assumption that all phenomena can be "reduced" to material properties. Conventional sociology and political science are similarly distorted by the premise that the subject-matter they treat consists of phenomena that at bottom are only causally (mechanically) connected. So viewed, the motivations of human beings, as well as their incentives and satisfactions, are fundamentally materialistic. If such characteristics as integrity, altruism, human solidarity, responsibility toward others, and to future generations, are to be found, they are simply a matter of personal idiosyncrasy. That a person's or an industry's primary motive should be profit for themselves alone; that no thought need be paid to costs to others (other cogs in the machine) and to nature (inert matter, to be exploited) are attitudes that are consistent with this general conception of reality.

But as we saw, physics itself has abandoned the mechanistic model of reality. This being so, it behooves other disciplines to take heed. Thus economics faces a similar need to reorient itself (as so do political science and sociology), by altering its values and updating its methodology. For, as dissidents point out, mechanistic or linear methods are totally inadequate to treat the present dynamic world system that involves numerous mutually interacting, often simultaneous, politico-socio-economic and other factors. The futurist Hazel Henderson has described the situation thus: the mature industrial societies' complexity and interdependence, their scale and centralization, and the unanticipated side-effects of the technology they have applied have become unmodellable and therefore unmanageable.

Specialists from various related disciplines are now contributing to rethinking the whole politico-socio-economic domain—an exercise induced by the acute dilemmas we face. In this process, economics is being placed in a broader perspective, so that in future it will no longer be the only or even the major source of wisdom in devising developmental policy. Quite apart from the shortcomings of present conventional economics, societal well-being can scarcely be comprehended by a single discipline. Instead, we need to study the political economy in its complex setting, including the natural support system. A holistic approach is in fact taking form, through inputs from political science, biology, systems analysis, futurism, sociology, physics, engineering, anthropology, ecology, psychology and holistic philosophy itself, the two latter implicating the very state of consciousness both of individuals and of society as a whole. Parenthetically, this approach naturally will draw on the respective insights and ideas of many of the leading-edge thinkers discussed in this book, from David Bohm to Ilya Prigogine, from Erich Jantsch to Ken Wilber.

In the now-classic critique of economics *Small is Beautiful,* by E. F. Schumacher, first published in 1973, the assumptions behind Western industry and economics were called into question, right down to their psychological and metaphysical foundations. (Schu-

The first economists denounced the status quo. . . . Under attack were the medieval economic institutions that had been retained by the emerging nation-states of Europe. The medieval centuries had left behind a strong distrust of individual pursuit of private financial gain. . . . The dominant social class . . . was a shifting mix of landed gentry, royalty, military leaders, and church officials. . . . But the medieval economic institutions were breaking down. Worldwide trade was becoming increasingly important. . . . Merchants and manufacturers were rising in importance despite the resistance of the traditional ruling classes. . . . Adam Smith was a moral philosopher and theologian who set out to prove the counterintuitive and socially subversive notion that unhindered private pursuit of personal gain would result in far more *social* gain than would regulation of individual economic activity. . . . [Economists] began as critics, not apologists. . . . But with the passage of time and the emergence of business leaders as the dominant class, "business economics" has to a large extent abandoned its critical mission for a largely apologetic defense of the new capitalist system. The result has been the close association of economics with commercial markets, businesses, dollar income, and profits.

Thomas Michael Power, *The Economic Pursuit of Quality [pp. 6-8]*

A crisis of manageability is now evident in most societies. Serious doubts are expressed even from conservative quarters about the capacity of existing authorities and institutions to cope with the stresses and strains visible in the major structures that shape the modern world.

R. B .J. Walker, *One World, Many Worlds: Struggles for a Just World Peace* [p. 13]

macher is the writer whose *A Guide for the Perplexed* was mentioned in Chapter 1.)

Schumacher deplored the single criterion of economics, namely, whether a thing yields a money profit to those who undertake it or not, which means that even simple, non-economic values like beauty, health and cleanliness cannot survive except where adjudged "economic." The adverse consequences of profit maximization are more evident today than ever. For instance, the marketplace in the United States offers a tremendous choice in models of telephone apparatuses but a great dearth of low- and middle-income housing. Commercialism is endlessly extended. According to one school of economics (in Chicago), private-interest maximization is just as applicable to the study of marriage and divorce as to the automobile industry and the inflation rate. It would expand economics into the traditional domains of sociology, political science, criminology, anthropology and law, and who knows what else (Lutz and Lux, 1988).

Schumacher deplored as self-defeating the practice of treating as mere income items those irreplaceable natural resources, which man has not made but simply found, and without which we can do nothing. In the preceding twenty-five years, the changes both in the quantity and in the quality of industrial processes had produced an entirely new situation—resulting not from failures but from what were thought to be the greatest successes. This had come about so suddenly that it was hardly noticed that society was "very rapidly using up a certain kind of irreplaceable capital asset, namely the *tolerance margins* which benign nature always provides," and were furthermore "already eating into the very substance of industrial man. . . . Ever-bigger machines, entailing ever-bigger concentrations of economic power and exerting ever-greater violence against the environment, do not represent progress: they are a denial of wisdom. Wisdom demands a new orientation of science and technology towards the organic, the gentle, the non-violent, the elegant and beautiful. Peace, as has often been said, is indivisible—how then could peace be built on a foundation of reckless science and violent technology?" (Schumacher, 1975, pages 18-34).

Schumacher believed that society has to take an entirely different course, evolve a new life style with new methods of production and a different pattern of consumption, including biologically sound agricultural and horticultural methods. He advocates evolving small-scale or relatively non-violent technology—"technology with a human face"—so that people might enjoy themselves while they work, instead of working solely for their pay packet; and that industry evolve new forms of organization and ownership.

An important influence upon Schumacher was the thought and the work of Mohandas K. Gandhi, who is remembered as the father of the Indian nation, but whom some regard more generally as the father of the idea of humanistic economic development. Gandhi himself had been affected by his reading of John Ruskin's *Unto This Last* (1866), wherein the British humanist criticized his country's political economy (Lutz and Lux, 1988). Schumacher was an advocate of humane economics. His thought may be described as decentralist, organic, holistic.

But meanwhile, most economists continue to preach the pursuit of *indiscriminate* growth as the panacea for all economic ills. More accurately, as Hazel Henderson puts it, they propose one moment that we save more and the next moment that we spend and consume more in a "jerky, contradictory stream" of directives issued in a desperate effort to control an uncontrollable economy, on the assumption generally that growth is good, and more growth is better. They are not concerned to ask: growth of just what? for whom? at what cost to the physical and social environment, and, more particularly, in terms of nonrenewable resources? at what cost to future generations? The conventional economic tool-kit contains no instruments for such distinctions, despite many authoritative studies that have conclusively shown that indiscriminate growth is calamitous.

A routine practice, incredibly, is to omit from balance sheets the costs of industrial production to society and to the natural environment:[1] costs concerned, to quote Hazel Henderson's telling list, are: "efforts to co-ordinate anarchistic economic activities and conflicting technological applications; to clean up the mess left by mass production and consumption; to ameliorate social problems and care for dropouts, addicts, disabled workers and other social casualties; to mediate conflicts and sustain even larger security forces against theft and crime; to keep the air breathable and the water drinkable" (Kumar, 1981, p. 166).

The GNP is economics' standard index of progress. But in fact this monetarized part of the economy represents less than 40 percent of the total productive economy, while the remainder, 60 percent, is composed of the whole natural support system as well as the unpaid work that people undertake without monetary recompense—such as

---

1. Indeed the GNP can be increased by methods of production which involve environmental destruction and social costs. Far from being deducted, these costs are *added* into GNP! (Elkins, 1986).

Capitalism and economics make a virtue out of covetousness and ambition, both in individuals and for the society as a whole. . . . The market respects only the bottom line, the net commercial value that can be obtained. If the commercial benefits of an activity outweigh commercial costs, there will be strong, almost irresistible pressure for someone to engage in it. Whatever the activity, it will be seen as a manifestation of the spirit of enterprise. . . . Even if the product . . . is distasteful or objectionable, the motivation for its production will be seen as understandable and acceptable. Thus, environmental catastrophes that kill hundreds or thousands are not seen as crimes or signs of moral failure; they are simply part of the costs of doing business.

Thomas Michael Power, *The Economic Pursuit of Quality* [pp. 201-202]

[Gandhi] foresaw, as soon as the British had left the country, an ongoing social and economic "revolution," a restructuring of the colonial economy that would emphasize self-reliant, egalitarian village economies in the rural areas. In contrast to Marx and Lenin, revolution had to be non-violent. Its aim was to change the social relationships. Work, both agricultural and industrial, had to be brought to the unemployed rural masses. It was the function of machines to serve, not replace people. . . . [He wrote,] "At the present the machine is helping a small minority to live on the exploitation of the masses." . . . [Gandhi's] successors first postponed the reform plans and then shelved them altogether. Inequality widened, the land tenure and education reforms never materialized, and the bulk of the rural population has remained in poverty.

Mark A. Lutz and Kenneth Lux, *Humanistic Economics* [pp. 304-305]

parenting, care of sick relatives and friends and voluntarism more generally. That 60 percent is in fact what makes possible and supports the 40 percent designated as GNP. Ironically, this large and indispensable component, known as the informal economy, is studied not by economics but by a whole group of other social disciplines. (Cf. Henderson, 1978, 1981 and 1985; also, Ross and Usher, 1986.)

There is a significant difference between the two types of economy: mass market and informal. Whereas the conventional or formal economy has the objective of profit maximization, the informal economy gives priority to human consequences—to the needs of the producers, the consumers and the local community. "A workers' cooperative will cut profits to the bone rather than put, say, half its members out of work—its objective is not to maximize profits but to provide productive work for its members and useful product or service for the community. Or take a community enterprise which could easily make a 20 percent return on capital by investing in the [urban] property market. But it will always opt for a 10 or 5 percent return, or less, if by so doing it can employ, for example, some youngsters locally" (George McRobie, in Ross and Usher, 1986, p. xiii).

In contrast to such mutual concern, the formal economy promotes simplistic distinctions between public and private, economic and social, production and consumption, and work and leisure. Such distinctions hinder understanding of both how we actually live and how we might want to live (Ross and Usher, 1986, p. 4).

In addition to the shortcomings earlier cited, there is another reason why the GNP is a deficient index: money does not reflect at all well actual production and consumption and exchanges of actual goods and services, owing to the fact that money supplies are manipulated by governments, and also because of the proliferation of "bewildering new forms of assets and trading methods." The latter phrase is from an article by Henderson and another futurist, Robert Theobald, who further state:

Today, the global financial system is based on this unreal system, which has become intrinsically unstable and which bears less and less relationship to any real society or natural resource base in the world (Henderson and Theobald, "Money vs. Wealth," *The Futurist*, March-April 1988).

Thirdly, the GNP tells us nothing about people's health, education and environmental conditions.

It should be understood that dissenters from conventional economics are not anti-commercial or anti-market. They understand that the commercial market mechanism "promotes a particular and valuable type of economic freedom. It maintains a discipline that encourages efficiency and discourages waste. It is an ingenious information-collection and distributor" (Power, 1988, p. 203). The utility of the market is confirmed by the fact that some of the centrally planned countries, notably the Soviet Union, are now gradually re-introducing it—in relation to pricing, trade, labor and capital, and even the notion of competition.

Although the market can be a valuable servant of human needs, it becomes an oppressor where it is tightly controlled in the interests of large-scale corporate enterprise. As the economist J. K. Galbraith has shown, this is its chief character in the so-called free market economies. It is money that speaks in the market, which is deaf even to the most essential needs of those without money.

Dissenters want a more balanced way of using the market mechanism. For example, Thomas Michael Power (1988) points out that only if we understand the limited role the commercial sector now plays and recognize the importance of the goods, services and resources developed outside of the world of commerce can we look in a balanced way at the total economy and choose where to draw the line limiting commercial activity. "Currently, the ideology of the market obscures a large part of the economy or relegates it to secondary importance. That ideological bias damages our economic well-being by limiting and frustrating our pursuit of quality" (p. 203).

By Their Fruits Ye Shall Know Them

The bulk of the world's consumption takes place in the high-income countries, which only have about one-fifth of the world's population but account for two-thirds of world consumption. Consumption is accelerated by the system's inherent encouragement of obsolescence, in turn demanded by its growth ethic. This and the problems caused by the massive accumulation of wastes by the high-income countries are the major (though not the only) causes of environmental degradation and global resource depletion (Ekins, 1987, p. 13).

There is an enormous gulf today between the "haves" and the "have-nots" of the world, a gulf that is widening, both within some of the world's wealthiest nations and between the rich and the poor nations. For example, in the United States in the past few years there has been an exponential growth both in the number of billionaires and the number of homeless people. In 1983 nearly half the world's people lived in countries with a GNP *per capita* of $400 or less, while one-sixth lived in countries with a GNP *per capita* of more than $5,500 (*World Bank Atlas*, 1986).

There are more hungry people in the world today than ever before, and their numbers are growing. Also rising are the number of people living in slums and shantytowns, who lack access to clean water and sanitation and hence are prey to diseases (the Brundlant Commission report, *Our Common Future,* 1987).

It is estimated that in 1980 some 730 million people in 87 poor countries lacked sufficient food for an active working life. Of these, some 340 million people lacked the minimum food to prevent serious health risks and stunted growth in children (World Bank, *Poverty and Hunger,* 1986).

According to the same study, about two-thirds of the undernourished lived in South Asia and one-fifth in Sub-Saharan Africa.

The Third World[2]

Most of the population of the poorer countries of the world is rural. A major cause of abject poverty is landlessness, or lack of access to land either through ownership or tenancy. The population/resource relationship has been worsening for some time, due to rapid population growth in poor countries, but rural landlessness is exacerbated by the concentration of ownership.

"In Latin America, the most extreme case," states Lester R. Brown, President of Worldwatch Institute (Washington, D.C.), in the Institute's *State of the World* report for 1987, "it is not uncommon for 5 percent of the populace to own four fifths of the farmland." In Asia, the countries of Bangladesh, India and Pakistan together now have 30 million landless rural households. In addition, 22 percent of the cultivated holdings are smaller than 0.4 hectares, not enough to support a family even when intensively farmed. As regards Africa, landlessness is a relatively new phenomenon, but one that is growing.

A grossly inequitable land tenure pattern is also found in Central

---

2. "The third world" is one of the three main categories of countries invoked today, the other two being the industrial market countries and the centrally planned economies, respectively. Other terms used for the third world are "less-developed countries," (LDC's), "developing countries," and "the South." With the exception of the high-income oil exporting countries (more accurately, those of this group that are still classed as third world countries, since some are not), third world countries have a low per capita income compared to the rest of the world, though they greatly vary in income, size, resources, and level of industrialization. Most are erstwhile colonial countries—countries which gained their independence sometime in the period since the end of World War II.

We find that from the 1970's to at least the mid-1980s, the income of the middle-income members of our [American] society has been declining, and that of the poorest of them declining even further. . . . These changes reflect a widening wealth and income gap between the rich and the poor. . . . In 1982 the richest 1 percent of American families had 27 percent of the wealth. Five years later this increased to 36 percent of the wealth. . . . In 1984 the top 40 percent of American families had 67 percent of the income and the lowest 40 percent of American families had 15.7 percent of the income, and that was the lowest percentage since 1947.

Mark A. Lutz and Kenneth Lux,
Humanistic Economics [p. 229]

More people suffer from hunger, malnutrition, and disease today [in about 1980] than at the end of World War II, both numerically and as a percentage of world population. . . . With population increases absorbing over half the economic gains made since 1960, with concentrations of power and wealth nesting higher and higher on the social pyramids, with domestic and foreign policies resistant to defining where business profit ends and social responsibility begins, and with mere fractions of colossal GNPs (a lion's share of which goes into military budgets) being consigned to the alleviation of human want, the gap between the 'haves' and the 'have-nots' widens and widens, both nationally and internationally. There are more children without schools to attend, more adult illiterates, more people in ill health and lacking in adequate medical services, more unemployed, more unable to satisfy the most basic of needs.

Burns H. Weston, in Feller *et al.*, eds.
1981 [p. 61]

America. Oxfam, America,[3] in *A Special Report, Fall 1985,* concerning Central America, states: "Land tenure only emerged as a major issue in the late 19th century, when Indians' communal land-

---

3. A non-profit relief and development organization active in many third world countries.

holdings were abolished in many areas to make way for coffee cultivation, and Indians were compelled to work for part of each year on
coffee plantations. Thus began a pattern that continued into the 20th
century: fertile, food-producing lands were taken over for the production of crops like sugarcane, cotton, bananas, and beef for export
to the United States and Europe. These products, including coffee,
are Central America's chief exports today, and food production for
domestic consumption has seriously declined in recent years." The
report goes on to point out that the enormous social inequities and the
pervasive hunger and ill health that affect the majority of Central
Americans, the rural poor, go far to explain the chronic unrest in that
part of the world.

Agriculture Minister Lerotholi, of Lesotho, a small African country, encapsulated the prevailing world situation when he stated in
1979 at the Agrarian Reform Conference in Rome:

> The world is tightly in the grip of elitism. . . . It cannot be the task of
> world bureaucracy and elitism alone to transform rural societies of the
> world unless the rural masses are represented (Gran, 1983, p. 1).

The extreme disparities, and the exploitation and marginalization
of the weak by the powerful elements of society, are at the root of
much of the conflict that rages today in the third world. In many
places people have been reduced to a state of utter destitution and
helplessness, an unprecedented condition for rural peoples who have
always known how to sustain themselves. Insult is added to injury
when their condition is attributed to their own ineptitude.

It is evident that the present path is disastrous not only for the poor
themselves but for everyone on the planet. In bringing about an
increasingly dual world, we are heading toward self-annihilation.
The alternative is a transformation of consciousness that recognizes
both the oneness and the plurality of the world in which we live.

Technical and Financial Assistance to Less-Developed Countries

The early 1950s, which began the historic decolonization process,
saw the rise within the young United Nations of the provision of
economic and technical assistance by the industrialized countries to
the newly-independent countries. In large part, this development was
motivated as much by self-interest as by altruism, for the industrial-

ized countries continued to need the primary commodities and raw material resources that they had long been securing from the erstwhile colonial countries. They also saw the necessity of priming the pumps, so to speak, in these countries, in order to open up the latters' markets for the their own exports.

The inauguration of technical and financial aid to the young nations, on a bilateral and multilateral basis,[4] brought into existence a new field of expertise, called "development economics." In recent years, the assumptions, concepts and policy prescriptions of development economics have been the subject of soul searching and revision with the benefit of hindsight.[5] However, the policy modifications so far are mainly in the rhetoric. The official donors and agencies continue, not surprisingly, to reflect the parameters of the system to which they owe their existence.[6]

It has long been acknowledged that the less-developed countries are at a serious disadvantage vis-à-vis the industrialized world. Their exports chiefly consist of primary agricultural and mineral products and (more recently) of semi-processed goods, such as electronic parts. These are exchanged for Western technology, machinery, food and finished products. The terms of trade are disadvantageous for the developing countries, due both to their lower wage levels and to the fact that prices are controlled and determined less by supply and demand than by their relatively weak political and economic position vis-à-vis the industrialized countries. What is more, further industrialization has not served to remedy the inequalities. The theory has been that industrialization would "trickle down" wealth to the masses, but in fact, inequalities have only widened.

In a hard-hitting essay entitled "Could We Study International Relations as if People Mattered?" Roy Preiswerk, a professor of international relations, states that sometimes the growth rate of inequality mimics the growth rate of the GNP, and he pointedly remarks: "International relations students should be concerned with

---

4. As through the International Bank for Reconstruction and Development, known as the IBRD or the World Bank, which came into existence at that time as one of the specialized agencies of the United Nations. It is financed by Western countries. Soviet-bloc countries have up to now not chosen to participate in its financing.

5. For an interesting and readable collection of essays by the outstanding pioneers in development, see the World Bank publication, *Pioneers in Development* (1984).

6. An excellent analysis of the nature of technical aid and its shortcomings in relation to truer human development is found in *Development by People* (1983), by Guy Gran.

growing internal [within less-developed countries] inequalities, because these most certainly are caused partly by the nature of external relations conducted by the countries concerned. Many recent studies on dependence, centre-periphery relations, structural violence, and imperialism provide us with conceptual frameworks for more research in this direction" (Feller, Schwenninger and Singerman, eds., 1981).

It is now recognized that the introduction of large-scale industrial projects in impoverished countries has been a mixed blessing at best. The capital intensity of such projects was often far out of gear with the endowments of capital and labor of the country concerned, and has in many instances had grievous consequences. "These models," writes Hazel Henderson, "[have led to] catastrophic urbanization, unsustainably resource-intensive production methods, costly centralized technologies requiring huge bureaucracies, unattainable levels of specialization, technological dependence, lost food self-sufficiency, and disruption of these countries' own cultures" (Henderson, 1981, p. 22).

Economic-development planner and Nobel Laureate Jan Tinbergen comments that the development strategy for underdeveloped countries has constituted an intensive learning process for all concerned. He advocates less emphasis on the creation and transfer of physical capital and more on education; less emphasis on foreign, capital-intensive technologies and more on appropriate, or adapted, less capital-intensive technologies, which in many cases implies a shift from large to smaller projects; and a shift from employment creation in cities to its creation in villages or small towns. In addition, he would de-emphasize external (intergovernmental) policies in favor of more internal policies "and, somewhat related, [a shift] from paternalism to self-reliance" (Meier and Seers, eds., 1984, p. 330).

The former Rector of the United Nations University (Tokyo), Dr. Soedjatmoko, stated that what the third world needs to achieve more independence and greater self-reliance, including less dependence on external supplies of energy, is to focus less on large tractors and more on two-wheel power tillers, less on automobiles and more on motor scooters and bicycles, less on nuclear power plants and more on simple solar water heaters (Lester B. Brown, 1984). But economist and Nobel Laureate Theodore Schultz has emphasized that investment in people is far more important than investment in machines (Lester R. Brown *et al.*, 1986).

The late noted economist/sociologist Gunnar Myrdal wrote that although their histories may vary widely, the developing countries all have in common one important failure: they have not carried out the egalitarian institutional reforms which are necessary to raise the consumption levels of the poor and thereby also their productivity. Land distribution reform is desperately needed, and the problem of corruption must be addressed. Other measures are equally imperative, such as population control and heath and education reforms. Myrdal also criticized the industrialized countries for their treatment of the third world, especially in the domains of trade and aid policies.

The governments of the third world generally plead for more transfers of capital and technology, increased trade, and a reaffirmation of national sovereignty, all of which are embodied in the resolution on the New International Economic Order (NIEO) adopted in May 1974 at a special session of the United Nations General Assembly. NIEO has been praised as an achievement due to what is called the collective self-reliance of the third world. "The term is misleading," points out Preiswerk. "What is really meant is increased bargaining power through Third World solidarity. Self-reliance has a deeper meaning: to rely on one's own forces at a local level whenever possible and to use inputs from the national, regional, or world levels only when local resources or knowhow are missing. Local self-reliance needs to be protected or at least tolerated by national governments. But if the representatives of these governments jointly ask for more foreign inputs, their action is counter-productive to self-reliance, not an expression of it. Studies of the feasibility of self-reliance as a development strategy, or as a new definition of development, must take a central place in international relations research" (Feller, Schwenninger, and Singerman, eds., 1981, p. 21).

According to sociologist Elise Boulding (1988), economics is only one dimension of the NIEO. Its members are equally interested in a discourse with the developed countries concerning their values, traditions, and ways of life that have up until now been written off by the latter as "backward."

Boulding observes that the third world is no more exempt from problems of corruption and greed than are the more industrialized countries, since they "frequently agree to arrangements that advantage their own elites at the expense of the general population. When governments of the South speak of wanting development as equals, that may not mean equal development within their own societies.

Idealism and self-serving behavior fight each other in the South as well as in the North" (Boulding, 1988, p. 24).

The consensus of these specialists is that the poorest countries cannot now and will not in the foreseeable future be able to move toward self-reliance without some external assistance, and that, equally important, the assistance must be of an appropriate nature in respect of the means used (the simplest and least costly), the people targeted (the poverty-stricken) and the focus (food production, sanitation, water supplies, health and schooling).

Our Common Future, the report of the World Commission on Environment and Development (1987), popularly known as the Brundtland Commission Report, underlines that external aid to the poor countries is imperative. Further, it points out that the reduction of poverty itself is a precondition for environmentally sound development, and that resource flows from rich to poor are a precondition for the eradication of poverty. It is alarming that, in consequence of third world debt repayment, there is a reverse net flow of resources, from the developing to the developed countries.

Lastly, concerning Africa in particular, a report for the Independent Commission on International Humanitarian Issues, *Famine—A Man-Made Disaster?*, similarly points out that the real answer to Africa's problems is long-term economic and social development enabling it to become self-sufficient. It advocates massive aid from external sources, essentially to small farmers.

It is evident that both of the present dominant economic systems, that is, the capitalist and the socialist, contribute to the mass poverty found in the third world. As Guy Gran, an international development consultant and adjunct faculty member of American University in Washington, explains in his book, *Development by People* (1983), the masses inevitably lose out under a capitalist culture "which legitimizes, encourages, and even glorifies the unlimited acquisition of wealth by an individual. . . . Comparable results inevitably come from a misnamed socialist culture that legitimates, encourages, and glorifies the unlimited acquisition of power by the state" (p. 7). Gran finds an alliance at the local level among local landlords, merchants, moneylenders and notables, who in turn cooperate with regional and national elites to maintain power and privilege, while beyond that there exists the triple alliance of national capital, the state and international capital. This broad alliance effectively directs and controls development in most third world societies.[7]

The Roots of Hunger

The World Bank's study, *Poverty and Hunger* (1986), concluded that a rapid increase in food production does not necessarily result in a diminution of widespread hunger, which can only be alleviated by redistributing purchasing power and resources toward those who are undernourished.

The report further states that notwithstanding the dramatic rise in yields of wheat and rice brought about by the Green Revolution,[8] the available data suggest that some 730 million people in the third world go hungry. The world has ample food; global food production has increased faster than the unprecedented population growth of the past forty years. But the hungry masses do not share in this abundance because of "a lack of purchasing power."

A similar picture is drawn by Lappé and Collins (1986), who document the further irony that many of the countries in which hunger is rampant export much more in agricultural goods than they import.

> While as many as 300 million Indians go hungry, the country exports everything from wheat to beef and government officials agonize over how to get rid of mounting "surpluses" of wheat and rice—24 million tons in 1985, more than double the entire world's annual food aid shipments in a typical year. . . . While Brazil has become the world's second largest food exporter (after only the United States), 86 million Brazilians do not have enough to eat. . . . Despite widening hunger, food exports from the Horn of Africa—Ethiopia, Kenya, Somalia, the Sudan, Tanzania, and Uganda—were worth nearly $1 billion more in 1983 than the food imported. . . . The Sahelian countries of West Africa are known for recurrent famines, but in most years they export more agricultural products than they import (pp. 11-12).

---

7. Gran also explores the process whereby the masses in the third world might be empowered or helped to develop local capacities, to become self-reliant, and to gain a voice in the global system.

8. The Green Revolution took place following the introduction in the 1960s of improved varieties of wheat and rice capable of greatly increasing yields, combined with the use of petrochemical fertilizers, pesticides, and, for the most part, irrigation.

Land has been absorbed increasingly for large-scale cash crops, since these bring the greatest return to producers, both domestic and foreign. Susan George (1983) explains that a cash crop can be non-edible, such as cotton, flowers, rubber; edible but without food value, as coffee and tea; or edible and with food value—anything from sugar to bananas to peanuts, even to wheat. "What distinguishes the 'cash crop' is who eats or uses it. *Bluntly stated, they are almost never the same people who produce it*" [Italics added] (p. 15).

There is for example the case of Mexico, described by Lappé and Collins (1986). Two-thirds of Mexico's population is chronically undernourished.

> In Mexico, poor farmers' primary crops are corn and beans, but the focus of Mexico's Green Revolution has been wheat. . . . Even the poor farmers who grew wheat were displaced by the big growers in Mexico's northwest, backed by generous government credit and an expensive government-built irrigation network (p. 52).

As a result of the Green revolution, the export of fruits and vegetables from northwest Mexico was greatly increased, involving heavy government investment in irrigation, and the beneficiaries were the nation's wealthiest farmers. Export earnings during the 1970s shot up a spectacular twelve-fold, while the amount used to import food fell from 12 to 9 percent. And of that already small share, four-fifths consisted of luxury goods—meat, feed grains and alcoholic beverages.

An even greater contraction of Mexico's food supply came as a result of the introduction of sorghum, "Mexico's real postwar boom crop." Sorghum, a feed grain, was unknown in Mexico in 1958, but by 1980, in response to the demand for livestock products by the top 15 percent of Mexicans (whose purchasing power enables them to consume half of Mexico's food), it covered twice the acreage in wheat. Millions of Mexicans are too poor ever to eat meat, and even poultry and dairy products are largely beyond their means.[9] The same situation obtains in Sri Lanka and in the Philippines with respect to local food production.

Poverty in poor countries has been exacerbated by the unequal distribution of land and other assets. Raising living standards is all

---

9. The authors state that over 40 percent of all grain worldwide goes to livestock, and only a fraction of the nutrients fed to livestock returns to humans.

the harder in the face of rapid population growth. These factors, combined with growing demand for the commercial use of good land, have pushed many subsistence farmers onto poor land and robbed them of any hope of participating in their nations' economic gains.

The same factors have promoted greater environmental stress. In the past, the cutting of forests for purposes of growing crops took place at a far slower pace. Forests were given time to recover. But the present configuration of factors and pressures causes forests to be destroyed ever more rapidly, often only to create poor farmland that cannot support those who till it (Brundtland Commission Report, 1987, pp. 29-30).

In turn, spreading deforestation and overcultivation are a major cause of the increasing incidence of natural disasters such as droughts and floods. Droughts have become decidedly more frequent in the past two or three decades in Africa, India and Latin America, while the incidence of floods has been increasing throughout Asia, parts of Africa, and the Andean region of Latin America.

The Causal Chain in Poor Countries[10]

Hunger and malnutrition, ill health, poor sanitary conditions, high rates of child mortality, population growth and environmental degradation all go hand in hand.

About a quarter of the world's population lacks clean drinking water and the means for sanitary human waste disposal. This is a major cause of disease and mortality in the third world.

The poorest countries face a drastically deteriorating environment. *These are all interrelated conditions.*

Take population growth and child health. The healthier the children, the greater their survival, the smaller the urge to have more children for the work and old-age support they contribute. The fewer children a woman bears, the more productive she can be (in agriculture, her main field of work). Slower population growth makes possible a better balance between resources and population.

Conversely, where children are stunted and retarded from malnutrition, their parents are overburdened and unable to be sufficiently productive for subsistence, let alone generating means for education

10. Based on "Investing in Children," by William U. Chandler, in *The State of the World 1986*.

Developing countries face . . . life-threatening . . . desertification, deforestation, and pollution, and endure most of the poverty associated with environmental degradation. The entire human family of nations would suffer from the disappearance of rain forests in the tropics, the loss of plant and animal species, and changes in rainfall patterns. Industrial nations face the life-threatening challenges of toxic chemicals, toxic wastes, and acidification. All nations may suffer from the releases by industrialized countries of carbon dioxide and of gases that react with the ozone layer, and from any future war fought with the nuclear arsenals controlled by those nations. All nations will have a role to play in changing trends, and in righting an international economic system that increases rather than decreases inequality, that increases rather than decreases numbers of poor and hungry.

Our Common Future [p. 22]

and development, and they feel impelled to have more children so that there may be more working hands. Populations burgeon and natural systems decline. Drought, disease and famine are perpetuated.

Such is the causal chain. Clearly, only an integrated strategy could ameliorate the conditions of dire poverty. Revegetating desiccated lands is an example of a strategy that addresses at once the three major problems of drought, drinking water and education. This would represent an investment in people.

Humanity's Common Dilemma

In 1983, the United Nations established the World Commission on Environment and Development and charged it with the task of proposing long-term environmental strategies for achieving sustainable development by the year 2000.[11] The World Commission issued its

---

11. Madame Gro Harlem Brundtland of Norway, then head of that country's Labor Party and now also Norway's Prime Minister, was appointed to chair the Commission, and Mansour Khalid, former deputy Prime Minister of Sudan, was appointed vice-chair. They together appointed the remaining members, twenty-one persons from nearly as many countries, including ten from the third world, four from the Soviet block countries, and William Ruckleshaus, former head of the Environmental Protection Agency of the United States.

first report, *Our Common Future,* in 1987. We have already referred to this important document, popularly known as the Brundtland Commission Report. Here are some of its findings.

● Poverty itself pollutes the environment. Those who are poor and hungry will often destroy their immediate environment in order to survive, by cutting down forests, causing their livestock to overgraze grasslands, and overusing marginal land. They will ultimately crowd into congested cities.

● It is crucial to sustain the ecosystems on which the global economy depends. This is a prerequisite for achieving beneficial international economic exchanges for all concerned.

● With respect more particularly to exchanges between the industrialized and the third world, it is imperative that the economic partners be satisfied that the basis of exchange is equitable—not unequal, or based on dominance of one kind or another. For many developing countries, neither the imperative of sustainability nor that of equitable exchange are met, and the present international system encourages rather than discourages disparities.

● All of us on this planet now share a common destiny—we shall die or survive together.

Militarization, and the Need to Redefine Security

Many countries, including not a few of the poorest ones, have been heavily militarizing themselves. Global military expenditures in 1985 totalled $940 billion, a sum which exceeded the income of the poorest half of humanity. "Stated otherwise, [the expenditures] surpassed the combined gross national products of China, India, and African countries south of the Sahara" (Brown, et al., 1986, p. 196). This is in spite of the fact that national security in military terms is an outmoded concept. Inasmuch as militarization can only be pursued at the expense of social, economic and environmental well-being, it is self-defeating, and is indeed a threat to national security instead of being a protection.

Soaring arms imports have been a major factor in the third world debt crisis. In turn, huge foreign debts, however incurred, are serious threats to the economic security of many third world countries. In the present century, military aggressors have repeatedly failed to win, while the prime losers have been civilians. Military interventions of

Between 1960 and 1981, [military outlays in the Third World] grew by some 7 percent per year, compared with 3.7 percent in the industrial world. . . . Over the past quarter-century, the international commerce in arms has soared, largely because of the militarization of the Third World economies that lack their own arms manufacturing capacity. Expenditures on arms imports have eclipsed those on other goods, including grain.

State of the World 1986 [p. 197]

Throughout history, governments have sought to develop and acquire more numerous and more effective arms. . . . But ultimately, unilateral advantages prove short-lived, fueling destabilizing arms races and degenerating into warfare. . . . The quest for the ultimate weapon has delivered the global community to an all-encompassing state of insecurity. . . . In the twentieth century, aggressors have won only 4 out of 10 wars; in the eighties, that ratio is down to 1 out of 10. Irrespective of the outcome of wars, the prime losers have been the civilians whom the military supposedly is protecting. Whether through direct war actions or war-induced starvation, civilians constitute a rapidly growing share of war victims; they accounted for 52 percent of all deaths in the fifties, but for 85 percent in the eighties. . . . [As Kenneth Boulding states] "National defense is now the greatest enemy of national security."

Michael Renner, *State of the World 1989* [p. 135]

the superpowers in third world conflicts have reached the point of diminishing returns (Renner, 1989).

Even for wealthy nations, maintaining a permanent war economy has seriously adverse consequences. "Both the United States and the Soviet Union . . . have spent enough on the military to cause a deterioration of vital infrastructure, a retardation of civilian research and development, and a loss of competitiveness" (Renner, 1989, p. 138).

It is increasingly understood that the greatest threat to survival is environmental degradation. Survival is impossible without breath-

Security can no longer be assured by military means—neither by the use of arms or deterrence, nor by continued perfection of the "sword" and the "shield". Attempts to achieve military superiority are preposterous. Now such attempts are being made in space. It is an astonishing anachronism which persists due to the inflated role played by militarists in politics. From the security point of view the arms race has become an absurdity because its very logic leads to the destabilization of international relations and eventually to a nuclear conflict. Diverting huge resources from other priorities, the arms race is lowering the level of security, impairing it. It is itself an enemy of peace. . . . The new political outlook calls for the recognition of one . . . simple axiom: security is indivisible. It is either equal security for all or none at all.

Mikhail Gorbachev, *Perestroika*
[pp. 127-128]

able air and drinkable water. Air pollution and acid rain are killing forests and humans alike. The growing hole in the ozone layer gravely threatens human health, agricultural productivity and marine fisheries. The global warming is potentially catastrophic for all nations. Against these threats and dangers, which respect no international boundaries, there are no military defenses; indeed, militarization and the global arms race exacerbate resource depletion and ecological imbalance. Thus environmental security critically depends on concerted actions and agreements on the part of the international community to limit or ban the production of substances inimical to the environment. This brings us to the more general question of norms of international behavior.

Norms of International Behavior

International law and norms of behavior are crucial for security and world peace, but as yet the world lacks a mechanism for their enforcement. National sovereignty still takes precedence, and in its very concept opposes the enforcement of trans-national standards of behavior.

Protected by the convention of absolute national sovereignty, many nation states perpetrate barbarities with impunity. Much of the repression goes hand in hand with the turmoil that stems from conditions of extreme social and economic injustice. Civil and political liberties are denied on a widespread scale. Forms of racism and sexism persist in many parts of the world. Amnesty International, an international network laboring impartially on behalf of victims of human rights violations, reports that the horrors of torture and political detention are everyday incidents in fully one-third of the world's governments.

In *A Commonsense Guide to World Peace,* professor of international law Benjamin B. Ferencz discusses the vital interrelationships of a whole chain of elements that must be forged for a more secure life for everyone. The links in the chain include the clarification of norms of international behavior; international cooperation; enforcement through economic sanctions or an international peace force; disarmament; improved economic and social conditions; the diminution of political unrest, consequent upon more equitable and better economic and social conditions.

An encouraging and little-known development, states Ferencz, is that international law is evolving rapidly. After a slow and erratic development international law has begun to flower only in the past two hundred years. But since the end of World War II, more international agreements have been concluded than in the previous four millennia.

The adoption of the United Nations Charter in 1945 represented the first time that the promotion of human rights, together with collective solution of economic and social problems, was accepted as a goal of international society. This was followed in 1948 by the Universal Declaration of Human Rights wherein the United Nations proclaimed the common aspiration of all people for freedom, justice and peace in a spirit of universal brotherhood, and specified many particular rights such as to life, liberty and security. Many other human rights instruments have since come into being, together with many agencies whose activities, spanning the globe, are designed to bring about a more equitable distribution of social advantages.

Yet it is still left to the nations to decide which customs they will adopt, and which declarations they will accept as governing their behavior. "Any system that allows competing parties to interpret existing codes solely on the basis of their own advantage is unworthy of respect, since it is practically no legal system at all," Ferencz declares. In *PlanetHood* (1988), Ferencz, in cooperation with Ken Keyes, Jr., has outlined what he believes to be the necessary steps for human survival on this planet. One is making the United Nations effective for the nuclear age.

The United Nations

The United Nations like its predecessor, the League of Nations, was obviously called into existence by the exigencies of our time. Its establishment in 1945 on the heels of World War II gave people new hope for a peaceful world. It is significant that today there exist no fewer than 20,000 international organizations, including some 18,000 non-governmental organizations, of which the overwhelming majority have come into existence during this century.

I think it is important to understand that the United Nations is a mirror of the world community and is only as effective as we allow it to be. Behind its Members (that is the member governments) is human society itself. For the first forty years of its life, the United Nations has not infrequently been misused and abused by member governments for narrow or ignoble purposes, to the detriment of the United Nations as a whole. But of late, in recognition perhaps of the fact that confrontations repeatedly fail and of the facts of countries' convergent interests and common stake in peace and stability, countries have increasingly turned to the United Nations to entrust it with far-reaching initiatives in the work for peace—as in respect of the conflict in Afghanistan, the Iran-Iraq war, the struggle for independence in Namibia, and in not a few other conflicts around the globe where the opposing sides have wanted its assistance. It has demonstrated its great potential. Fittingly, the United Nations Peacekeeping Forces were awarded the 1988 Nobel Peace Prize.

The accomplishments of the United Nations are far from inconsiderable. They have included the following:

● The United Nations played a decisive role in the process of decolonization, which has changed the political complexion of the globe and given vast populations control over their destiny.

● It authoritatively defined human rights and devised monitoring and other mechanisms for encouraging greater respect for them.

● It has codified international law.

● In partnership with its specialized agencies, it has established guidelines for a wide range of concerns including the environment; population; the law of the sea; the safeguarding of the rights of the hitherto disadvantaged segments of society, such as women, children, the aging and the handicapped; terrorism; drug abuse; and the incidence of AIDS.

● It has raised consciousness of global economic imperatives.

● In the political field, it has repeatedly acted to limit and control armed conflicts.

● It has emphasized the general objectives of arms limitation and disarmament, the self-determination of peoples and the promotion of human rights (United Nations, G.A., Forty-Third Session, Supplement No. 1, A/43/1, October 1988). The United Nations together with its agencies in fact provides our planet a veritable laboratory for the monitoring, diagnosis and coordination of the multiple facets of human and planetary affairs.

The major mandate of the United Nations at its establishment was to oversee the maintenance of international peace and security. However, the United Nations Charter contains no clause mandating the institution of a supra-national arm. The world was obviously not ready for such an idea forty-odd years ago.

Scholars have long since pointed out significant flaws in the United Nations Charter—indeed, some of these flaws were recognized right from the start. Each of the member states (of which there are 159 at present), regardless of territorial size, population and resources, has one vote, "a manifestly undemocratic, unfair and unrealistic voting procedure," to quote Ferencz's characterization of it. In addition, the five Permanent Members of the Security Council, namely, China, France, the Soviet Union, the United Kingdom, and the United States, each has the power of veto, which means that the Security Council, the enforcement arm of the United Nations, can only function if there is unanimity among its most powerful members. "This fatal flaw," states Ferencz, " has remained uncorrected simply because those with the power of final decision were not prepared to relinquish it—even if it meant undermining the effectiveness of the organization on which other nations and all people had pinned their hopes for world security" (1985, p. 59).

Work by individuals and organizations on the improvement or reform of the United Nations Charter has been carried on for years, but much remains to be done to make the United Nations a more useful instrumentality for world peace, including the elimination of the two above-mentioned flaws.

Before the United Nations can become the guarantor of international peace and security, nations must be willing to cede to it a supranational role for peace-keeping. This would require transforming the United Nations from only a *league* of nations whose state loyalty overrides loyalty to the wider community, into a *federation,* wherein loyalty to each state is balanced by loyalty to the wider community— into an effective world government with adequate checks and balances. However daunting a prospect this may be, it is, according to some respected thinkers, both feasible and imperative, given our nuclear weaponry and our material and social interdependence. Among others, Ferencz and Keyes (1988) maintain that this is a feasible goal; they cite the striking parallels between the present situation with respect to the United Nations and the difficult and dangerous situation in America at the time, two hundred years ago, when the United States constitution was hammered out.

Redefining National Sovereignty

Clearly the world is still very much wedded to the notion of absolute national sovereignty. Yet it has become apparent that the nation state is too small for the big problems in the present interdependent world and too big for the small problems.

"National governments are turning rigid in some parts of the world," writes Franz Shurmann, "flabby in others, and all too often are gigantic institutionalized bodies of vested interests, bereft of ideas and ideals. More to the point, they are being rent by vast global changes that they cannot control and their ideologies cannot explain" (Anderson, ed., 1983, p. 47).

In fact, national sovereignty is already far from absolute, having been considerably eroded by the interdependence of nations in respect of military security, economic and social conditions, and the environment. Other supra-national factors are the trans-national corporations, which wield far more power than many national governments. For they now control one-third of gross world production, 40 percent of all world trade, and in some sectors of the economy, notably commodities, up to about 90 percent of trade (Ekins, ed., 1986, p. 340).

There is an ever more pressing need for a United Nations that has the reources and energies to be open to new realities and aspirations. There is no reason, for example, why anyone should be satisfied with the way people are represented only through the formal sovereign equality of the General Assembly or the overtly hierarchical order of the Security Council and the World Bank. There is more and more justification for creating a third forum open to people rather than only to political and economic elites.

R.J.B. Walker, *One World, Many Worlds* [p. 169].

There are amazing parallels between our situation with the United Nations today and the dangerous situation in the United States two centuries ago. Tom Hudgens in his book *Let's Abolish War* points out that the Continental Congress under the Articles of Confederation:

1. Had no independent taxing powers.
2. Could not regulate interstate and foreign commerce.
3. Had no powers of direct enforcement of its laws.
4. Was ineffective in foreign affairs.
5. Had no chief executive.
6 Had no binding court of justice. . . .

As George Washington and Benjamin Franklin would testify, there is no one simple way to hammer out a new constitution. It takes an open-minded willingness to consider all points of view, to lay aside one's prejudices and psychological certainties, and to be patient enough to listen and search until effective answers are found and agreed upon. Just as success in 1787 required that various states be satisfied, in like manner we must create a reformed U.N. that meets today's needs and interests of the nations of the world.

Benjamin B. Ferencz and Ken Keyes, Jr., *PlanetHood* [pp. 101-104]

The structure of the states system is implicated in all kinds of
. . . problems, from a failure to cope with ecological collapse
to the abuse of human rights. Taken together, all these problems
put into question the underlying ethical, cultural, and political
legitimacy of the state itself. Short-term concerns with particular missiles also raise very serious questions about how and
why people live together in the way they do. After all, if one of
the most basic justifications for the state has involved its ability
to ensure the security needed to pursue a good life within its
borders, the fragility of national security in a nuclear age puts
the old distinction between citizen and foreigner, us and them,
onto very flimsy foundations indeed.

> R.B.J. Walker, *One World, Many*
> *Worlds* [p. 47]

If global struggles are inescapable, and if a just world peace
must therefore be a struggle for One World, it must also be
remembered that both present structures and future aspirations
are encountered and articulated on the basis of many different
experiences, many different histories. The pursuit of a just
world peace and new forms of solidarity must be rooted in an
equal respect for the claims of both diversity and unity. One
World must also be Many Worlds.

> R.B.J. Walker, *One World, Many*
> *Worlds* [p. 5]

The Brundtland Commission Report states: "The global commons
cannot be managed from any national centre: The nation state is
insufficient to deal with threats to shared ecosystems. Threats to
environmental security can only be dealt with by joint management
and multilateral procedures and mechanisms" (p. 301).

If we are to loosen our attachment to absolute national sovereignty,
we need to develop the perception that there is no contradiction
between self-interest and the interest of the greater world community,
that indeed the two necessarily go hand in hand. Nor need we fear
eradicating our nationhood. Gerald and Patricia Mische (1977) argue
persuasively that if greater priority were to be given to the good of

humanity as a whole; if certain legal power presently located on national levels were shifted to a world level, the results would *not* be the eradication of nations. Neither would there be a *loss* of national sovereignty. Instead, true sovereignty would be *augmented*. Patricia Mische (1985) further argues that, as global interdependencies increase, the reluctance to share sovereignty in a common security system means national sovereignty is left *more* vulnerable.

It would seem, then, that two fundamental requirements today that need to be achieved and balanced one with the other are these: on the one hand, people want autonomy in their own affairs and to be self-reliant; on the other, the planet needs a transnational mechanism, with effective checks and balances, to attend to and co-ordinate transnational concerns.

On Disarmament

Since 1961, when the United States and the Soviet Union concluded a statement on Agreed Principles for Disarmament Negotiations, the acknowledged goal of the United Nations has been general and complete disarmament under strict international control. The two superpowers both recognized that each stage of disarmament needs to be accompanied by increasing the effectiveness and capability of the United Nations to maintain peace among Member States. It was envisaged that at the end of the disarmament process, national arms and armies would have disappeared and all states would be completely dependent upon the effectiveness of global community mechanisms for their security (Keys, 1982).

The question of disarmament has in point of fact received intensive study at the United Nations for many years, work in which a number of particularly able and dedicated disarmament leaders have been involved.[12] However, disarmament was stymied by the two superpowers' mutual suspicion and fear and the problem of verification.

A historic landmark, as we well know, was the agreement, in December 1987, between the United States and the Soviet Union on

---

12. Keys writes: "The size and intensity of the UN's effort [on disarmament] is an unknown story. . . . The important work and proposals of disarmament leaders such as Alva Myrdal and Inga Thorsson of Sweden, Alfonso Garcia Robles of Mexico, William Epstein of Canada, General Carlos P. Romulo of the Philippines are relatively unknown. Also unknown is the strength of the annual appeals of the UN membership to the superpowers to cease and desist for the sake and safety of everyone."

the elimination of all intermediate-range nuclear weapons. It is safe to say that this agreement is a result of the existing material and other constraints being experienced by both parties, including the facts concerning the real nature of security along lines earlier described.

This agreement was but a first small step toward mutual reductions in armaments. But watching the event on TV screens, human beings around the globe unquestionably experienced a new sense of hope; what is rational would perhaps take precedence over what is madly irrational; there might be a reprieve at long last from years of gloom and doom—from being hurtled down a steep incline toward extinction.

Many efforts directed toward reining in the arms race continue in different quarters. They include envisioning how to set in motion the conversion process from a military to a civilian economy and the important grassroots peace movement (which is discussed below).

An essential element for disarmament however is still missing, and that is a trans-national peace-keeping force.

Towards a Transnational Peacekeeping Force

The United Nations still lacks a commonly sanctioned peace-keeping force which alone would enable it adequately to fulfill its major mandate to maintain international peace and security. Unless and until one comes into being, states will not be able to disarm beyond a certain point. With zero lead-time for nuclear missiles, governments can but maintain constant mobilization and cannot avoid giving precedence to military security over human values and domestic priorities. (Cf. Gerald and Patricia Mische, 1977.)

But a supra-national peacekeeping force will not come into being as long as nations are heavily armed. It would make no sense—the force could not be strong enough to maintain international peace in such conditions.

What is the solution to this Catch-22 problem? It would seem to depend on the momentum of the new impulse toward armaments reduction. But the arms reduction momentum will in turn be influenced by the progress made in addressing the psychological, political, ideological and cultural *causes* of the arms race. In this circular process many different agents and actors are already or will be involved; all of us can indeed contribute, in some degree and in one or another way, to furthering the needed process.

The Technological Dimension

Technology is a major link between science and the societal realm. As we well know, society has applied modern technology to everything, from agriculture to industry, from lethal weaponry to health, from genetics to space exploration. Technology's impact on society depends on how appropriately it is applied. Appropriate technology has been defined as one which conserves resources, is kind to the environment, is good to work with and creates socially useful products (Ekins, ed., 1986). Unfortunately, applications at present are largely based on financial/competitive considerations, notwithstanding the fact that the non-financial considerations are extremely significant.

Many alternative or "soft" technologies are already available, or are being developed, that could permit us to discontinue reliance upon polluting and dwindling fossil fuels and to shift instead to solar and other non-polluting and renewable energy sources, or from the "hard" to the "soft" energy path, in the parlance of energy specialists. Indeed appropriate technology is available or could be developed to resolve most of society's practical problems, including population control, armaments verification, and food security.

However, the present world system operates not to foster but rather to impede benign use of technology. Indeed, it positively favors an exploitative use of technologies. According to the scholar R. B. J. Walker (1988), in the context of the states system, technologies "amplify dangers that are already present in the structure of fragmentation and in superpower dominance. In the context of the world economy, they reproduce and intensify patterns of unequal development that are central to the way the world economy is organized" (p. 43).

At the present time we are undergoing yet another great technological revolution—one of the greatest in the history of humankind. According to Manuel Castells (Mendlovitz and Walker, eds., 1987), this revolution, whose core stems from its ability to generate and process information, is transforming our societies from their very roots. "Microelectronics process information in increasingly powerful, yet decreasingly costly, miniaturized circuits. Computers use microelectronics to process, and eventually generate, information at an ever greater speed and accuracy. . . . Telecommunications transmit and interconnect information, bringing together, at a decreasing

cost and with increasing carrying capacity, all information-processing machines (including human beings), regardless of distance and
(almost) of time. . . . And (possibly the most relevant technology for
the future) genetic engineering decodes the information system of
living matter in order to reprogam it" (pp. 79-80).

Castells maintains that capitalism has undergone a significant
change in which high technology has played a major role, not as a
cause but as a tool. This has permitted capitalism to recover "some of
its dynamism and much of its social control by shrinking the number
of people benefiting from the system and reaching out to almost the
entire planet to connect all segments of potential beneficiaries of this
leaner, more aggressive, more determined type of capitalism"
(Mendlovitz and Walker, eds., p. 81).

Castell enumerates a series of measures undertaken in tandem by
governments and private business that together are bringing about the
new model of economic policy. These include monetary measures
aimed at dismantling the welfare state; the reduction of wages, social
benefits and other labor costs; disinvesting massively from those
sectors, regions and companies that become less profitable, and investing in new products and activities, generally in high-technology
manufacturing, corporate services, miscellaneous consumer services, and real estate; increasing internationalization of the economy,
taking advantage of the most favorable locations for production,
management, and control of the markets, within a system interconnected world-wide; relative control of world prices of raw materials
and energy from the center; and the internationalization of the
world's financial markets caused by deregulation and advances in
information-processing technologies.

The more automation enters the process of production and management, the less low wages play a role in the comparative advantages of a given location. "One of the greatest paradoxes of the
effects of automation on employment is that the most directly hurt are
the Third World countries whose incipient process of industrialization, however exploitative, is based upon the differential cost between unskilled labor in the core and in the periphery" (Mendlovitz
and Walker, eds., 1987, p. 86).

Technology is impacting in a major way on productivity and labor
requirements. For example, in the 1980s the automobile industry
underwent a major change as a result of the use of robots and other
innovations, and it will undergo more change as it shifts from an

The 1953 discovery of the structure of DNA and the 1973 development of recombinant DNA (gene-splicing) techniques promise to change irretrievably the familiar landscape of agricultural development. . . . From 1920 to 1950, agriculture in industrial countries was dominated by mechanical technologies that dramatically increased the amount of food produced per worker and per hour. Shortly after World War II, the mechanical age gave way to the chemical age as farmers worldwide began to adopt artificial fertilizers and synthetic chemical pesticides. Biotechnologies shift the focus of research toward crop plants themselves. . . . Biotechnologies may offer cheaper and quicker ways to improve Third World staples . . . than the costly innovations of the mechanical and chemical eras. . . . Technical hurdles must be overcome and environmental risks evaluated before . . . [the biotechnological] potential can be realized. But more troublesome from the standpoint of Third World agriculture is the degree to which the private sector will dominate agricultural biotechnologies.

Edward C. Wolf, "Raising Agricultural
Productivity," *State of the World 1987*
[p. 151-154]

[World population] remains divided in many ways—by state, class, ethnicity, race, gender, and ideology. But it is involved in material and communications processes that are organized on a worldwide basis. . . . Contemporary innovations make it clearer than ever that the world in which we struggle is not simply given . . . but is made by people. . . . Contemporary global structures often involve connections between the elites of particular societies rather than between those societies as a whole. . . . We undoubtedly live in a global "system"; but few people feel or act as if they live in a global "community." Indeed, it is not at all clear what a global community could or should look like.

R.B.J. Walker, *One World, Many
Worlds* [pp. 11-12]

electro-mechanical industry to an electronics-plastics industry, dramatically increasing productivity and reducing employment in production. This in turn becomes a bargaining factor between management in the automobile industry and labor, in favor of management.

The new technologies, especially telecommunications, play an essential role in the internationalization of the economy, which is a particularly important feature of the new model of accumulation. "Only through the integrated system of telecommunications and computers is it possible to both integrate and decentralize production, distribution, and management in a world-wide, flexible, interconnected system" (Mendlovitz and Walker, eds., 1987, p. 84).

Castells observes in summary: "Thus the economic uses of automation translate labor saving into job suppression, and work flexibility into union busting. Uneven development on a world scale translates the impulse for technological innovation into an insurmountable technological gap for dependent, impoverished Third World countries. The new media reinforce the tendency toward social isolation and turn the electronic home into an individualistic inner space. . . . The most powerful innovative technologies are appropriated and kept secret, to be geared toward warfare. . . . While new technologies are based upon free flows of information, hidden bureaucracies tend to utilize them for scrutinizing people to program their lives" (p. 120).

What can be done to avert or reverse these calamitous ways of using technology? Castells's proposal is similar to others we have mentioned: not to devise alternative *technology* but rather to struggle for an alternative *society*. "What we require, most urgently, is a social restructuring able to match, and to control, the techno-economic restructuring underway" (p. 121).

18

Toward a More Holistic Economy

Introduction

Will it be possible, *how* will it be possible to reverse the present unsustainable world course? How can we put an end to indiscriminate growth, stop the further erosion of our natural support system, reverse the steady drift toward a dual world of haves and have-nots, a polarization that threatens the survival of both?

It will not be easy to put the world on a proper course, given the environmental degradation and economic confusion that now prevail. The (Washington-based) Worldwatch Institute's 1988 report on the *State of the World* (by Brown and Wolf) observes that getting on a sustainable path depends on a reordering of priorities, a fundamental restructuring of the global economy, and a quantum leap in international cooperation on the scale that occurred after World War II. Unless such a goal becomes a central concern of national governments, the continuing deterioration of the economy's natural support systems will eventually overwhelm efforts to improve the human condition. At the same time, this and a subsequent report present many practical suggestions for action, including developments already underway.

It is encouraging to realize that the problems we face are provoking so many positive responses on international, regional, national, institutional, business, and grassroots levels. We will sketch several of them in this and in the next chapter.[1]

---

1. For specifics in respect of energy and resource conservation, reversal of ecological decline, equity questions, redesign of economies, and so forth, see the aforementioned reports of the Worldwatch Institute.

Changes in Industry

According to futurists Hazel Henderson, Alvin Toffler and John Naisbitt, mature industrial economies have reached a logical point in their evolution when a basic change becomes inevitable. It consists of a shift from economies that seek to maximize material production, mass-consumption and planned obsolescence based on non-renewable resources and energy, to economies that minimize waste, recycle materials, employ renewable resources and energy, and aim at sustained-yield, long-term productivity. Hazel Henderson calls this the transition to the Solar Age, because it entails gradually winding down reliance upon fossil fuel "capital" in favor of *renewable* forms of solar energy.[2] She sees the economic transition as a generic part of a deeper and broader transition to a new world culture.

The transition is characterized by the advent of new forms of industry and the related new technologies. The new technologies, such as solar energy collectors, wind generators, organic farming, local food production and processing, and waste recycling are smaller in scale and decentralized, more flexible and responsive to local conditions, and designed to increase self-sufficiency. They are far gentler to the environment but they are no less sophisticated than the older technologies (Cf. Capra, 1983, p. 399).

In Alvin Toffler's book *Previews and Premises* (1983), two fundamental changes taking place in industrial production are described: demassification of production and distribution, and the expansion of production for use rather than for exchange. "This is a profound change, an historical change . . . and our conventional economists have hardly begun to notice it yet" (p. 17).

Toffler calls these industries the "Third Wave." They differ radically from mass (Second Wave) industries in types of products, environmental implications, kinds of people in them, organizational

---

2. As remarked in Capra (1983), the fossil fuels of course *also* had their ultimate source in the sun. In fact, all the energy of which we dispose except nuclear energy has its ultimate source in the sun, which has been the planet's main energy source for billions of years. Wood, coal, oil or gas as sources of energy represent energy originally radiated to the Earth from the sun and converted into chemical form by photosynthesis. Wind energy is dependent upon a flow of air as a result of heat from the sun. Hydro energy is part of the continuous water cycle sustained by solar radiation. Unconventional sources of energy are becoming more and more competitive with conventional non-renewable sources, especially when social costs are included in the calculations. Many are already in use, and many suitable technologies for unconventional energy are being developed.

Ozone depletion, climate change, and oceanic pollution simply cannot be solved at the national level. . . . Scientific cooperation is one aspect of environmental protection that has advanced in recent years. Most notable is the International Geosophere-Biosphere Program . . . [which was established in 1986] . . . International environmental cooperation has come furthest in Western Europe, where a score of countries are squeezed into a small area and trade pollutants back and forth across their borders via winds and rivers . . . In 1979, a U.N.-sponsored Convention on Long-Range Transboundary Air Pollution was agreed to by 35 countries in Eastern and Western Europe and North America . . . On April 30, 1982 . . . the Convention on the Law of the Sea was signed by 119 nations, 35 of which ratified it. . . . [The] United Nations Environment Programme led the effort to create the Vienna Convention for the Protection of the Ozone Layer, adopted in 1985 to provide a mechanism for CFC controls. . . . In 1987, the Montreal Protocol was established [to freeze CFC production at 1986 levels] and has now been signed by 35 countries. . . . The International Council of Scientific Unions and the World Meteorological Organization are coordinating international research on climate change. . . . Some have called for an international "Law of the Atmosphere" parallel to the Law of the Sea. . . . [Now] ripe for discussion of new international conventions or protocols are the preservation of bio-diversity, the slowing of deforestation, and perhaps even family planning.

State of the World 1989 [pp. 16-20]

structures, style and culture, and, at the deepest level, the knowledge they entail.

Second Wave industries used brute force technologies—they punched, hammered, rolled, beat, chipped and chopped, drilled and battered raw materials into shapes we needed or wanted. . . . The Third Wave industries operate at an altogether deeper level. Instead of banging something into shape, we reach back into the material itself and reprogram it . . . instead of extending brute force, the new technologies extend human mental power (p. 20).

Third Wave industries include electronics, lasers, optics, communications, information, genetics, alternative energy, ocean science,

My use of the word "politics" is in its broadest sense, not the narrower definition of party and electoral politics, which is now breaking down as old consensuses splinter in all industrial democracies. I am talking about all the newer "politics by other means," the more fundamental politics of: redefining issues and reshaping questions; restating old "problems"; re-visioning alternative futures; alternative life-styles; reweaving the split between work and leisure, the "public" and "private" sectors, money and wealth, "success" and well being, psychic riches and deeper human satisfaction. I am talking about the new "issue politics," which is supplanting geographical politics, not in its narrow, vengeful form but in the broader issues: the politics of planetary awareness and ecological understanding, and the new demands growing out of it: global laws concerning equitable resource use, new conflict-resolution mechanisms, universal human rights, freedom of information and media access, a New International Economic Order, and a global framework of accountability for multinational corporate enterprises and the impacts of science and technologies.

> Hazel Henderson, *The Politics of the*
> *Solar Age: Alternatives to Economics*
> [p. xix]

[The] shift of focus from the inert and inorganic to a deeper knowledge of the organic complexity and dynamism of bioecological systems constitutes my definition of the postindustrial revolution. The new scientific enterprise will also involve a shift from our focus on "hardware" to "software"; for example, the concept of production will no longer . . . conjure up . . . visions of a factory, a machine, or any hardware at all. We will more carefully model . . . production in its larger social and ecological dimensions . . . review diverse options, scan ecological systems . . . before any investments are committed. . . . There are substitutable organic ways of meeting human needs of which we have hardly dreamed.

> Hazel Henderson, *The Politics of the*
> *Solar Age* [p. 148]

space manufacture, ecological engineering and eco-system agriculture, "all reflecting the qualitative leap in human knowledge which is now being translated into the every day economy" (p. 21).

These new technologies and the related new industries, combined with the changing roles of producers, consumers and third parties, add up, declares Toffler, to a great upheaval and restructuring of the economy.

John Naisbitt, in *Megatrends* (1984), discusses trends in the United States, but almost everything said applies to other developed countries. He notes especially: (1) a shift from an industrial society to one based on information; (2) a move "in the dual directions of high tech/high touch, matching each new technology with a compensatory human response"; (3) the recognition that the national economy must be regarded as part of a global economy, not as isolated and self-sufficient; (4) a restructuring of our society from short-term considerations and rewards to longer-term; (5) discovery of the ability to act innovatively and to achieve results, from the bottom up; (6) a shift from institutional help to more self-reliance in all aspects of life; (7) recognition that "the framework of representative democracy has become obsolete in an era of instantaneously shared information"; (8) a shift from a dependence on hierarchical structures in favor of informal networks.

We have already noted that the present global system uses technology in such a way as to reinforce the already uneven development, with an especially adverse effect upon the least developed of the third world countries.

Henderson and Theobald both suggest that it behooves governments, in adopting policies, to broaden their horizons and not rely on the tools of an obsolete type of economics, especially since such innovations as "futures research, scenario building, game theory, cross-impact studies, technology assessments, and social and environmental impact studies [are available] . . . policy tools [which] go beyond economics and assess real resources, technologies, and the behavior of people" ("Money Vs. Wealth," *The Futurist*, March-April 1988, p. 34).

Henderson (1981) had long predicted the present transition from a centralized, capital-intensive method of production to a more decentralized and a more refined and benign type of industry. The problem, she says, is *not* one of growth versus no-growth but, rather, a matter of what is growing, what is declining, and what must be maintained.

"Thus, neighborhood- and community-based enterprises are mush-rooming as viable alternatives to both multinationals and large state-operated enterprises both in the Western countries and in the Eastern bloc" (p. 101).

We must understand that a critique of growth as such does not imply a rejection of all growth *per se*. Nor does it imply a lack of concern with poverty and economic development. Nor does it imply a drastic decline in living standards. What it implies is moving toward a conserver rather than a consumer economy, which means *inter alia* that certain areas would need to be developed and expanded to give the economy social and ecological sustainability (Ekins, ed., 1986).

Changes in the Character and Purpose of Work[3]

The prognosis concerning the solar era is that it will have a radical-ly different notion of the meaning of employment and the nature of work. The major factor behind this view is the advent of automation, as opposed to mechanization. "In the early and middle years of industrialism, the technological thrust was towards mechanisation, toward the introduction of machines that worked with people to produce more than the people could by themselves. The machines may have destroyed traditional skills and communities, and required the migration of labour from country to town, but they kept labour very much in the picture and actually added to its economic value what it could produce, and therefore to its bargaining power. . . . Now, however, the thrust of technology is not towards mechanisa-tion, a composite of labour and machines, but towards automation, which, far from enhancing the value of labour, does away with it almost altogether, except for a highly-skilled technocratic elite" (Ekins, ed., 1986, pp. 84-85).

Employment in the capital-intensive, highly automated, mass-pro-duction sector in industrialized countries has for some time been

---

3. This and the two subsequent sections are largely based on Ekins, ed. (1986). The latter book in turn is based on some fifty expert papers, by authors from different parts of the world, that were prepared for the first two conferences—in 1984 and 1985—convened by The Other Economic Summit (TOES), "an independent, international initiative, seeking to develop and promote a New Economics, based on personal development and social justice, the satisfaction of the whole range of human needs, sustainable use of resources and conservation of the environment."

declining markedly and is so bound to continue. These enterprises have only two alternatives: either to continue to become more automated for the sake of competitiveness—which would result in the further decline of employment—or to fall behind in competitiveness, which would also bring a declining trend in employment.

Analysts conclude that in virtue of the two factors, namely, international competition and automation, full employment is a thing of the past. And this, in turn, implies that conventional employment will not, in future, any longer be the chief means of distributing income and ensuring people's livelihood.

Castells, for example, states that new technologies could and should be used to redefine the social nature of work. "Paid working time should be reduced dramatically for everybody, so that everyone has the possibility of being employed. Productivity increases, allowed by widespread automation, could provide substantial pay for less working time, even allowing for a fair increase of private profit for employers in a capitalist economy" (Mendlovitz and Walker, eds., 1987, p. 122). There is however one important proviso: this policy would have to be generalized at the international level. "Otherwise, competition between countries and companies will wreck the economic foundation of those engaged in the path of social change" (p. 122). Castells also points out that this is not an unheard-of idea, since in fact it happened in Western Europe as a result of legislation in the second half of this century, when blue-collar workers' pay went up considerably while their working time went down.

Economist James Robertson sees two new categories on the horizon, namely, leisure and ownwork (in Ekins, ed., 1986).

Robertson observes that advanced small-scale technologies will help to bring productive work back into the home and neighborhood, and enable local work to meet a greater proportion of local needs. The fields of work concerned are energy and food production, information technology (including home computers), building, plumbing, decorating, electrical work, furnishing and clothing, and even hardware manufacturing with small, inexpensive, versatile robots.

The mass-production era brought about a radical change in the character and purpose of work. People became dependent on others for employment, and indeed towns and districts all over the world lost much of their autonomy. The large-scale settings made the work situation very impersonal, and tended to discourage workers' sense of personal responsibility for the outcome of their work. Centralization also meant that many people have had to commute to work over long distances to places far removed from their family, friends and community.

Still another feature of mass employment has been that men as employees have enjoyed a higher status and pay than women. Although in more recent times, many more women have entered the arena of paid work, the conventional masculine bias still downgrades the work of women.

The employment society also downgrades all those not employed for pay, including retired people, teen-agers not yet eligible to join the labor market, and unemployed people of working age. All informal work, no matter how useful, is downgraded.

Robertson observes that, with decentralization, work will become more independent, more within the personal and local control of workers, more intrinsically interesting, more informal, more balanced as to masculine and feminine values, and more inclusive in the sense of giving everyone opportunites for useful work.

Less Industrial Specialization, Especially in the Third World

In the industrial era, localities and regions have tended to specialize—for example in coal-mining, steel-making, ship-building, fruit-growing, coffee-growing, fishing, tourism, or glass-making. But for the third world countries especially, specialization has spelled vulnerability. James Robertson writes, "For many people and in many places the desirable limit to economic specialisation has now been reached, if not passed. The relative costs and benefits of specialisation and self-reliance now tend to favour the latter" (in Ekins, ed., p. 92).

Scaling Down Export-Import Relations

International trade and competition are at present so intensive as to render every participant dependent on everybody else's choice. This applies even to rich countries. All are trapped in an unwholesome race which mandates growth at any cost. The solution dissenters propose is to scale down export-import relations. This would decrease countries' vulnerability to crises and collapses abroad, and would permit opening up a whole new range of choices in shaping domestic development.

Delinking from the international market is a very different solution from that of protectionism, which aims at making specific industries unfairly competitive in the international market.

> [Delinking] is the gradual but systematic withdrawal from international trade in those areas where a country has the skills and resources to be self-reliant, so that it becomes able to satisfy its domestic market from its own production, and regains political control over its own course of development. In addition, it does not then contribute via its purchasing power to conditions that exploit people or the environment abroad (Ekins, ed., 1986, p. 83).

However, bringing about this change might, for a certain transition period, require "protectionism for the sake of self-reliance and reconversion for the sake of export 'disarmament'" (Sachs, in Ekins, ed., 1986, p. 336).

For third world countries, the strategy would be one of selective dissociation from the North. "Imports from the North create consumption without inducing growth, and force export production to expand to pay for the increasingly expensive imports. Export production is the stronghold of the national power elite, and diverts valuable resources in terms of land, capital and technology away from the needs of the population at large" (Ekins, ed., 1986, p. 337).

Global economic change would, in sum, consist of several interrelated components: decentralization, facilitated by new technological developments in both the industrialized and the less-developed countries, increased self-reliance, less dependency (especially in respect of economic essentials such as staple foods and energy supplies), decreased international trade, and reduction of causes of international tension and possible conflict. All this requires mutual or complementary or convergent objectives on the part of the industrialized countries, on the one hand, and the third world, on the other, as well as between domestic and international concerns (Ekins, ed., 1986).[4]

---

4. Convergent aims of this nature have already given rise to several development action campaigns in recent years. These are detailed in Sach's essay.

19

How Shall We Characterize the New Era?

The egocentric ideal of a future reserved for those who have managed to attain egoistically the extremity of 'everyone for himself' is false and against nature. . . . The outcome of the world, the gates of the future, the entry into the super-human—these are not thrown open to a few of the privileged nor to one chosen people to the exclusion of all others. They will open only to an advance of all together, in a direction in which all together can join and find completion in a spiritual renovation of the earth. . . . No evolutionary future awaits man except in association with all other men.

Pierre Teilhard de Chardin,
The Future of Man

A New Trend in Politics and Political Science

We have yet to discuss the present evolution of thought in the specific realm of politics and political science.

In his book, *New Age Politics, Healing Self and Society* (1978), Mark Satin listed the following names for the emergent new politics, together with their respective authors:

"Anarchic Capitalism"—William Irwin Thompson, cultural historian

"Cooperative Capitalism"—Joe Falk, community organizer

"Enlightened Humanism"—John Maher, organizer of ex-felons

"Global Humanism"—Richard Falk, professor of international law

"The New Localism"—David Morris and Karl Hess, political economists

"Participatory Divinity"—David Spangler, spiritual philosopher

"Personalism"—Nikolai Berdyaev, religious philosopher

"The Politics of the Person"—Theodore Roszak, cultural historian

273

"Radical Humanism"—Erich Fromm, psychologist

"Synergic Politics"—Jim Craig, management consultant, and Marge Craig, healer.

This list suggests a markedly holistic trend at the cutting edge of political thought.

Satin describes "new age" politics as a new way of looking at the world. Different writers have suggested various epithets for the emergent period, such as post-mechanistic, post-liberal, post-Marxist, post-industrial, post-modern, the solar age. Most recently, in view of the dramatic shifts in communist policies, one hears the term "post-communist" or "post-cold-war" era. Political scientist Richard A. Falk of Princeton University alludes to the present "transitional decade of reaction against the dying, obsolescent order evolved in the West by way of state power, technological innovation, consumerism, and the prevalence of military and paramilitary modes of conflict resolution" (Mendlovitz and Walker, eds., 1987, pp. 369-370).

As we have been saying, society creates its own world, its own reality. In the past, this creation has been largely unconscious. But we seem to have reached the point when we want to become conscious of this fact, to situate ourselves, to grasp better what it is we *do*, what it is we *need* to do in order to shape societal order. At the present juncture in our planetary affairs, this impulse seems to stem in large part from the societal impasse. Our problems are of such global proportions that they challenge us severely, and may cause us to undergo nothing less than a transformation of consciousness.

In the past two decades there has appeared a new breed of holistic scholars in international affairs (of which Richard Falk, above-mentioned, is one). They are engrossed in the task of conceiving a new world order consonant with their philosophy, and of elaborating models and strategies for bringing about such an order. Thus in the 1970s there was the World Order Models Project (WOMP), which involved groups of scholars associated with principal regions and/or actors of the world (Latin America, Africa, Japan, Europe, Soviet Union, India, United States, with indirect representation for China for the network of transnational actors). The values agreed upon as suitable criteria for world order appraisal were minimization of collective violence; maximization of economic well-being; maximization of social and political justice; and maximization of ecological quality (Falk, in Feller, et al., eds., 1981, p. 41). Some of the same scholars are involved in a newer grouping called the Committee for a Just World Peace (established in 1985), which apparently has many of the same concerns as did WOMP. It is motivated by the conviction that while this is a time of great danger, it is also a time of transformative opportunities, and it is particularly interested in understanding the relationship between the global structures and processes that affect people everywhere and the social movements that have arisen in specific situations in response to seemingly specific problems (Mendlovitz and Walker, 1987).

According to Falk, in the past scholarly thinking has been marked by ever narrower specialization or focus on smaller and smaller segments of reality. In contrast, the new world-order thinking reverses this tendency and seeks an understanding of the world political system as a whole. Falk has observed that many students of world order look more to the humanities and to religious thought than to the social sciences for intellectual help, since "behavior cannot be understood in any purely rational reductionist interpretation that limits its observations to external planes of existence" (Feller et al., eds., 1981, p. 47).

Grassroots Movements for Social Change

An extraordinary development in recent years is the rise of numerous grass-roots social movements, such as the spiritual, environmental, feminist, and "men's liberation" movements; the human potential, simple living, appropriate-technology, and business-for-learning-and-pleasure movements; the humanistic-transformational education movement and the nonviolent-action movement (Satin, 1978).

Hazel Henderson, who herself is the founder of many public interest groups, believes that citizen groups and movements—whether concerned with human rights, corporate accountability, economic justice, consumer and environmental protection, holistic health, appropriate technologies, simple living, personal growth, and greater awareness of the interdependence of the human family—are an effective force for greater global equity (Henderson, 1978 and 1981). They are a grass-roots response to an unacceptable state of societal affairs.

All these social movements have arisen in response to the perceived failures of the industrial age, and as an alternative to the bureaucracies and hierarchies typical of large-scale social organization and decision making (Cf. Naisbitt, 1984, Lipnack and Stamps, 1986, and Ferguson, 1987). These movements are a critical social form for our time. Their networking activity is an integrative process (Ferguson, 1987). They arise in different parts of the world and in different circumstances. They are part of the struggle against specific problems and global processes, such as militarization and ecological degradation, war, poverty, hunger, repressive regimes, violation of human rights and all kinds of discrimination practiced in many different places (Mendlovitz and Walker, eds., 1987).

In the past, movements against the existing social order (socialist, nationalist and democratic alike) were directed toward the seizure of state power or toward gaining the ability to seize such power in a particular territory. But history shows that approaches which rely on violence are fruitless—that the means cannot be divorced from the ends—and to oppose violence with violence is to betray the whole undertaking. Some of the new movements have demonstrated the possibilities of engaging in social transformation without violence (Mendlovitz and Walker, 1987).

Grass-roots movements are directed at reconstructing values, communities and political participation. The individuals concerned believe that they *can* make a difference. And there is ample evidence that they *do* make a difference (Mendlovitz and Walker, eds., 1987).

Struggle for a Global-Local Perspective

A slogan of "new age" political activists is, "Think globally, act locally." This is surely a transformative aspiration. At the same time, its practical implementation, given today's circumstances, is not simple. That is to say, powerful global economic institutions and processes impact tremendously upon local affairs. Activists have to decide whether to work to transform the global structures, or to empower people at the local level, or to attempt to do both simultaneously.

An interesting essay (by Chadwick F. Alger and Saul H. Mendlovitz) exploring the relationship between activism at the global and local levels is to be found in Mendlovitz and Walker (1987). In discussing the way activists in the United States deal with the global-local connection, it states that the vast majority of these activists are not concerned with global matters or issues and that, relatively speaking, only a small minority have a globalist perspective. The latter can in turn be divided into two broad categories: those who have chosen to focus their activity on local problems and ignore global issues; and the relatively rare activists (one must regard them as inspiring pio-

Marxist and liberal interpretations of human endeavor, with their exclusive reference to external relationships, are jointly flawed by their attempt to explain the failure of societal arrangements. . . . Marxists await revolution as the dynamic in which victims seize the means of production so as to reorganize society along non-exploitative lines. Liberals, on the other hand, seek only to institutionalize moderation in the state so that abundance can serve as the dynamic providing everyone with sufficiency. . . . Both outlooks are overly optimistic, secular, materialistic, and rationalistic, awaiting societal fulfillment in historical time without inner transformation or divine intervention. Both underestimate the religious or spiritual dimension of human personality.

Richard Falk [in Feller, et al., eds.,
1981, pp. 46-47]

The strength of existing structures, and the threats posed by their main lines of policy . . . generate exemplary actions of resistance by individuals and groups. The purpose of such resistance is symbolic communication beyond the framework of lawful activity. Resistance implies negation, and it expresses both the urgency of the challenge and the impotence of mainstream responses. . . . It is exhilarating to notice how universalistic these forms of resistance, spontaneously enacted in grass-roots settings, have become in tone and symbolic content, despite the unevenness of the situation that exists in various countries and regions. The song of the Swedish Great Peace Journey ". . . we are gentle, angry people" expresses the paradoxical attitudes that underlie a decisive rejection of what is and an equally decisive refusal to fight fire with fire.

Richard A. Falk [in Mendlovitz and
Walker, 1987, pp. 370-371]

neers) who try to integrate and actually to involve themselves in both types of issues. In so doing, they endeavor to address local people's immediate needs and deprivations and at the same time perceive themselves as working on issues that have global dimensions—that are integral to achieving a better world. This type of activist tends to be primarily concerned, not with organization and structures, but with *processes:* non-violent, participatory, non-sexist, non-racist, self-reliant processes.

As we have seen, many crucial issues today, such as systems of production, the arms race, violence, racism, and sexism, cannot be labelled as only local or only global; their impact and manifestations are *both* global and local. The authors of the above-mentioned essay come to the conclusion that in fact global and local activists are increasingly converging upon a common agenda, and that in reality the global place is but a vast array of local places. They believe that "a sensitive and understanding alliance between those who call themselves localists and those who call themselves globalists would provide a powerful base for a transformational movement aimed at creating a more human and just world" (p. 361).

International Nongovernmental Organizations

Another significant development (which is distinct from but closely related to that of the social movements) is the proliferation of international non-governmental organizations (INGOs). Elise Boulding (1988) devotes a chapter of her book *Building a Global Civic Culture* to this phenomenon. The number of INGO's grew from 176 in 1909 to some 18,000 in 1988. They have national sections in states belonging both to the NATO and the Warsaw Pact blocs. It has taken a good deal of ingenuity, but these organizations have managed to serve the interests of the larger community, thereby transcending these political blocs.

The major goal of the INGOs, whatever their specific purpose, is international understanding, peace and security for the whole world. The areas of their activity are indeed very diverse, ranging from science to trade, from the arts to helping women farmers in countries of the South improve crop yields.

INGOs' networks link people across the world irrespective of cultures and political systems. They provide "local-global linkage from hometown to hometown across continents" (Boulding, 1989, p. 37). They are channels for the flow of scientific and cultural contacts between East and West where governmental contacts are lacking. They provide major programs of education, training and social investment in human welfare infrastructures of the South when there is an absence of such help from the North.

A great many INGOs are represented at the United Nations. That is to say, those concerned with matters within the competence of the

> Non-governmental organizations (NGOs) are non-profit citizens' voluntary organizations organized nationally or internationally. . . . Some are active in information and education; others are operational and are engaged in technical projects, relief, refugee and development programmes.
>
> Examples of NGOs are: professional, business and cooperative organizations; foundations; trade unions; religion, peace, and disarmament groups; youth and women's organizations; development, environmental, and human rights groups; research institutes and associations of parliamentarians.
>
> *The United Nations and Non-Governmental Organizations*[1]

Economic and Social Council of the United Nations can avail themselves of official consultative status with that body, and such status permits them also to hold consultations with the United Nations Secretariat.

INGOs lobby nation-states for constructive foreign policies. They have long played a particularly significant role at the United Nations in regard to disarmament through the NGO Disarmament Committee, consisting of representatives of all INGOs with arms control and disarmament concerns (Boulding, 1988). Observers believe INGOs should and will in future attain to a more formal position in the United Nations structure.

"Global Thinking" in the Soviet Union

How about the communist countries? Are the present remarkable developments in the communist world related in any way to the holistic trend described above? The answer is decidedly in the affirmative. In the Soviet Union, where the developments concerned were initiated, the changes represent a response to severe economic and other problems that have cumulatively developed in the course of years. Mikhail S. Gorbachev inaugurated a degree of liberalization,

---

[1]A brochure produced by the Department of Public Information/NGO Executive Committee in cooperation with the United Nations Department of Public Information.

especially a relaxing of the controls of the press and the introduction of certain democratic measures. This resulted in an upsurge, a revelation, of strong, pent-up desires on the part of the population for civil and political freedoms. The series of developments in question have been sudden and astonishing, and have impacted upon the whole climate of international relations, affecting both the rest of the communist bloc and the so-called free world, and posing new challenges to all concerned.

How these changes and challenges—to different governments, blocs of countries and ethnic groups, for example—will work themselves out will be of great general interest, but this subject is beyond the scope of the present book. What is especially interesting for our theme, however, is the *nature* of the new socio-political thought in the Soviet Union—more accurately, the twin, interrelated movements, *glasnost* (openness) and *perestroika* (reconstruction). For these undoubtedly parallel in significant ways the evolutionary developments that we have described elsewhere. Thus, the editor-in-chief of *Communist Magazine* (Moscow), I. T. Frolov, is quoted in the Brundtland Commission report (p. 39) as saying:

> Mankind is on the threshold of a new stage in its development. We should not only promote the expansion of its material, scientific, and technical basis, but, what is most important, the formation of new value and humanistic aspirations in human psychology, since wisdom and humaneness are the 'eternal truths' that make the basis of humanity. We need new social, moral, scientific, and ecological concepts, which should be determined by new conditions in the life of mankind today and in the future.

In the Soviet Union the socio-political reorientation was initiated, as we know, not outside official channels but from the top. Mikhail Gorbachev himself, in his book *Perestroika*, makes an impassioned plea for new thinking in his country and in the world. He explains that the new political thinking in the Soviet Union is based on the recognition of a contradictory but interconnected, interdependent and, essentially, integral world. "The fundamental principle of the new political outlook," he writes, "is very simple: nuclear war cannot be a means of achieving political, economic, ideological or any other goals. This conclusion is truly revolutionary, for it means discarding the traditional notions of war and peace. . . . For the first time in history, basing international politics on moral and ethical norms that are common to all humankind, as well as humanizing interstate relations,

> There is a great thirst for mutual understanding and mutual communication in the world. . . . And if the Russian word "perestroika" has entered the international lexicon, this is due to more than just interest in what is going on in the Soviet Union. Now the whole world needs restructuring . . . fundamental change. The restructuring is a must for a world overflowing with nuclear weapons; for a world ridden with serious economic and ecological problems; for a world laden with poverty, backwardness and disease; for a human race now facing the urgent need of ensuring its own survival. We are all students, and our teacher is life and time . . . through RESTRUCTURING in the broad sense of the word, the integrity of the world will be enhanced.
>
> Mikhail Gorbachev, *Perestroika*
> [p. 240]

has become a vital requirement" (pp. 126-127). Furthermore, Gorbachev maintains that the United Nations is the most appropriate forum for seeking a balance of the interests of states, which is essential for the stability of the world.

Another interesting book, *Breakthrough* (Gromyko and Hellman, eds., 1988), affords a remarkable glimpse into the thinking of prominent scholars in the Soviet Union about perestroika and glastnost. It is also a first in that it was written jointly by American and Soviet scholars. Let us look at some of the extraordinary assertions in this book.

Fyodor M. Burlatsky, professor of philosophy and vice president of the Soviet Political Science Association, states that perestroika means that all aspects of the Soviet political life must be democratized—the electoral system, the judicial processes, the guarantees of basic human rights (this book, incidentally, predated the Soviet Union's electoral reforms and elections in 1989). Burlatsky and Academician Alexander I. Belchuk allude to the movement of society toward decentralization, a movement which will involve the people whose support will be essential for economic rebirth. Again, academician and director of the Institute of Experimental Medicine (Leningrad) Natalia Bekhtereva emphasizes the importance of individual participation, not only for the sake of good government, but to overcome a sense of powerlessness and to realize that the individual can make a difference.

The American and Soviet authors of this book jointly adopted the term *global thinking* to describe their common outlook, which is being called forth in response to the intensifying interdependencies of nations and, above all, by the nuclear imperative. They state further that global thinking begins with the beauty and the simplicity of the unity principle discovered by the cosmonauts and astronauts during their flights in space.

Anatoly A. Gromyko, director of the Institute of Africa Studies in the Soviet Union, writes, "We ought to recognize each other's humanity, as we move to solve today's complex problems dealing with political relations, economics, and social life" (Gromyko and Hellman, eds., 1988, p. 6).

Breakthrough avers that from the view of the spaceship it is not possible, as it previously was, to place blame on someone invisible across the sea or across the mountains. Ales Adamovich, Professor and Corresponding Member of the Byelorussian Academy of Sciences, joins Gromyko in declaring that we cannot blame others for ozone damage or soil erosion or injustice, since "everyone is responsible for everything." In a joint essay, Jerome Frank, American psychiatrist, and Andrei Y. Melville, member of the Academy of Sciences of the USSR, say that it is simply not true that all contradictions and conflicts among social groups and cultures can be explained by an evil to be found outside one's own society, but never inside.

Breakthrough declares that the new thinking requires a radical change, entailing basic alterations in everything we think and do, and assuming personal and historical responsibility for everything on the planet. We are all responsible, and together we can all help to solve any problem. "Thinking globally requires discovery of the right relationship between the individual and the global community. Neither is insignificant. There has to be a healthy relationship between the community, the social order, the whole, and the individual" (p. 8).

What is more, these scholars agree that humankind is evolving; it is "emerging from a chain reaction of cause and effect that stretches back for billions of years. Now this species has the power to affect its own evolution by conscious choice" (p. 11). We are "at a threshold," not only because of the nuclear threat, but because our planet is circled by unprecedented new means of communication.

The people know more now than ever before. Radios, televisions, computers, telephones, and copiers have spread across the globe in a century. No generation ever had these to add to newspapers, magazines, and the arts. Ours is a time of unlimited possibility for exchange, interaction between cultures, travel, and learning (p. 11).

The book expresses the deep conviction that to achieve change it is important to engage people in active participation. The American social scientist Kenneth E. Boulding opines that the challenge in both countries is to find citizens who will move the world across a phase boundary from unstable to stable peace. And thus *Breakthrough* ends with a strong plea for action by everyone for peace-building.

The Emergence of Wholeness as a Guiding Principle in Thought and Action

As we know all too well, the present planetary scene is characterized by divisiveness of every kind—intellectual, emotional and institutional. At the same time, it is amply evident, as I believe we have shown, that the idea of wholeness is re-emerging in a new way in different contexts. This paradox may be described as a karmic rebalancing, bringing into play a cosmic law which somehow—unfathomably—comes into operation at all levels of existence to re-establish balance and harmony wherever and whenever they are disturbed.

In the scientific realm, as the limits of mechanism were being reached, perspectives on wholeness began to re-emerge, and physics and biology have revealed the fallacy of reductionism. In the politico-socio-economic realm, we have witnessed the progressive intensification of linkages and interdependencies in material, economic, ecological, technological, military, political and other respects. But while the world is thus interconnected, it is hardly unified. The global problems have aroused a response in many different quarters. For instance, a reaction is underway against the extremes of centralism and giantism and in favor of such values as self-reliance, greater economic equality, more appropriate uses of technology, ecological sustainability, work enjoyment and creativity. Again, in the sphere of international relations, due to the recognition that peace and security cannot be attained in the absence of economic and social justice, the assurance of human rights and adequate international cooperation and sharing, holistic approaches are increasingly advocated. The establishment of the United Nations and its thirty-odd specialized agencies and programs arose out of the impulse towards inclusivity which transcends nationalism. A similar impulse underlies the phenomenal proliferation of international non-governmental organizations—which link together all continents, nation-states, communities and households in networks based on the common interests of their members.

Furthermore, the whole world was affected by the wondrous image of Planet Earth as viewed from outer space. By the accounts both of the U. S. astronauts and the Soviet cosmonauts, at the moment of seeing our tiny planet against the vastnesses of space, they instantly *know* its beauty, uniqueness, wholeness, preciousness and fragility. They instantly perceive, too, that boundaries of all types are far more shallow and specious than they appear in conventional thought. Inner and outer space seem simultaneously to merge in their consciousness.

> What strikes me, is not only the beauty of the continents..but their closeness to one another . . . their essential unity (Soviet cosmonaut, Yuri Gagarin).

> From where you see it, the thing is a whole, and it is so beautiful (Apollo 9 astronaut Russell Schweickart) (Gromyko and Hellman, eds., 1988, p. 7).

All in all, we are challenged as never before, I believe, to reconcile our own particularities—nationality, ethnicity, local issues—with other people's particularities. In fact, a good many individuals already identify first with their status of human being, superseding their particular geographic provenance and their sex, as well as the culture and religion into which they were born. These individuals are interested in the health of the whole planet, not just their little corner. Insularity, parochialism, chauvinism hold no appeal for such people, for they represent a new cast of mind and a new state of consciousness. The schools of humanistic and transpersonal psychology that have arisen in the West, movements that are concerned with exploring consciousness, are surely co-relative developments, as is the growing enthusiasm for the synthesis of the world's religions and myths.

How, then, are we to characterize the incoming era? We may identify it by not a few different names, as is being done. But however identified, it will be marked above all, I would say, by the emergence of a new awareness of wholeness as a guiding principle for every domain of thought and activity. For many this will conduce (it is already happening) to an expansion of consciousness that results in a more inclusive, a more universal, type of worldview and spirituality.

Wholeness in the Field of Education

A basic imperative of our times obviously is to extend genuine global vision and values into the educational sphere, so that the new generation will see things whole, and thus avoid some of our mistakes.

Education at the present time unfortunately reflects the reductionistic, utilitarian bias of the prevailing culture. The heavy emphasis is on careerism, conformity, technical and basic skills, and on achieving success (Massanari, 1988). According to Allan Bloom's widely discussed criticism, higher education in America has failed democracy and impoverished the souls of today's students. He laments the relativism and historicism that prevail on university campuses. The different departments operate in isolation from each other, so that the student is denied any integrative learning experience. The result is that students mill about in a value vacuum.

At present science and the humanities are still walled off from each other, and the barriers cannot come down until specialist defenses are replaced by a more inclusive educational philosophy. Western academics will have to acknowledge that the recent evolution in human thought brought about by science requires that education attend once more to ethical convictions, spiritual values and the meaningfulness of life. It is ironic that intellectuals in the Soviet Union, a country which officially embraces atheism, are now invoking eternal truths, while educators in America cling to "value neutrality"!

Peace education—an endeavor called into existence by the dire exigencies of our time, which has received legitimation only recently, after years of devoted work by its pioneers—especially demands a trans-disciplinary or holistic approach. For peace is much more than the absence of war. It is a positive value. It cannot be brought about merely by external reorganization. It is a state of consciousness, a perception of the need for harmony with the essential nature of things, a sense of the unity of humankind—a unity which is not only biological or even cultural, but is rooted in the deeper reality which includes all life, and our beloved earth itself.

A leading peace educator who has pioneered in this field, Betty

Reardon of Teachers College, Columbia University, has stated it very well: "An education that is concerned more with instruction than with learning, with quantity more than quality, is especially lamentable at this particular time in our history, when we are on the point of a possible quantum leap toward a significant new stage in the human experience, a coming of age of the human species and of human society: and the achievement of positive peace. The capacity and inclination to make peace, to bring about a nonviolent and just social order on this planet, would be the primary indicator of a maturing of our species" (Reardon, 1988, p. 56).

What students around the world need is an educational environment imbued with an understanding of the commonality of knowledge and experience that promotes seeing the interrelationship and the complementarity of science, philosophy, art and spirituality and that relates personal life to the social welfare. Students need also to understand the orders of nature and their relationship to and meaningful role vis-à-vis nature. "Where there is a spirit of free inquiry, there is no real conflict among the different modes of knowing; rather, there is damage to the whole person when the aesthetic and the intellective are severed from one another. Once we appreciate that the various modes of knowing, whether scientific or humanistic, are conjoined in all of us (with or without formal expression), we can begin to understand how scientific knowledge, for example, can undergird our search for a world of harmonious relationships, rather than furnish a means for the exploitation of others. It is possible to teach in such a manner that each field of knowledge and realm of experience can be related to a wider context within which diverse perspectives integrate and illumine one another, and thus reveal a meaningful, value-laden ground for human action." This is a statement I elicited from Emily B. Sellon, a wise teacher of mine, she to whom this book is dedicated.[2]

---

2. Emily B. Sellon was co-editor, with the late Fritz Kuntz, and editor, after his death in 1972, of the excellent journal *Main Currents in Modern Thought* (November 17, 1940-November 17, 1975), whose stated aim was to present contributions that pointed "toward a unified vision of the world, by bringing into view the universal principles and modes of knowing in terms of which all cultures, ancient and modern, Eastern and Western, find their unique expressions."

A Postscript on the Intersection of Religion, Perennial Philosophy, Science and Society

Each of us is both the product of a long evolutionary journey and a self-organizing, self-evolving participant in the unceasing process of unfoldment. Some have called that unfoldment a Divine Plan—a Divine Plan which is indeterminable in its detailed realization but not in its character and direction. For instance, Alfred Hofmann, the discoverer of LSD and psilocybin and author of many scientific works in the chemical-pharmaceutical field, has written:

> It seems evident, but here begins belief, that the primitive cell began following a plan. . . . A plan represents an idea, and an idea is spirit. . . . If even for the cell, the smallest unit of living organisms, an accidental origin is not imaginable, then less is this the case for the innumerable higher forms of life, for all the higher organisms of the plant and the animal kingdom. . . . In the same way as [a] cathedral emanates the idea and spirit of its architect, in every living organism the idea and the spirit of its creator become visible. The highest developed, the most differentiated, and the most complex organism of evolution is the human being, which means that human beings express more of their creator than all the other creatures (Hofmann, 1988, p. 9).

Western culture has held individual freedom as primary, but freedom for what? Our erroneous concept of freedom is that it consists in limitless satisfaction of personal appetites. This type of "freedom" in truth leads to profound dissatisfaction, and indeed is tantamount not to freedom but to bondage to the appetite for pleasure. Freedom obviously cannot be *awarded* to anyone, least of all by governments. Freedom means the ability to choose, but choices must be informed. Thus each individual must *win* a degree of freedom by following, by expressing, the higher laws of his or her nature. For, as we earlier argued, freedom and necessity or law are a pair of inseparable polarities. The epitome of freedom, known in all the religious traditions by various terms—for instance, enlightenment, liberation, nirvana, moksha, satori—is described as an experience in which the subject feels united with every other being and with everything that exists. It is a state wherein the experiencer equates his or her own good with that of others. Although mystical union is rare, something of the experience of unity is known to many who have stumbled onto the fact that what is most fulfilling is an endeavor with a larger purpose than merely personal gain. By a seeming paradox, to make the choice of the greater whole is the best way to express one's personal freedom, even one's uniqueness. Perhaps that is what Teilhard de Chardin meant when he employed the phrase "convergence differentiates."

In systems theory parlance, human societies are dynamic systems in the third state. A society's environment, in Ervin Laszlo's phrase, is both natural and social: "It is in part the biosphere and its various ecologies . . . and in part the sociosphere, made up of other societies and their infrastructures. . . . Unlike specific organizations . . . the networks of relations that bind individuals in entire nations, states and cultures cannot be designed; they emerge in the course of history. The degree of complexity attained in a modern society, though modest in comparision with an organism, exceeds by far that which its human members could achieve by purposeful design" (1987, p. 89).

As an autopoietic system our society can become destabilized and experience critical junctures, "bifurcations." These junctures are pregnant with chaos (which is *not* a total absence of order, as we saw) and regression, on the one hand, and with the possibility of a quantum leap to a higher level of order and functioning, on the other. The outcome is indeterminable, but nevertheless it is the result of the actions of the members of the system. I am not certain if systems theory speaks of the power of intentions and thoughts. But perennial philosophy (like depth and transpersonal psychology) recognizes that thought power is possessed by all. And it is probably the most potent power we have, for it is able to change the course of history and the lives of individuals.

The present state of world imbalance is the cumulative consequence of what has been thought and done over a long period of time—a mix, as we saw, of tremendous scientific and technological achievement, on the one hand, and serious shortcomings in terms of self-understanding and values, on the other. At any rate, the industrial era has now culminated in a crisis of global proportions.

Meanwhile, a *second* industrial revolution is now upon us—again a consequence of human creative genius in the fields of information, communication and automation. How appropriately will these new technologies be applied? Will they be subverted by the elite? Will the information revolution impede or obviate the future possibility of totalitarianism, with its brutalities and repression?

It would seem, when we reflect upon it, that the deeper significance of the industrial era may have been a totally contingent one: the profound intensification of societal interconnectedness and interdependence. For it is this existential condition that now forces us to revise our idea of reality, to re-examine our premises, values and relationships.

20

Order Amid Chaos

The imperative of every new age is a newly integrated world-view, a new synthesis of past wisdom and future aspirations and ideals. It is by responding to the periodic challenge of history that man can keep advancing on the road of evolution. And this response can become a creative advance only by bringing together in a comprehensive Weltanschauung *the latest findings in our knowledge of* fact and existence *on the one hand and freshly-won insights in the realm of* essence and value *on the other.*

Haridas Chaudhuri, *Being, Evolution and Immortality*

I have argued that several remarkable, simultaneous and interrelated global developments are impacting profoundly on human affairs— on thought, action and values in the economic, social and political realms— and on human consciousness and spirituality. As a simultaneous set, these unfoldments are unprecedented. What is more, they are strikingly convergent in that they all seem to bring to the fore, in new ways for our time, the holism of existence, the reality of wholeness.

In light of these developments, I would like to adduce, in this concluding part of our exploration of wholeness, the presentiments of three thinkers of the relatively recent past, because in retrospect they are seen as prophetic.

The Harvard sociologist Pitirim Sorokin[1] believed that we were in midst of a decline of what he termed the "Sensate" form of culture and society—a culture for whom reality and value are confined to that which can be seen, heard, touched, tasted and smelled; a culture that tends to cultivate scientific knowledge of the physical and biological

---

1. Sorokin's monumental 4-volume work *Social and Cultural Dyanamics* was written in 1937-1944.

properties of sensory reality, and to neglect religion and theology; a culture whose dominant ethic is invariably utilitarian and hedonistic. Sorokin felt that the Sensate Culture had brilliantly discharged its creative mission, especially in the fields of science, technology, fine arts, politics and economics, but that it was now in decay. He saw us as between two epochs—the dying Sensate Culture of our magnificent yesterday, and the coming culture of the creative tomorrow, a new Integral Order (Sorokin, 1975). Sorokin argued that none of our familiar ideologies, including capitalism, socialism, communism, collectivism, aristocracy and democracy, represent absolute values, and he held that even the nation-state and private property had outlived their period of greatest service to humankind.

The second prophetic thinker I have in mind is the Catholic paleontologist-mystic Pierre Teilhard de Chardin, several of whose works were initially published posthumously in the late 1950s. As Sir Julian Huxley wrote in his Introduction to *The Phenomenon of Man*, Teilhard effected a threefold synthesis—of the material and physical world with the world of mind and spirit; of the past with the future; and of variety with unity, the many with the one. Teilhard, too, envisioned a great transition. He believed that "the ills from which we are suffering have their seat in the very foundation of human thought," but also that we are entering the greatest period of change the world has ever known—a change involving the whole structure of human consciousness and the start of a fresh kind of life. In both *The Phenomenon of Man* and *The Future of Man*, Teilhard attested to his deep conviction about man's ultimate role and responsibility. In the latter book, he contrasts his view of human progress with those who fail to perceive this truth. To those he labels the "immobilists," the "passionless," the "inertia-ridden," the "pessimistic" camp, nothing changes. For them, "Human suffering, vice and war, although they may momentarily abate, recur from age to age with an increasing virulence. Even the striving after progress contributes to the sum of evil. . . . For the sake of human tranquility, in the name of Fact, and in defence of the sacred Established Order, the immobilists forbid the earth to move. Nothing changes, they say, or can change" (1964, pp. 11-12).

Teilhard expounded the nature of the change he perceived. "It is most striking that the morphological change of living creatures seems to have slowed down at the precise moment when Thought appeared on earth. . . . If we are to find a definitive answer to the question of the entitative progress of the Universe we must do so . . . by envisaging a world whose evolutionary capacity is *concentrated upon and confined to the human soul.* . . . What is the difference between ourselves, citizens of the twentieth century, and the earliest human beings whose soul is not entirely hidden from us? Organically speaking, the faculties of those remote forebears were probably the equal of our own. . . . To all appearance . . . the individual instrument of thought and action may be considered to have been finalized. But [in another dimension the] great superiority over Primitive Man which we have acquired, and which will be enhanced by our descendants in a degree perhaps undreamed-of by ourselves, is in the realm of self-knowledge; in our growing capacity to situate ourselves in space and time, to the point of becoming conscious of our place and responsibility in relation to the Universe" (p. 16).

Preceding these two influential thinkers by about half a century was H. P. Blavatsky. When crass materialism and imperialism were the order of the day in the West, she boldly challenged the assumptions of materialistic science and also the narrow theology of her time, and advanced concepts of consciousness, mind and matter that are increasingly corroborated today at the cutting edges of science and by depth and transpersonal psychology. Blavatsky was centrally concerned, among other fundamental questions, with the grand theme of cosmic and planetary evolution. (Notice that evolution preoccupied, in one way or another, all three of the seminal thinkers here mentioned.) I have already discussed Blavatsky's far-reaching propositions about involution/evolution, and shown that the presently emergent co-evolutionary theory corroborates, as far as it goes, the ideas she advanced. In place of the West's belief in the superiority of the white races (over even the venerable Chinese and Indian peoples), she expounded the unity of humankind, not merely in biological but in far deeper, cosmic terms. I think one may fairly say that today's singular impulse toward a synthesis of knowledge—a new appetite to integrate the insights of religion, philosophy and science— owes much to Blavatsky and the theosophical movement which she co-founded.[2]

---

2. The Theosophical Society was established initially in New York in 1875 and developed into an international theosophical movement which is dedicated to the encouragement of the synthesis of religion, philosophy and science and the realization that humanity is one and indivisible.

The Theosophical Society, while reserving for each member full freedom to interpret those teachings known as theosophy, is dedicated to preserving and realizing the ageless wisdom, which embodies both a world view and a vision of human self-transformation. This tradition is founded upon certain fundamental propositions:

The universe and all that exists within it are one interrelated and inter-dependent whole.

Every existent being—from atom to galaxy—is rooted in the same universal, life-creating Reality. This Reality is all-pervasive, but it can never be summed up in its parts, since it transcends all its expressions. It reveals itself in the purposeful, ordered, and meaningful processes of nature as well as in the deepest recesses of the mind and spirit.

Recognition of the unique value of every living being expresses itself in reverence for life, compassion for all, sympathy with the need of all individuals to find truth for themselves, and respect for all religious traditions. The ways in which these ideals become realities in individual life are both the privileged choice and the responsible act of every human being.

Central to the concerns of theosophy is the desire to promote understanding and brotherhood among people of all races, nationalities, philosophies, and religions. Therefore, all people, whatever their race, creed, sex, caste, or color, are invited to participate equally in the life and work of the Society. The Theosophical Society imposes no dogmas, but points toward the source of unity beyond all differences. Devotion to truth, love for all living beings, and commitment to a life of active altruism are the marks of the true theosophist.

The Theosophical World View[3]

Now Blavatsky postulated periodicity as a fundamental principle, second only to the unity of existence itself. In her schema, periodicity underlies and is reflected in the universal progression of all existents toward a higher life. She emphasized—and here is the point to which I would draw attention—that while change is constant and ubiqui-

---

3. A pamphlet published by the Theosophical Society in America.

tous, it is not random, and *never contravenes inner law.* (This is the conviction that underlies the Chinese view of change as embodied in the *I Ching.*) The cosmic dynamics are never merely random or blind or mechanical but, on the contrary, are an expression of inner law; moreover, inner law is not a blind, mechanical, deterministic law, but living and intelligent. It is a lawfulness that conduces to the convergence of necessity and creativity in nature and in human life, individually and collectively; a lawfulness that permits and promotes a progression at all levels to a higher life. She identified this most fundamental law as that known as "karma."

We have examined the doctrine of karma, and also the chaos theory of science, which strikingly parallels karma in several ways. Both karma and chaos theory, as pointed out, rest on the holistic principle, and pertain to the resolution of the tension between forces of instability and imbalance, on the one hand, and those of harmony and creativity, on the other. But it is the law of karma that here interests us. As noted, karma is the law of action and reaction, the cosmic and moral law that re-establishes balance and harmony wherever these are disturbed, and does so in a way that is not static but oriented toward the future. I would like now to apply the karmic principle to our present societal situation, and to show how remarkably planetary conditions illustrate the working of this law.

The present planetary scene seems anarchic and chaotic, characteristics which are generally understood to oppose order. But the doctrine of karma states (and chaos theory proposes) that even destabilizing events are subject to universal law. The dynamics that are observed operating in societal affairs today illustrate this teaching. There is marked disorder. At the same time, the problems are global and dynamically interrelated. What does this globality and interrelationship of outwardly diverse problems spell but inner law? As we earlier saw, mass poverty is closely connected with the short-sighted way more affluent segments of the population have pursued prosperity. There is fateful interconnection between industrial production of the raw-materials-intensive and energy-resources-intensive kind and the degradation of the environment. The environment is also degraded from necessity by those suffering from poverty. The pressures on land, especially in the poorest countries, result in a high incidence of natural disasters in those countries. In such regions as Africa's Sahel, we see the tragic and vicious cycle of poverty leading to environmental degradation, which leads in turn to even greater poverty. Desertification, a major threat to life on this planet, comes about as a result of complex interactions between humans, land and climate.

If development impacts on environment, environmental degradation, conversely, can dampen or reverse economic development. And perhaps the greatest threat to the earth's environment, to sustainable human progress and indeed to survival, is the potential for nuclear war. The latter possibility is in turn reinforced by the turmoil that goes hand in hand with abject poverty. Interconnected equally are world instability and the arms race, the latter itself inducing poverty. Similarly interlinked are poverty, international debt, inflation and the prevailing problems of competition in production, marketing and trade. In short, the different problems are both global and interconnected; they reinforce each other and constitute a major global crisis.

These characteristics of globality and interconnectedness attest, to repeat, to an internal order. It is an order that obviously embraces and interrelates the physical, the emotional, the mental and the moral or spiritual levels of societal existence. By virtue of its ineluctible operation our wrongs are now coming up to meet us everywhere, to paraphrase a famous line of Christopher Fry's in *A Sleep of Prisoners*. It is thus an order that we can ignore only at our peril. In the measure that we take appropriate action—which, as we are increasingly coming to understand, must include a fundamental change of consciousness on the part of a sufficient number of individuals—the inner rebalancing laws will have served as a timely warning and spur to a new era. Otherwise—that is, if the challenge and the opportunity are not met—we will undergo regression by virtue of the same cosmic laws.

The planetary scene may be described in another way. It is a situation wherein every commission and omission of ours, in any domain (be it chemistry, biology, ecology, economics, human rights or hot or cold war-making) and in any locality, sooner or later impact on all domains and localities.

The karma doctrine implies that all phenomena are infinitely interconnected in consciousness. This moral and spiritual truth, heretofore known only by saints and sages through direct insight, is now revealed to all through actual global conditions—conditions that are proof of the dynamic wholeness of the world and of a meaningful inner order.

Earlier we quoted a Soviet scholar's memorable pronouncement that *"everyone is responsible for everything."* His words remind me of a passage in an essay on karma written many years ago by the English Buddhist-theosophist, Christmas Humphreys. Humphreys recalls that according to the law of karma, each disturbance of harmony starts from some particular point and can only be restored by the reconverging to that same point of all the forces which were set in motion from it. He continues:

> That point is each of us. Hence utter and complete responsibility of every man for all that each man thinks and wills and does. There is therefore no escape from karma and it is useless to project our insufficiency beyond the ambit of our skin. We are self-responsible and everyself-responsible *(sic!)*, with the enormous dignity for every individual which flows from that tremendous truth. If I seem to be at times the plaything of fate, a pawn being played by a force I cannot control, this is, in the wider view, illusion. I made things as they are or helped to make them so. I can unmake them as and when I choose to begin, and no power on earth or God in heaven can stop me (Hanson, ed., 1971, p. 30).

It is as if the holism of existence were being illustrated to us on a planet-wide canvas by some mysterious force behind the scenes. But that force is of course terrestrial humanity itself. Ours is the freedom of choice. Wisdom, both ancient and modern, tells us that we are the authors of our own destiny, both individually and collectively. Now we have new evidence supporting this truth: global interdependence. It is ourselves that have brought this situation about, through our knowledge, invention, motivations, values and activities over a period of some centuries.

In pragmatic terms, the situation is this: rich and poor countries alike are constrained to live together on this finite planet; we are presently carelessly and dangerously impairing our natural support system; population growth, especially in the poorest countries, is exponential; we possess weapons that could extinguish all life on this planet; and, finally, but not least, we have all the means we need to resolve our self-made dilemma. The technology is available, and we also have the powers of reason and compassion needed to reverse our course. The question is mainly of mobilizing the will to change.

Unquestionably, a critical number of sufficiently enlightened people acting in concert *could* set the relevent inner forces in motion with sufficient momentum to lift human society into a new orbit—thereby benefiting all life on our planet. Will it happen? No one can predict with certainty what choices people will make. What is clearly evi-

FOURFOLD HAPPINESS

Happiness, which is the object of all human endeavor, involves fourfold joy: natural, transcendental, creative, and dialectic. Natural joy consists just in existing, in breathing the breath of life, in enduring as an integral part of the natural order. . . . The transcendental joy is the joy of immediate existential contact with the eternal, or the nontemporal dimension of Being . . . the joy which flows profusely from the Fount of all being. . . . But the nontemperal is inseparable from the creative. Being is inseparable from becoming. . . . The affirmation of the creative aspect of Being is the root of creative joy. . . . Fourthly, there is the dialectical joy. It is the joy of surmounting obstacles and conquering opposition. In affirming the world as creative self-expression, an encounter with the forces of ignorance and inertia, with the forces of darkness and evil, is only to be expected. . . . The joy of squarely facing opposition, or overcoming resistances, is the dialectical joy. All suffering incidental to such an heroic approach is transmuted into an element of the overruling harmony of dialectical joy.

Haridas Chaudhuri, *Mastering the Problems of Living*

dent, however, is the emergence of a new type of consciousness on Planet Earth, one which gives rise to a universalism that transcends religion, race, culture and sex. This vision is as yet to be found only among a small minority, but these individuals are spread widely over the terrestrial landscape. Theirs is an outlook which is at once inner directed and imbued with a sense of relatedness to the here-and-now—a sense of concern, compassion, responsibility and creative intentionality. The activism which it fosters cannot be characterized as altruism or pragmatism: it is the way of self-fulfillment; a caring which is its own reward.

There is yet another aspect to this movement in consciousness. Notwithstanding that the impulse toward wholeness has been eclipsed by separative tendencies in a large and powerful portion of human society, it has always been present and viable. Our own neglect of this dynamic only ensured that sooner or later we would reencounter it all the more forcibly.

Epilogue

Walt Whitman sang of the Ensemble, not just of parts, and he sang of all days, not just of a day. In his time, he embraced the Whole—in his inimitable poet's way—and looking thus at the objects of the Universe, he found no particle of any but had reference to the soul.

The cosmic process is impartible and mind-pervaded. In our day, science has uncovered this truth—in its own inimitable way. From the cosmos—the dynamic matrix, the "mind stuff"—issue alike infinitesimal "particles" and human beings, all capable of intercommunicating, not only locally but also, instantaneously, beyond space-time.

Emanating from and pervaded by boundless Reality, the manifested universe is all of a wholeness, life within life, interpenetrating, impartible. Yet each life is specific and special—at once unique and reflective of myriad lives.

This is true even here on our tiny Planet Earth, swimming in the vastnesses of space. What are size and distance when every point of entry can lead to the center where all knowing converges, where the inner is the outer, and the outer the inner?

Each of us is both unique and a microcosm of the Whole: each is at once scientist/artist/mystic. Hence, each is equipped both to contribute something of value to the co-creation and to unite and be one with the Whole.

References

Amidon, Elias V., and Elizabeth J. Roberts. 1987. "Gaian Consciousness," *ReVision*, vol. 9, 2.

Anderson, Walter Truett (ed.). 1983. *Rethinking Liberalism*. New York: Avon Books, Discus.

Arber, Agnes. 1967. *The Manifold and the One*. Wheaton, Il.: Theosophical Publishing House, A Quest Book.

Augros, Robert, and George Stanciu. 1987. *The New Biology*. Boston: Shambhala.

Barborka, Geoffrey, A. 1972. *The Divine Plan*. Madras, Adyar: Theosophical Publishing House.

Barnett, Lincoln. 1968. *The Universe and Dr. Einstein*. New York: Bantam.

Barnstone, Willis (trans.). 1972. *The Poems of St. John of the Cross*. New York: New Directions.

Bateson, Gregory. 1980. *Mind and Nature—A Necessary Unity*. New York: Bantam.

—— and Mary Catherine Bateson. 1988. *Angels Fear*. New York: Bantam.

Blavatsky, H.P. 1888. *The Secret Doctrine*. Collected Writings 1888, 3 vols., 1979. Madras, Adyar: Theosophical Publishing House.

——. 1877. *Isis Unveiled*. Collected Writings 1877, 2 vols., 1972. Wheaton, Il: Theosophical Publishing House.

——. 1889. Second edition, 1946. *The Key to Theosophy*. Pasadena, Calif.: Theosophical University Press.

Bloom, Allan. 1987. *The Closing of the American Mind*. New York: Simon and Schuster.

Bohm, David. 1983. *Wholeness and the Implicate Order*. London: Routledge, Ark Paperbacks.

Bohm, David, and F. David Peat. 1987. *Science, Order, and Creativity*. New York and Toronto: Bantam.

Boulding, Elise. 1988. *Building a Global Civic Culture*. New York and London: Teachers College Press, Columbia University.

Bradley, T.H. 1914. *Essays in Truth and Reality*. London: Oxford University Press.

Breck, A.D. and W. Yourgrau (eds.). 1974. *Biology, History, and Natural Philosophy*. New York: Plenum/Rosetta.

Briggs, John P., and F. David Peat. 1984. *Looking Glass Universe*. New York: Simon & Schuster, Cornerstone Library.

Brown, Lester R. 1986. "Redefining National Security," *State of the World 1986*. New York and London: W.W. Norton & Company.

———. 1987. "Analyzing the Demographic Trap," *State of the World 1987*. New York and London: W. W. Norton & Company.

Brown, Lester R. and Edward C. Wolf. 1988. "Reclaiming the Future," *State of the World 1988*. New York and London: W. W. Norton & Company.

Bruteau, Beatrice. 1979. *The Psychic Grid*. Wheaton, Il.: Theosophical Publishing House, A Quest Book.

Campbell, Joseph. 1972. *The Hero with a Thousand Faces*. Princeton, N.J.: Princeton University Press, Bollingen Series XVII.

Capra, Fritjof. 1977. *The Tao of Physics*. New York: Bantam.

———. 1983. *The Turning Point*. New York: Bantam.

Carroll, Raymond. 1985. *The Future of the United Nations*. New York, London, Toronto, Sydney: Franklin Watts, An Impact Book.

Chandler, William U. 1986. "Investing in Children," *State of the World 1986*. New York and London: W. W. Norton & Company.

Chang, Garma. 1971. *The Buddhist Teaching of Totality*. Pennsylvania: Pennsylvania University Press.

Chaudhuri, Haridas. 1974. *Being, Evolution & Immortality*. Wheaton, Il.: Theosophical Publishing House, A Quest Book.

———. 1975. *Mastering the Problems of Living*. Wheaton, Il: Theosophical Publishing House, A Quest Book.

———. 1977. *The Evolution of Integral Consciousness*. Wheaton, Il.: Theosophical Publishing House, A Quest Book.

———. 1981. *Integral Yoga*. Wheaton, Il.: Theosophical Publishing House, A Quest Book.

———. 1984. *Modern Man's Religion*. San Francisco: Cultural Integration Fellowship.

Cranston, Sylvia, and Carey Williams. 1984. *Reincarnation—A New Horizon in Science, Religion, and Society*. New York: Crown Publishers, Julian Press.

Denton, Michael. 1986. *Evolution: A Theory in Crisis*. Bethesda, Maryland: Adler & Adler.

Dillistone, F.W. 1986. *The Power of Symbols in Religion and Culture*. New York: Crossroad.

Dossey, Larry. 1982. "Space, Time & Medicine," *ReVision*, vol. 5, 2.

Einstein, Albert. 1977. *Out of My Later Years*. Secaucus, New Jersey: The Citadel Press.

Eisler, Diane. 1987. *The Chalice and the Blade*. New York: Harper and Row.

Ekins, Paul (ed.). 1986. *The Living Economy*. London and New York: Routledge & Kegan Paul.

Ellwood, Robert. 1980. *Mysticism and Religion*. Englewood Cliffs, N.J.: Prentice-Hall.

———. 1982. *Many Peoples, Many Faiths*. Englewood Cliffs, N.J.: Prentice-Hall.

———. 1986. *Theosophy*. Wheaton, Il.: Theosophical Publishing House, A Quest Book.

Fagg, Lawrence W. 1985. *Two Faces of Time*. Wheaton, Ill.: Theosophical Publishing House, A Quest Book.

Feller, Gordon, S.R. Schwenninger, and D. Singerman (eds.). 1981. *Peace and World Order Studies, A Curriculum Guide*, Third Edition. New York: Transnational Academic Program, Institute for World Order.

Ferencz, Benjamin B. 1985. *A Common Sense Guide to World Peace*. London, Rome and New York: Oceana Publications.

——— and Ken Keyes, Jr. 1988. *PlanetHood*. Coos Bay, Or.: Vision Books.

Ferguson, Marilyn. 1987. *The Aquarian Conspiracy*. Los Angeles: J.P. Tarcher.

George, Susan. 1983. *How the Other Half Dies*. Totowa, New Jersey: Rowman & Allanheld.

Gleick, James. 1988. *Chaos*. New York: Penguin.

Goodwin, B. C. 1989. "Organisms and Minds as Dynamic Forms," *Leonardo*, vol. 22, 1.

Gorbachev, Mikhail. 1988. *Perestroika*. New York: Harper & Row, Perennial Library.

Govinda, Lama Anagarika. 1976. *Creative Meditation and Multi-Dimensional Consciousness*. Wheaton, Il.: Theosophical Publishing House, A Quest Book.

Gran, Guy. 1983. *Development By People*. New York: Praeger Publishers.

Green, Elmer and Alyce. 1984. "Biofeedback and Tranformation," *The American Theosophist*, Special Issue, Spring.

Grof, Stanislav. 1986. "New Paradigm Thinking in the Life Sciences," *ReVision*, vol. 9, 1.

——— (ed.). 1986. *Ancient Wisdom and Modern Science*. Albany, N.Y.: State University of New York Press.

Gromyko, Anatoly, and Martin Hellman (eds.). 1988. *Breakthrough*. New York: Walker and Company.

Hanson, Virginia (ed.). 1971. *H.P. Blavatsky and the Secret Doctrine*. Wheaton, Il.: Theosophical Publishing House, A Quest Book Original.

——— and Rosemarie Stewart (eds.). 1981. *Karma, The Universal Law of Harmony*. Wheaton, Il.: Theosophical Publishing House, A Quest Book.

Happold, F.C. 1966. *Religious Faith and Twentieth-Century Man*. London: Penguin.

———. 1981. *Mysticism*. London: Penguin.

Haraway, Donna Jeanne. 1976. *Crystals, Fabrics, and Fields: Metaphors of Organicism in Twentieth-Century Developmental Biology*. New Haven and London: Yale University Press.

Harman, Willis, and Howard Rheingold. 1984. *Higher Creativity*. Los Angeles: Jeremy P. Tarcher.

———. 1986. *Newsletter of the Institute of Noetic Sciences*, Spring.

———. 1988. *Global Mind Change*. Indianapolis, Indiana: Knowledge Systems, in cooperation with the Institute of Noetic Sciences.

Harris, Harold (ed.) 1976. *Astride the Two Cultures, Arthur Koestler at 70*. New York: Random House.

Head, Joseph and S.L Cranston (compilers and eds.). 1979. *Reincarnation: The Phoenix Fire Mystery*. New York: Julian Press/Crown Publishers.

Henderson, Hazel. (1978) 1980. *Creating Alternative Futures*. New York: Perigee Books, published by G.P. Putnam's Sons.

———. 1981. *The Politics of the Solar Age—Alternatives to Economics*. New York: Anchor Press/Doubleday. Also, Indianapolis, Knowledge Systems, Inc. (1989).

Herbert, Nick. 1985. *Quantum Reality*. New York: Anchor Press/Doubleday.

Hofmann, Albert. 1988. "The Transmitter-Receiver Concept of Reality," *ReVision*, vol. 10, 4.

Humphreys, Christmas. 1971. *Walk On!* Wheaton, Il: Theosophical Publishing House, A Quest Book.

Huxley, Aldous. 1970. *The Perennial Philosophy*. Harper & Row.

Jantsch, Erich. 1980. *The Self-Organizing Universe*. Pergamon Press.

Johnson, Raynor C. 1954. *The Imprisoned Splendour*. Wheaton, Il.: Theosophical Publishing House, A Quest Book.

Jones, Roger S. 1982. *Physics as Metaphor*. New York and Scarborough, Ontario: New American Library, A Meridian Book.

Keys, Donald. 1982. *Earth At Omega*. Boston: Branden Press.

Koestler, Arthur. 1959. *The Sleepwalkers*. New York: Grosset & Dunlap, The Universal Library.

———. 1967. *The Act of Creation*. New York: A Laurel Edition, Dell Publishing Co.

——— 1973. *The Roots of Coincidence*. New York: Vintage Books, Random House.

Kumar, Satish (ed.). 1981. *The Schumacher Lectures*. Harper & Row.

Lappé, Frances Moore and Joseph Collins. 1986. *World Hunger*. New York: Grove Press, A Food First Book.

Laszlo, Ervin. 1987. *Evolution, The Grand Synthesis*. Boston & London: Shambhala: New Science Library.

Lemkow, Anna. 1981. "Of Holism, Freedom, and the Creative Meeting of Opposites," *ReVision*, vol. 4, 2.

LeShan, Lawrence, and Henry Margenau. 1982. *Einstein's Space & Van Gogh's Sky*. New York: Macmillan Publishing Co.

Lipnack, Jessica and Jeffrey Stamps. 1986. *The Networking Book: People Connecting with People*. New York: Methuen.

Lovelock, James. 1979. *Gaia: A New Look at Life on Earth*. London and New York: Oxford University Press.

———. 1988. *The Ages of Gaia: A Biography of Our Living Earth*. New York: Norton.

Loye, David. 1983. *The Sphinx and the Rainbow*. Boulder & London: Shambhala, New Science Library.

———. 1986. "New Paradigm Thinking in the Social Sciences and Business," *ReVision*, vol. 9, 1.

Lutz, Mark A. and Kenneth Lux. 1988. *Humanistic Economics*. New York: Bootstrap Press.

Margenau, Henry. 1987. *The Miracle of Existence*. Boston & London: New Science Library, Shambhala.

Massanari, Ronald L. 1988. "Re-Visioning Education," *ReVision*, vol. 2,2.

Maturana, Humberto R. & Francisco J. Varela. 1987. *The Tree of Knowledge*. Boston & London: New Science Library, Shambhala.

Meier, Gerald M. and Dudley Seers (eds.). 1984. *Pioneers in Development*. A World Bank Publication. New York: Oxford University Press.

Mendlovitz, Saul H. and R.B.J. Walker (eds.). 1987. *Towards a Just World Peace*. Butterworths.

Mesarovic, Mihaljo and Eduard Pestel. 1976. *Mankind At the Turning Point*. The Second Report to the Club of Rome. New York: New American Library, A Signet Book.

Mische, Gerald and Patricia. 1977. *Toward A Human World Order*. New York/Ramsey, N.J.: Paulist Press.

Mische, Patricia. 1985. *Star Wars and the State of Our Souls*. New York: Harper & Row.

Morowitz, Harold J. 1975. "Biology as a Cosmological Science," *Main Currents in Modern Thought*, Retrospective Issue, November 17, 1940-November 17, 1975, vol. 32, 2-5.

———. 1987. *Cosmic Joy & Local Pain*. New York: Charles Scribner and Sons.

Naisbitt, John. 1984. *Megatrends*. New York: Warner Book.

Nasr, Seyyed Hossein. 1987. *Islamic Art and Spirituality*. Albany, N.Y.: State University of New York Press.

Needleman, Jacob (ed.). 1974. *The Sword of Gnosis—Metaphysics, Cosmology, Tradition, Symbolism*. Baltimore, Maryland: Penguin Books.

———. 1976. *A Sense of the Cosmos—The Encounter of Modern Science and Ancient Truth*. New York: E.P. Dutton.

———. 1982. *The Heart of Philosophy*. New York: Alfred A. Knopf.

Nicholson, Shirley. 1985. *Ancient Wisdom—Modern Insight*. Wheaton, Il.: Theosophical Publishing House, A Quest Book.

O'Regan, Brendan. 1987. "Healing, Remission and Miracle Cures," Institute of Noetic Sciences, Berkeley, Special Report.

Osborn, Arthur. 1969. *The Cosmic Womb*. Wheaton, Il.: Theosophical Publishing House, A Quest Book.

Parrinder, Geoffrey. 1987. *Encountering World Religions*. New York: Crossroad.

———. 1976. *Mysticism in the World's Religions*. New York: Oxford University Press.

Peat, F. David. 1987. *Synchronicity, The Bridge Between Matter and Mind*. New York: Bantam Books.

Penfield, Wilder. 1975. *The Mystery of the Mind*. Princeton: Princeton University Press.

Perry, Whitall N. 1986. *A Treasury of Traditional Wisdom*. San Francisco: Harper & Row.

Polanyi, Michael. 1962. *Personal Knowledge*. Chicago: The University of Chicago Press.

Polanyi, Michael, and Harry Prosch. 1975. *Meaning*. Chicago: The University of Chicago Press.

Pollard, Jeffrey W. (ed.). 1984. *Evolutionary Theory: Paths into the Future*. Chichester, New York: John Wiley and Sons.

Portmann, Adolf. "Colors of Life," *Main Currents in Modern Thought*, Retrospective Issue, November 17, 1940-November 17, 1975, vol. 32, nos. 2-5.

Power, Thomas Michael. 1988. *The Economic Pursuit of Quality*. Armonk, New York and London: M.E. Sharpe, Inc.

Prem, Shri Krishna and Sri Madhava Ashish. 1969. *Man, The Measure of All Things*. Wheaton, Il.: Theosophical Publishing House.

Prigogine, Ilya and Isabelle Stengers. 1984. *Order Out of Chaos: Man's New Dialogue with Nature*. New York: Bantam Books.

Purucker, G. de. 1974. *Fountain-Source of Occultism*. Pasadena, Ca.: Theosophical University Press.

Ravindra, Ravi. 1984. *Whispers from the Other Shore*. Wheaton, Il.: Theosophical Publishing House, A Quest Book.

Reardon, Betty A. 1988. *Comprehensive Peace Education*. New York and London: Teachers College Press, Columbia University.

———. (ed.) 1988. *Educating for Global Responsibility*. New York and London: Teachers College Press, Columbia University.

Renner, Michael. 1989. "Enhancing Global Security," *State of the World 1989*. New York and London: W.W. Norton & Company.

Rosen, Steven. 1982. "Wholeness and Psi: The Implications of David Bohm's Concepts for Parapsychology." *theta*, vol. 10, 4.

Ross, David P. and Peter J. Usher. 1986. *From the Roots Up*. New York: Bootstrap Press.

Ross, Nancy Wilson. 1966. *Three Ways of Asian Wisdom*. New York: Simon and Schuster, 1966.

Satin, Mark. 1978. *New Age Politics—Healing Self and Society*. Vancouver: Whitecap Books with Fairweather Press.

Schmookler, Andrew Bard. *The Parable of the Tribes*. Berkeley, Los Angeles, London: University of California Press, 1984.

Scholem, Gershom G. 1973. *Major Trends in Jewish Mysticism*. New York: Schocken Books.

Schroedinger, Erwin. 1954. *Nature and the Greeks*. Cambridge: Cambridge University Press.

Schumacher, E.F. 1975 (originally published in 1973 by Blond and Briggs, London). *Small Is Beautiful*. Harper & Row, Perennial Library.

———. 1978. *A Guide for the Perplexed*. Harper Colophon Books, Harper & Row.

Schuon, Frithjof. 1953. *The Transcendent Unity of Religions* (Peter Townsend translator). New York: Pantheon.

Sheldrake, Rupert. 1981. *A New Science of Life—The Hypothesis of Formative Causation*. Los Angeles: J.P. Tarcher.

———. 1987. *Noetic Sciences Review*, Spring.

Sloan, Douglas (ed.). 1984. *Toward the Recovery of Wholeness: Knowledge, Education, and Human Values*. New York and London: Teachers College Press, Columbia University.

Smith, Andrew P. 1984. "Mutiny on the Beagle," *ReVision*, vol 7, 1.

Smith, E. Lester (ed.). 1975. *Intelligence Came First*. Wheaton, Il.: Theosophical Publishing House, A Quest Book.

———. (ed.). 1975. *The Universal Flame*. Madras, Adyar: Theosophical Publishing House.

Smith, Huston. 1977. *Forgotten Truth—The Primordial Tradition*. Harper Colophon Books, Harper & Row.

———. 1984. *Beyond the Post-Modern Mind.* Wheaton, Il.: Theosophical Publishing House, A Quest Book.

Smuts, Jan Christian. 1926. *Evolution and Holism*. New York: Macmillan.

Sorokin, Pitirim A. 1975. "Three Basic Trends of Our Times," *Main Currents in Modern Thought, Retrospective Issue*, November 17, 1940 - November 17, 1975, vol. 32, nos. 2-5.

Spanier, John. 1985. *The Games Nations Play*. Washington, D.C.: Congressional Press.

Swimme, Brian. 1984. *The Universe is a Green Dragon—A Cosmic Creation Story*. Santa Fe, New Mexico: Bear & Company.

———. 1986. "The Cosmic Story," *ReVision*, vol. 9, 1.

Tart, Charles T. 1987. *Waking Up*. Boston: New Science Library, Shambhala.

Teilhard de Chardin, Pierre. 1964. *The Future of Man*. New York: Harper & Row.

———. 1965. *The Phenomenon of Man*. Harper Colophon Books, Harper & Row.

Thomas, Lewis. 1975. *The Lives of a Cell*. New York: Bantam.

Tillich, Paul. 1969. *My Search for Absolutes*. New York: Simon and Schuster.

Toffler, Alvin. 1985. *Previews & Premises*. New York: Bantam Books.

Walker, R.B. J. 1988. *One World, Many Worlds: Struggles for a Just World Peace*. Boulder: Lynne Rienner Publishers. London: Zed Books.

Weber, Renée. 1986. *Dialogues with Scientists and Sages: The Search for Unity*. London and New York: Routledge & Kegan Paul.

———. 1975. "The Good, the True and the Beautiful," *Main Currents in Modern Thought*, Retrospective Issue, November 17, 1940—November 17, 1975, vol. 32, nos. 2-5.

Weisz, Paul B. and Richard N. Keogh. 1977. *Elements of Biology*, Fourth Edition. McGraw-Hill Book Company.

Whitehead, Alfred North. 1967 (Lowell Lectures, 1925). *Science and the Modern World*. New York: Free Press.

Wilber, Ken. 1977. *The Spectrum of Consciousness*. Wheaton, Il.: Theosophical Publishing House, A Quest Book.

———. 1980. *The Atman Project*. Wheaton, Il.: Theosophical Publishing House.

———. 1981. *Up From Eden—A Transpersonal View of Human Evolution*. New York: Anchor Press/Doubleday.

———.1981. *No Boundary—Eastern and Western Approaches to Personal Growth*. Boulder & London: Shambhala.

——— (ed.). 1982. *The Holographic Paradigm*. Boulder & London: Shambhala.

———. 1983. *Eye to Eye, The Quest for the New Paradigm*. Garden City, New York: Anchor Books, Anchor Press/Doubleday.

——— (ed.). 1984. *Quantum Questions—Mystical Writings of the World's Great Physicists*. Boston & London: Shambhala.

Williams, Jay G. 1978. *Yeshua Buddha*. Wheaton, Il.: Theosophical Publishing House, A Quest Book.

Wood, Ernest. 1967. *The Seven Rays*. Wheaton, Il.: Theosophical Publishing House, A Quest Book.

———. 1973. *Seven Schools of Yoga*. Wheaton, Il.: Theosophical Publishing House, A Quest Book.

World Bank. 1986. *The World Bank Atlas, 1986*. Washington, D.C.

———. 1986. *Poverty and Hunger*. Washington, D.C.

World Commission on Environment and Development. 1987. *Our Common Future*. New York: Oxford University Press.

Zimmer, Heinrich. Edited by Joseph Campbell. 1971. *Philosophies of India*. Princeton, N.J.: Bollingen /Series XXVI, Princeton University Press.

Zonneveld, Leo (ed.). 1985. *Humanity's Quest for Unity* (proceedings of a United Nations/University for Peace Teilhard Colloquium). Netherlands: Mirananda and Wasenaar.

Zukov, Gary. 1979. *The Dancing Wu Li Masters, An Overview of the New Physics*. New York: William Morrow and Company.

———. 1989. *The Seat of the Soul*. New York: Simon and Schuster.

Index

Abraham, Ralph, 112

Absolute, the: an essential consensus concerning, 24-25; significance of for unity, 25; transcends all religions, philosophies, ideologies, and theories, 28; statements about, 49; a belief of all religions, 181; provides ultimate meaning in daily life, 200; and the higher values, 219.

Activism: as self-fulfillment, 298

Activists: and the global-local connection, 276-278

Adamovich, Ales, 282

Advaita philosophy, 26

Aeneas, 180

Aid to poor countries, 239-243; disadvantageous position of poor vis-à-vis industrialized countries, 240; inequalities within poor countries, 241; questionable value of large-scale projects, 241; and self-reliance, 241, 242, 243; treatment accorded poor countries, 242; New International Economic Order

(NIEO), 242; recommendations in *Our Common Future*, 243, 247; aid to Africa, 243. *See also* Hunger; Third world; Economics; Technology

Ain Soph, 24, 26

Akasa, 116

Alger, Chadwick F., and Saul H. Mendlovitz, 276

Allah, 24, 25, 175

Amidon, Elias V., and Elizabeth J. Roberts, 109

Amnesty International, 251

Aquinas, St. Thomas, 37, 50

Arber, Agnes, 182, 184

Archimedes, 59

Aristocracy, 292

Aristotelian logic, 9, 30

Aristotle, 59, 87

Arnold, Sir Edward, 213

Art: Nature's, 146-148; in science, 82-84; in the Islamic faith, 175; of living, 215

Aryans, 193

Ashish, Sri Madhava, 133, 211

Augros, Robert, and George Stanciu, 106, 124, 145

Aurobindo, Sri, 28, 130

Autopoiesis, 139

Bacon, Roger, 59
Barborka, Geoffrey A., 16, 132
Bekhtereva, Natalia, 281
Belchuk, Alexander I, 281
Bell, J.S., 71
Bell's Theorem. *See* Quantum physics
Belousov-Zhabotinsky reaction, 114
Bendit, Phoebe D., 167, 168
Berdyaev, Nikolai, 273
Bernal, J.D., 100
Berry, Thomas, 108, 203
Bertalanffy, Ludwig von. *See* Von Bertalanffy
Bhagavad Gita, 174
Bible, the, 35
Biofeedback, 155-156
Biology: still in its infancy, 95-96, 100, 144; preponderantly mechanistic, 96; overlapping many fields, 96-97; assumes accidental origin of life, 97; dissenters in, 99; compared with physics, 99, 100; its data reveal the impartibility and holism of life, 101-108; mechanists' self-contradictions, 140; morphogenetic fields, 141-145. *See also* Life, origin of; Living nature; Evolution; Molecular biology; Genetics; Gaia; Systems approach
Blake, William, 90, 132
Blavatsky, H.P., 16, 25, 28; on numberless universes, 98; regarding a cosmological biology, 99, 108, 116, 126; on evolution, 128-132; 132 n,
133, 148, 192, 206, 213, 214, 293; on change and inner law, 294-295
Bloom, Allan, 285
Bodhi. See Mystical union.
Bohm, David: on knowledge, values, and society, 11, 17, 19, 20, 70, 71, 72-73, 75, 80, 99; on knowledge, 42, 148; on wholeness and the implicate order, 86-91, 220; on the good, 221; on insight, 221 n, 230; and F. David Peat, 89, 145, 159
Bohr, Niels, 66, 69, 70, 86, 204
Boulding, Elise, 242-243, 278
Boulding, Kenneth E., 283
Bradley, F.H. 219
Brahman, 24, 25
Brain: and the self, 34; and mind, 149-156; as computer, 151, 152; and the psi faculties, 163; states of and paranormal perceptions, 164, 166
Broglie, Prince Louis de. *See* De Broglie
Brown, Lester R., 237; *et al:* on militarization, 249; on getting onto a sustainable economic path, 263; on international cooperation on environment, 265
Bruntland, Madame Gro Harlem, 247 n
Bruteau, Beatrice, 43
Buddha, the, 21, 47, 180, 194
Buddha-nature, 25, 183-184
Buddhism, 175-176; the Middle Way, 189, 209, 214

Buddhist temples, 190
Burlatsky, Fyodor M., 281

Campbell, Joseph, 179, 180, 191
Capitalism, 243, 260, 292
Capra, Fritof, 69, 70, 77, 86, 108, 154, 264
Cartesian dualism, 61
Castells, Manuel, 259, 260, 262, 269
Category error, 52, 178
Causality: in the biological realm, 143; in Newtonian science, 157; and indeterminism, 158, 159; in the interdependent society, 158-159; in the systems approach, 160
Chandler, William U., 246 n
Chang, Garma, 211
Chaos science, 115-119, 295; and holism, 117, 118, 119
Chaudhuri, Haridas, 28, 49, 50, 192, 195, 219; on the Absolute, 27; on dogmatism, 27; on man's nature, 36; on the two inseparable dimensions of reality, 138; on happiness, 298
Christ, 21. *See also* Jesus
Christ-nature, 25, 183-184
Christianity, 174, 194
Committee for a Just World Peace, 274
Communism, 292
Complementarity. *See* Quantum physics
Complexity, sciences of, 112-113
Confucius, 194

Consciousness: as viewed in mechanism and nondualism, respectively, 32; and the implicate order, 88; primacy of, 98, 166; irreducible to matter, 149-152, 156
Copernicus, 87
Cousins, Norman, 154
Craig, Jim and Marge, 274
Creationists, 122, 178; conflict with evolutionists nullified in nondualism, 132
Crick, Francis, 7, 127

Darwin, Charles Robert, 113, 121, 122, 123, 129, 142
De Broglie, Prince Louis, 66, 204
Delphic injunction, 36, 37
Democracy, 292
Denton, Michael, 125
De Purucker, G., 132
Descartes, René, 60, 61, 62, 62 n, 79, 79 n, 205
Dirac, Paul, 66
Disarmament, 257-258, 279
Dissipative structures, 114, 136, 139
Dobzhansky, T., 105, 123
Dogmatism, 28, 51
Dossey, Larry, M.D., 152
Dynamic systems science, 116 n

Earth, as a living whole, 108-109, 284. *See also* Gaia hypothesis
Eccles, Sir John, 34, 150, 153
Economics: in historical perspective, 228-229; mechanis-

tic character and values of, 229-237; and crisis of manageability, 230, 331; E.F. Schumacher's critique of, 230, 231, 232, 233; criterion of profit maximization, 230, 232; a holistic reorientation, 230; indiscriminate growth as panacea, 233; and social costs of production, 233; deficiencies of the GNP index, 233, 233 n, 234, 235; and the informal economy, 234, 235; and the market, 235-236; and gross economic and social inequalities, 236-237; requirements for getting on a sustainable path, 263; The Other Economic Summit (TOES), 268 n. *See also* Technology; Industry; Environment; Third world; Aid to poor countries; Politics

Eddington, Sir Arthur, 19, 204

Education, wholeness in the field of, 285-286

Eigen, Manfred, 134

Einstein, Albert, 20, 66, 73, 74, 75, 76, 77, 143; on science and religion, 201, 204

Eisenbud, Jules, 165

Ekins, Paul, 268 n

Eliade, Mircea, 179

Ellwood, Robert, 98, 132, 171, 172, 190, 196, 198

Emerson, Ralph Waldo, 25

Environment, 230, 232, 233, 234, 236, 247; international cooperation on, 265

Epistemology, 47

Epstein, William, 257 n

Evolution: as roughly outlined by the organization of living matter on earth, 102-108; Darwinian theory of, 122; neo-Darwinism, 123-126; from the perspective of perennial philosophy, 128-132; and consciousness, 131; as a holistic process, 128-131; *co*-evolution, an emergent paradigm, 132-137; central to the thought of Sorokin, Teilhard, and Blavatsky, 291-295. *See also* Life, origin of; Systems approach; Genetics; Order: through fluctuations; Morphogenetic fields; Form: Sheldrake's theory

Falk, Joe, 273

Falk, Richard, 273, 274, 275, 277

Faraday, Michael, 65

Ferencz, Benjamin B., 251, 252, 253; and Ken Keyes, Jr., 254, 255

Ferguson, Marilyn, 156

Firsoff, W.A., 98

Force field(s), 65, 143, 143 n. *See also* Morphogenetic fields

Form(s): unique expressions, 29; vehicles for life, 29; primacy of over components, 105; organicists' approach to, 141; theory of causative formation, 144; traditional religious, 182-183, 184-185. *See also* Morphogenetic fields

Frank, Jerome, 282

Freedom and wholeness, 287-288

Freedom-determinism controversy, 64

Frolov, I.T., 280

Fromm, Erich, 274

Fry, Christopher, 296

Fundamentalism, religious, 25, 195, 196

Gaia hypothesis, 108-109

Galbraith, J. K. 236

Galileo, Galilei, 60, 61, 62, 87, 89

Gandhi, Mohandas K., 233

General Systems Theory, 81, 109. *See also* Complexity, sciences of

Genetics: and neo-Darwinism, 124, 125

George, Susan, 245

Glasnost, 8, 280

Gleick, James, 116, 117, 118, 119

Global thinking, 282

God, 24, 25, 174, 175; esoteric understanding of, 182, 183-184; affirmative and negative ways to, 188-189, 194, 195

Godhead, 24

Goodwin, Brian C., 142, 143, 144

Gorbachev, Mikhail: military superiority an anachronism, 250, 279, 280, 281

Gould, Stephen Jay, 124

Govinda, Lama Anagarika, 24, 189, 215, 216; on the preciousness of form, 29; on

transcending either/or logic, 31; on the complete human being, 31; on man's oneness, 36; on intuitive knowledge, 46, 51, 116, 159; on the integration of Eastern and Western religious values, 188

Gran, Guy, 240 n, 243, 244 n

Grassroots movements for social change, 275-276, 277. *See also* Activists and the global-local connection

Green, Elmer and Alyce, 155, 165

Grof, Stanislav, 165

Gromyko, Anatoly A., 282

Happold, F.C. 48, 180, 181

Haraway, Donna Jeanne, 144

Harman, Willis, and Howard Rheingold, 156

Harrison, Ross G., 144

Hastings, Arthur, 165

Haynes, Renée, 163

Healing, 154. *See also* Medicine; World Health Organization

Heisenberg, Werner, 66,70, 80, 86, 204

Heitler, Walter, 86

Henderson, Hazel, 230, 233, 235, 264, 266, 267, 275; and Robert Theobald, 267

Herbert, Nick, 86

Hierarchy: traditional, 16-18; contrasted with mechanistic order, 17; and reductionism, 18-19; in the organization of "inanimate" and "animate matter" on earth, 102-108;

and evolution, 106, 128-129. *See also* Systems approach

Hinduism, 35, 173-174, 209, 214; asserts the unity of its countless gods, 174

Hippocrates, 166

Historicism, 25, 285

Hologram, 80, 90

Human being(s): two vastly different conceptions of, 33, 149; human relations, 35; as multi-dimensioned, 34-35; as microcosm, 36-37; as evolving at three levels, 130; and self-knowledge and capacity to situate ourselves, 293

Human society: crisis of, 13; and state of consciousness, 14; present evolution of, 282; intersection with religion, perennial philosophy and science, 287-289; present karmic re-balancing, 295-298

Humphreys, Christmas, 215, 297

Hunger: 244-248; and the Green Revolution, 244-245, 244 n. *See also* Third world; Aid to poor countries

Huxley, Aldous, 22, 25, 36

Huxley, Sir Julian, 292

Huyghens, Christian, 60, 61

Ibn Arabi, 166

I Ching, 295

Idolatry and proscription of images, 175

Implicate order. *See* Bohm, David; Quantum physics

Industry, changes in: transition to post-industrial era, 264-271; related changes in the character and purpose of work, 268-270; and industrial specialization, 270; and international trade, 270-271

Integration and differentiation, dual properties in nature, 104-105

International law, 250-251; evolving rapidly, 251

International nongovernmental organizations (INGO's), 278-279. *See also* United Nations

International organizations, 252

Islam, 174-175, 194

Jantsch, Erich, 100, 111, 112, 133, 134, 135, 136, 139, 141, 230

Jeans, Sir James, 19, 204

Jesus of Nazareth, or Christ, 174, 180, 194; and God, 183-184. *See also* Christ

John, St., of the Cross, 47

Johnson, Raynor C., 45, 141, 147

Johnston, Charles M., M.D., 14, 199

Jones, Roger S., 77, 82, 84, 85

Judaism, 174, 194

Jung, C.G., 181

Kabbalah, 26

Karma: 35, 116, 158; connotations, meaning and implications for the individual and society, 209-216; literal meaning of the term, 209;

ethical connotations of, 210, 211; karma and interplane correlations, 211; a cosmic, moral and metaphysical force, 211; implies universal order, 212; and the significance of choice and freedom, 212-213; and society's collective values, intentions, and action, 213; and the individual and society; 213; and reincarnation, 214-216; ultimate meaning of, 216; as present rebalancing process in science and society, 283-285; present societal conditions and, 295-298

Katchalsky, Aharon, 112

Kepler, Johannes, 60, 61, 62, 87

Knowing: modes of, 41-48; sensual mode, 43-44; reason, 44-45; reason and ontological questions, 45; intuition, 46; spiritual insight, 46; mystical experience, 46; mystical union, 46-48; mystical perception as the source of religion, philosophy and art, 48-49; the interrelationship of the modes of, 49-53. *See also* Knowledge

Knowledge: and values, 10-15; 219; nature and ingredients of, 42; unmapped regions of, 206

Koestler, Arthur, 61, 62, 82, 105, 107

Koran (or Qur'an), 35, 175

Korzybski, Alfred, 16

Krippner, Stanley, 165

Kuhn, Thomas, 80, 84

Lamarck, Chevalier Jean-Baptiste de, 121, 122

Lao Tse, 21, 47, 194

Lappé, Frances Moore, and Joseph Collins, 244, 245

Laszlo, Ervin, 107, 110, 288

Leibnitz, G.W., 22, 60

Lerotholi, Minister of Agriculture, Lesotho, 239

LeShan, Lawrence, and Henry Margenau, 34 n

Liberalism, 277

Liberation. *See* Mystical union

Life, origin of: implausibility of neo-Darwinist theory on, 126-127; ultimately a mystery, 126; and an underlying generative order, 127; origin by design, 127, 137; as an inherent principle of the universe, 137

Living nature: organization of on earth, 101-108; self-reference, 138-140; mentalist activities in, 140-141; intrinsic purposiveness in, 145-146; artistry in, 146-148

Logical empiricism, 9

Lovelock, James, 108

Lutz, Mark A., and Kenneth Lux, 234, 238

Maher, John, 273

"Man," Sanskrit root of, 44

Margenau, Henry, 52, 81, 149, 150

Margulis, Lyn, 108

Marxism, 277
Mathematics: role in science, 60; in nonlinear systems, 117
Maturana, Humberto, 112, 134, 139
Maxwell, Robert, 65
McClintock, Barbara, 99
McRobie, George, 235
Mechanism: values of and their consequences, 10-15; fosters fragmentations, 11; in industry, 11-12; the emergent trend away from, 15; reductionist view of the human being and of the mind, 33; is still entrenched, 63-64; sees the universe as a dead machine, 64; was outmoded by physics itself, 65-66; in biology, 96-99, 140; in medicine, 152; and category error, 178; in economics, 229-230; in education, 285. *See also* Reductionism
Medicine, and the body-mind relationship, 152-155
Melville, Andrei Y., 283
Mendlovitz, Saul H., 276
Michelson, Albert Abraham, 73
Militarization, 248-250; military imports by third world countries, 248, 249; national defense at odds with national security, 248, 249, 250; and environment, 249-250. *See also* United Nations; Disarmament
Mills, Joy, 23, 212
Mind: reductionistic view of, 5, 33; inseparability from matter, 98, 166; and brain, 149-156
Mische, Gerald and Patricia, 256; Patricia, 257
Moksha. See Mystical union
Molecular biology: and the secret of life, 97; and organisms *per se,* 99-100; and theoretical biology, 100. *See also* Genetics; Biology
Monod, Jacques, 150
Morley, Edward Williams, 73
Morowitz, Harold, 8, 101, 150
Morphogenetic fields, 141-145; and origin of species, 142. *See also* Organicism; Biology
Morris, David and Karl Hess, 273
Moses, 180
Muhammad, 175, 194
Murphy, Gardner, 165
Myrdal, Alva, 257 n
Myrdal, Gunnar, 242
Mystical union, 46-48; goal of religions, 172; a union of freedom and necessity, 288
Myth(s): religious, 177-181; and fact, 177, 178; universality of, 179-181; of the heroic journey, 180-181

Naisbitt, John 267
Nation-state, the, 292
National sovereignty: and international law, 251, 252; and norms of nations' behavior, 251; redefining of, 254-257
Needham, Joseph, 144
Needleman, Jacob, 21, 50, 98

Newmann, John von. *See* Von Newmann

Newton, Sir Isaac, 60, 62, 63, 81, 205

Nicholson, Shirley, 132

Nirvana. See Mystical union

Nondualism, 26-29; and world peace, 29, 32; unites all dualities, 29-32

Nonlocality, 71

Occult science, 206, 207

Ontology, 47

Open system, defined, 111

Opposites: as mutually-defining polarites, 29-32; united in a higher unity, 30-32; in religion(s), 187-189; in Eastern and Western thought, 187-188

Order(s): spectrum of, 89; through fluctuation, 113-115; and chaos theory, 115-119, 160; and self-organization, 137; in the biological realm, 142; and determinism and chance, 159; in the aesthetic realm, 160

Organicism, 142

Organisms, attributes of, 138-139; universal consciousness or selfhood, 139-140; organicists' approach to, 141

Osborn, Arthur, 164

Our Common Future, 243

Oxfam America, 238, 238 n

Pallis, Marco, 184, 197

Parabrahm, 24

Paradigm, 80

Parasychology. *See* Psi faculties

Parrinder, Geoffrey, 194

Paul, St., 35

Pauli, Wolfgang, 66, 204

Peace Education, 285-286. *See also* World Peace

Peat, F. David, 89, 145, 158, 159, 160, 166

Penfield, Wilder, 150, 151, 153

Perennial philosophy, the, 22-24; tenets summarized, 38-40; and core wisdom tradition, 22, 23, 23 n, 193; various names for, 23; and religion, 183; intersection of with religion, science and society, 287-289

Perestroika, 280, 281

Periodicity: in science, 60; a fundamental principle of existence, 294

Philo, 166

Philosophy, 5; and the present societal crisis, 13; and science, 19-21; character of today, 21, 45

Physics: its three branches, 67; modern physics, 67-77; and reality, 79, 81; and consciousness, 81; picture of the world of, 81, 83; and truth, 84-86; its sublime unifications in the twentieth century, 91-92; and parapsychology, 164; and mysticism, 204-205

Planck, Max, 66, 204

Plotinus, 48-49

Polanyi, Michael, 84

Politics and political science: a new trend in, 273-274; holistic scholars, 274-275; in the Soviet Union, 279-283; political ideologies, 291-292. *See also* Grassroots movements; Economics; Technology; Karma

Popper, Sir K.R., 34, 150

Portmann, Adolph, 146, 147, 148

Positivism, 13

Power, Thomas Michael, 231, 234, 236

Preiswerk, Roy, 240

Prem, Sri Krishna, and Sri Madhava Ashish, 211

Pribram, Karl, 150

Prigogine, Ilya, 112, 113, 114, 115, 134, 136, 230

Private property, 292

Progoff, Ira, 52

Prometheus, 180

Prophets of Israel and Judah, 194

Psi faculties, 163-168; and the mind-brain problem, 163; and the inseparability of mind and matter, 166-167; and spiritual vision, 167-168

Psychoneuroimmunology, 154

"Pure" objectivity, 4, 42, 79, 80

Purucker, G. de. *See* De Purucker.

Puthoff, Harold, 165

Quantum physics, 67-73; elementary particles, 68; paradoxical features of: complementarity, uncertainty principle, nonlocality or Bell's Theorem, 69-71; the way it challenges mechanism, 72-73; its metaphoric nature, 82; interpreting quantum reality, 86; and the implicate order, 88-91

Reality: subjective nature of, 3; and cultural and historical factors, 3, 291-292; as misconceived by mainstream professionals, 4-10; reductionist view of, 5; implications of reductionist assumptions concerning, 6; not merely actuality, 24; no final modes of, 43; self-created, 42, 160, 210, 213, 216, 274, 297; and types of knowledge as yet dismissed by mainstream science, 206; and the higher values, 219. *See also* Absolute, the

Reardon, Betty A., 285-286

Reductionism. *See* Mechanism

Reincarnation, 151, 214, 214 n, 215

Relativism, 25, 285

Relativity: 73-77; special theory of, 74-76; general theory of, 76-77; and undivided wholeness, 87-88. *See also* Physics; Time and Causality

Religion(s): and the present societal crisis, 13; working definition and goal of, 171; envisage an ultimate reality, 172; diversity of, 172-176; parallel teachings in, 176; symbolic or mythic expression in, 177-179; exoteric and esoteric strands of, 182-185; inner unity of, 187-192; and Truth, 187, 191; contradictions in, 187-189; empathizing with various, 190; as different paths up the same mountain, 190-192, 193; purpose of comparative study of, 192; towering figures of, 194; as sources of conflict, 194; non static, 194; familial relationships among, 194-195; today's trends in, 195, 196, 197; a new form of spirituality, 197-198; and science, 201-207; interseciton of with perennial philosophy, science and society, 287-289. *See also* Karma; Mystical union; Unity

Renner, Michael, 249
Rheingold, Howard, 156
Rhine, J.B., 164, 165
Rig Veda, 193
Robertson, James, 269, 270
Robles, Alfonso Garcia, 257 n
Romulo, Gen. Carlos P., 257 n
Rosen, Steven M., 165
Ross, Nancy Wilson, 183
Roszak, Theodore, 273
Ruskin, John, 233

Santiago school of biologists, 139
Satin, Mark, 273, 274
Satori. See Mystical union
Scholasticism, 59
Scholem, Gershom, 183

Shroedinger, Erwin, 66, 83, 204
Schultz, Theodore, 241
Schumacher, E.F., 16, 17, 21, 230, 231, 232
Schuon, Frithjof, 178, 182, 184
Science: The rise of modern, 57-63; nature of the scientific movement, 58-63; and mathematics, 60; and the elimination of qualitative values, 61; method of, 63, 81, 82; mechanism in the eighteenth and nineteenth centuries, 63-65; an aesthetic and creative activity, 82-84; its symbolic language, 82; and the humanities, 84; revision of procedure in, 90-91; far-reaching significance of, 92-93; and religion, 201-204; and mysticism, 204-207; and perennial philosophy, 205; intersection with religion, perennial philosophy, and society, 287-289
Scientism, 4, 21, 80
Secret Doctrine, The, 99; a monumental treatise on evolution, 128; comments about, 130
Sellon, Emily B., 131, 161, 166, 286
Shankaracharya, Sri, 26
Shaw, Robert, 112
Sheldrake, Rupert, 144
Sherrington, Charles, 150
Shinto shrines, 190
Shurmann, Franz, 254
Smith, Andrew P., 125, 127

Smith, E. Lester, 152
Smith, Huston, 4, 10, 21, 23, 53, 80, 191, 203
Smuts, Jan Christian, 101, 130, 134
Socialism, 292
Society for Psychical Research, 164
Socrates, 194
Soedjatmoko, Dr., 241
Sorokin, Pitirim, 28, 194, 291, 291 n, 292
Spangler, David 273
Sperry, Roger, 99, 150
Srimad Bhagavatam, 193
Stanciu, George, 106, 124, 145
Sunyata. See Mystical Union
Supernatural, 6
Synchronicity, 158; as the sympathy of all things, 166
Systems approach, the, 109-112; and reductionism, 112; and the perennial philosophy, 138. *See also* Complexity, sciences of
Szent-Gyorgi, Albert, 124

Tao Te Ching, 35-36
Tao, the, 24
Targ, Russell, 165
Tart, Charles T., 33, 165
Technology: 259-262; appropriate technology defined, 259; and present world system, 259; the present technological revolution, 259-262; related changes in capitalism and economic policy, 260, 262; impact of its present change
on the third world, 260-262. *See also* Industry; Economics; Third world; Aid to poor countries
Teilhard de Chardin, Pierre, 101, 130, 203, 288; prophecy regarding human consciousness, 292
Theobald, Robert, 235, 267
Theophrates, 166
Theosophical movement, 293
Theosophical Society, 293 n
Theosophical world view, 294
Theosophy, 35, 98, 209, 214
Third world, the, 237-247; defined 237 n; grossly inequitable land tenure in, 237, 238, 239, 242, 245; environmental degradation in, 245, 246; population growth, 245; droughts, 246; and capitalism and socialism, 243; a causal chain in, 246-247; and the present technological revolution, 260-262. *See also* Aid to poor countries; Hunger; Economics; Technology
Thom, René, 112
Thomas, Lewis, 109
Thompson, D'Arcy, 105
Thompson, William Irwin, 273
Thorpe, W.H., 150, 153
Thorsson, Inga, 257 n
Tillich, Paul, 181, 198, 199
Time and Causality, 157-162. *See also* Causality; Synchronicity; Karma
Time; and space, 159; and timelessness, 162
Tinbergen, Jan, 241

Toffler, Alvin, 264
Torah, 174
Toynbee, Arnold, 181; on religions, 194
Truth: nature of statements about, 28, 43, 49, 187; desire for and inner morality, 50; its assimilation, 50; oneness of, 193; together with goodness and beauty, an attribute of the universe, 222
Turiya. See Mystical union

Ultimate Reality. *See* Absolute, the
Uncertainty principle. *See* Quantum physics
United Nations, 239, 247, 252-258; accomplishments of, 252-253; flaws in and reform of United Nations Charter, 253-254, 255; and disarmament, 257; and a transnational peacekeeping force, 258, 278, 279, 281, 283
Unity: in the deepest sense, 25; a universal drive toward, 104; as sympathy of all things, 166; among individuals, with nature and with art, 217-218; search for, 218, 220; and the global society, 220; and the higher values, 220-221; today's challenge to transcend particularities, 284; *See also* Perennial philosophy; Nondualism; Opposites
Upanishad, 174
Uribe, Ricardo, 134, 139

Values: Value neutrality, 7, 8, 10; instrumental values, 7, 10; need to reclaim the higher, 50; truth, goodness, beauty, justice, freedom, peace and progress as categorical imperatives, 222; of the industrial era, 228-236; of Soviet intellectuals, 280-283; in education, 285; of political ideologies, 291-292
Varela, Francisco, 112, 134, 139
Vitalism, 144, 144 n
Void, the, 24, 115, 116. *See also* Chaos science
Von Bertalanffy, Ludwig, 81, 99, 109, 110, 111, 113, 141
Von Newmann, John, 112

Waddington, Conrad, 124, 134
Wald, George, 33, 99
Walker, R.B.J., 196, 231, 255, 256, 259, 261
Wallace, Alfred Russel, 121
Weber, Renée, 115
Weiner, Norbert, 112
Weiss, Paul, 134, 144
Weston, Burns H., 238
Whitehead, Alfred North, 57, 58, 59; on mechanistic cosmology, 68, 85, 134, 178
Whitman, Walt, 299
Wholeness: key to understanding of self, universe, and existence, 3-40; and truth and reality, 24; primacy of in quantum physics, 71; and the implicate order, 86-91; corroborated by physics, 92;

corroborated by biological data, 102-106; and chaos, 115-119; and parapsychology, 165; of religion(s), 187-192; a new awareness of, 283-285; of Planet Earth, 108-109, 284; in education, 285-286; and freedom, 287-288; of today's planetary conditions, 295-298

Wilber, Ken, 16, 21, 51, 114, 131, 156, 199, 204, 206 n; on direct apprehension of Being, 207, 230

Williams, Jay G., 177, 179

Wisdom, 6; and theory, 21; as healing, 22; not an object in space-time, 22

Wittgenstein, Ludwig, 9

Wolf, Edward C., 261

World Bank, 240 n

World Commission on Environment and Development, 247; its report, *Our Common Future*, 248, 256

World Health Organizaiton (WHO), 154-155

World Order Models Project (WOMP), 274, 275

World Peace, requirements for, 251, 256

Zeeman, Christopher, 112

Zimmer, Heinrich, 177

Zoroaster, 194

QUEST BOOKS
are published by
The Theosophical Society in America,
Wheaton, Illinois 60189-0270,
a branch of a world organization
dedicated to the promotion of the unity of
humanity and the encouragement of the study of
religion, philosophy, and science, to the end that
we may better understand ourselves and our place in
the universe. The Society stands for complete
freedom of individual search and belief.
In the Classics Series well-known
theosophical works are made
available in popular editions.
For more information
write or call.
1-708-668-1571

We publish books on:
Health and Healing ● Eastern Mysticism
Philosophy ● Reincarnation ● Religion
Science ● Transpersonal Psychology
Yoga and Meditation

Other books of possible interest include:

Beyond Individualism *by Dane Rudhyar*
A literary journey from ego-hood to Self-hood.

Being, Evolution, and Immortality *by Haridas Chaudhuri*
East's insight into being; West's discovery of evolution.

Beyond the Post-Modern Mind *by Huston Smith*
Beyond reductionist philosophy and materialistic culture.

Culture, Crisis, and Creativity *by Dane Rudhyar*
The myth of our cultural omnipotence and omniscience.

The Enlightened Society *by John L. Hill*
Future of humanity experiencing psycho-spiritual evolution.

Fullness of Human Experience *by Dane Rudhyar*
How creation's cyclic nature affects our psychic evolution.

Jungian Synchronicity *by Alice O. Howell*
Appreciating equivalence of signs and ages in your psyche.

Rhythm of Wholeness *by Dane Rudhyar*
A study of the continuous process of being.

Spectrum of Consciousness *by Ken Wilber*
Psychotherapies and the non-duality of spirit.

Spirals of Growth *by Dwight Johnson*
Possibilities for development inherent in the human mind.

Available from:
The Theosophical Publishing House
P.O. Box 270, Wheaton, Illinois 60189-0270